"Lesley Paterson is one of the most mentally tough professional athletes I know, and Simon Marshall knows why. Their special sauce has finally been bottled, and the strategies described in *The Brave Athlete* promise to help athletes of all abilities become dirty fast."
—**TIM DON,** WORLD CHAMPION TRIATHLETE

"Forget marginal gains; Dr. Simon Marshall understands the most important part of performance: the athlete's mind. His expertise is an invaluable resource to help athletes master theirs."
—**DAVID BAILEY,** PHD, HEAD OF PERFORMANCE AT BMC RACING TEAM

"My training background and philosophy evolved under the coaching of Lesley and the mental slapping of Simon."
—**JESSICA CERRA,** PROFESSIONAL CYCLIST

"I have admired Dr. Simon Marshall's talent as a scientist and a communicator for more than two decades. In *The Brave Athlete* he brings this talent to the fore as he translates psychological science into meaningful strategies to help athletes become more confident, motivated, and calm."
—**DR. KIRSTEN DAVISON,** PROFESSOR OF PUBLIC HEALTH, HARVARD UNIVERSITY

"This book will take you deep inside yourself so that you can identify what you thought were your limits and, with Simon and Lesley's help, smash them to smithereens."
—**BOB BABBITT,** HOST OF BABBITTVILLE RADIO, USA TRIATHLON HALL OF FAME INDUCTEE

"Simon and Lesley get to the heart of what it takes to be a brave athlete. It's about creating a mindset that goes to bat for you rather than against you. *The Brave Athlete* is an invaluable guide to help you sort out your head. Plus it's funny. Really bloody funny."
—**FLORA DUFFY,** WORLD CHAMPION TRIATHLETE

"Marshall and Paterson, in some kind of post-Western duo, limn their own version of Wyatt Earp and Doc Holliday. Only the guns and whiskey are replaced with doctoral degrees and world titles. In *The Brave Athlete* they challenge the reader to draw swords on the psychic battlefields of sport but do so with the gift of Continental mirth and compassion."
—**SCOTT TINLEY,** TWO-TIME IRONMAN WORLD CHAMPION, AUTHOR, AND TEACHER

"Simon and Lesley bring years of training at the world-class level, in multiple sports, together with years of working in academia—all in the real world."

—**JANEL HOLCOMB,** PROFESSIONAL CYCLIST AND COACH

"I always struggled with my inner self and demons during races. Simon taught me not only how to deal with those demons, but also how to manipulate them in such a way to take my racing to an entirely different level."

—**KYLE HUMMEL,** IRONMAN 70.3 AGE-GROUP WORLD CHAMPION

"Lesley has shown me the ability to suffer like no other with the strategies outlined in this book. With these skills neither family or sport is jeopardized, bringing a much-needed balance to my life."

—**BRANDON MILLS,** AGE-GROUP MOUNTAIN BIKER

"The formula for *The Brave Athlete* is a winner and can be applied to any challenging situation."

—**DR. JACQUELINE KERR,** PROFESSOR OF FAMILY MEDICINE AND PUBLIC HEALTH, UNIVERSITY OF CALIFORNIA AT SAN DIEGO

"Working with Lesley and Simon has been one of the biggest life-changing experiences."

—**MAURICIO MÉNDEZ,** XTERRA WORLD CHAMPION AND IRONMAN 70.3 CHAMPION

THE BRAVE ATHLETE

TO ALL THE CONFIDENT, MOTIVATED,
WELL-BALANCED, AND HAPPY ATHLETES . . .
THIS BOOK ISN'T FOR YOU.

CALM THE F*CK DOWN

AND RISE TO THE OCCASION

Simon Marshall, PhD
Lesley Paterson

an imprint of Ulysses Press
PO Box 3440
Berkeley, CA 94703
www.velopress.com

Library of Congress Cataloging-in-Publication Data

Names: Marshall, Simon (Simon J.), author. | Paterson, Lesley (Triathlete), author.
Title: The brave athlete: calm the f*ck down and rise to the occasion / Simon Marshall, PhD, & Lesley Paterson.
Other titles: Brave athlete: calm the fuck down and rise to the occasion
Description: Boulder, Colorado: VeloPress, 2017. | Includes index.
Identifiers: LCCN 2017005951 (print) | LCCN 2017008297 (ebook) | ISBN 9781937715731 (pbk.: alk. paper) | ISBN 9781937716912 (ebook)
Subjects: LCSH: Sports—Psychological aspects. | Athletes—Psychology.
Classification: LCC GV706.4 .M358 2017 (print) | LCC GV706.4 (ebook) | DDC 796.01/9—dc23
LC record available at https://lccn.loc.gov/2017005951

Art direction: Vicki Hopewell
Cover design: Kevin Roberson
Handlettering: Molly Jacques
Illustrations: Chi Birmingham
Photos: Cover photo, Matt Wright; p. 341 (top), David Friend; p. 341 (bottom), Larry Rosa

21/10 9 8 7 6

CONTENTS

FIGHT *Get stuck in with new battle skills*

PREFACE

[Enter Lesley, sobbing.] "And he can go f*ck himself!" And so ended Lesley's career as a professional triathlete at the tender age of 20. Coached by physiologists and bean counters with sport science degrees, she had come to know the dark side of the new paradigm of scientific coaching. Getting ignored by coaches after a bad race, receiving performance feedback as an Excel spreadsheet, or simply being told that she was never going to be a good swimmer or cyclist left her void of inspiration and motivation. This emptiness, combined with the energy spent sustaining mindless hours of slogging up and down pool lanes, roads, and trails, brought her to a tipping point. She had been competing at an international level since age 14, but she found herself disillusioned and emotionally disconnected from her sport. She felt her coaches treated her as a pair of legs and lungs with little regard for the thoughts and feelings of a young woman. She wasn't so naïve to assume that results didn't matter. Of course they did. But who was doing the work to find out what it takes to get the best out of the athlete? Facing a seemingly insurmountable philosophical rift, she retired—still swearing, but exhausted. What a perfect time to get married. Ahem.

Meanwhile I (Simon) was busy completing too many college degrees in sport psychology and trying to help athletes do things faster, higher, and stronger by making better use of their heads. After working with athletes in lots of different sports, I realized that my rigorous academic training hadn't prepared me to deal with real people. Nothing was ever as simple or as clear as the college courses and textbooks made out. Many of the techniques handed down from the ivory towers turned out to be utter nonsense when I tried to use them on real athletes. Even worse, athletes weren't always honest about what worked and what didn't. So I retired. I moved out of sport psychology and into the academic faculty of behavioral medicine at a big university. There we were—a retired athlete and a retired sport psychologist, and now married—still discussing how to best help athletes reach their potential. Clearly, we had unfinished business.

We pooled our knowledge and experience to create our own philosophy for training athletes—one that treats the athlete as a whole person and not just a data point, and one that relied on evidence- and practice-based mental techniques that actually worked. We focused on the issues that the training books never really addressed—how to improve your psychological and emotional strength to better help you cope, improve, and thrive in sport. Except athletes don't ask for help to improve their psychological and emotional strength. Instead, they say things like "In the end, I just sort of give up," "I just need to harden the f*ck up," "I don't cope well with injury," "I work out all the time, but I still feel fat," or "I don't do well under pressure." These were the types of problems we wanted to solve.

Our first case study would be wifey herself, Lesley Paterson. We wanted to walk the talk. Lesley came out of retirement and started enjoying her sport again. She teamed up with Vince Fichera, a San Diego cycling coach with similarly unorthodox training methods and opened her new mental toolbox. Within five years, she won three world titles in off-road triathlon and was an Ironman® 70.3 champ. Holy crap, this shit was working! I became so inspired and excited by our new approach that I left the safety net of a tenured professorship to focus on building Brave Athletes full time.

We started Braveheart Coaching and, over the years, we've now coached athletes of all abilities, ages, and levels of motivation. We've coached husbands and wives, teens, grandparents, and even entire families. We've coached neo pros, age groupers, and professional world champions; people struggling under the weight of mental illness; people in unhappy relationships; loved-up newlyweds; and people dealing with debilitating physical illnesses or chronic disease. People who are just sick and tired of being sick and tired. And we've learned from all of them an important lesson: An athlete's backstory is the starting point for building bravery. We've witnessed first-hand the transformative effect that endurance training has on the mind and body. It begins a lifestyle that not only makes you fitter and faster, but leads to increased self-awareness and personal growth, setting the stage for real breakthroughs in what is possible, enriching both life and sport.

Now, after more than 20 years of coaching, consulting, and competing in endurance sports, we've written it all down. This is our book of special sauce. Whether you're a newbie training for your first 5K, an experienced amateur looking for better results, or a pro trying to become more consistent in races, this book is designed to help you deal with the thoughts and feelings that are currently holding you back. Each chapter focuses on a common psychological or emotional challenge that we've encountered over the course of our careers. These challenges are presented in the same way that athletes describe them. You will probably recognize yourself in at least one of them. We will uncover the psychology of each roadblock and give you advice on what you can do about it. We want to give you the tools you need to become a brave athlete.

INTRODUCTION

At some point in our lives, we've all been told, "Be brave." You probably first heard it from your mom or dad as you stood sobbing with a skinned knee, or when you realized that the large needle that the nurse was holding was headed for *your* arm. Being brave is about facing physical or mental discomfort with courage. And courage is the ability to act despite having thoughts and feelings that scream at you to run, hide, or freeze.

Being brave is not about acting without fear or anxiety.
In fact, far from it. BEING BRAVE is
about feeling fear and getting stuck in anyway.

Only under very specific circumstances would you throw yourself headfirst into danger *without* fear: (1) There is too little time to think about what the dangers actually are, (2) you've grossly underestimated the danger in the first place, or (3) you're f*cking nuts. For some, it's a little bit of all three. Regardless of how brave you prove yourself to be, you should almost always expect to feel like a scaredy-cat sometimes. It's entirely normal.

In this book we're going to use fairly loose definitions of bravery and fear. This is not just because of the blindingly obvious truth: Being an endurance athlete doesn't actually require you to face real danger—you know, the kind in which fate hangs in the balance and lives are at stake. Real bravery is reserved for the people who put their own lives at risk to help others. Our goal is not to cheapen this virtue, but rather to acknowledge that **we should all do stuff that scares us, however small, and this takes a very personal form of courage.**

It turns out that doing stuff that scares us is surprisingly good medicine for the brain. As you start to accumulate experiences of dealing with scary stuff, your brain thanks you by physically changing to become better prepared. Yes, your brain starts literally reorganizing itself to react in a more "we got this" way. Scientists call this "neuroplasticity," but we call it "hardening the f*ck up." Think about that the next time you're stuffed into Lycra and on the verge of crapping your pants before a race.

We all feel fear, but how we respond reflects our own life experiences and how we manage the expectation of emotion that comes from thinking about the future. For example, some athletes are excited for competition because they know exactly what lies ahead, whereas others are excited because, well, ignorance is bliss. Some are paralyzed by the thought of competition, despite never actually having done a race. Others are experienced athletes who selectively draw on a single traumatic event to drive anticipation of what must surely happen next.

The bottom line is that we all come to the table with baggage. Yes, even you. For this reason, the brave athlete's heart is always bandaged. Whether you're a first-timer buckling under the weight of "feeling like an idiot" or a top pro struggling with the emotional roller coaster of chronic injury, this book is about helping you get through it. You might even be one of those athletes who's in calm waters, at least for now. No issues, no problem. In that case, think of this book as your mental flu shot. Brush up on a few skills or learn a few tricks to stop the excess (emotional) baggage piling up. Why not also take the time to develop some empathy for your fellow athlete's experience of suffering and awkwardness? As Reverend John Watson, the Scottish author and theologian, once said: "Be pitiful, for every man is fighting a hard battle." In contemporary and less sexist parlance, this simply means that you need to be kind because everyone is dealing with their own shit that you probably know nothing about. So quit sippin' the Haterade and start lovin' instead of judgin'. (And in return, we promise never to talk like that again.)

It might come as a surprise to some (and very good news to others), but talent is vastly overrated. Your physique, your responsiveness to training, and your personal records (PRs) have little to say about how brave you are. To be a brave athlete, you need a special set of skills. Not Liam Neeson–level skills, but skills nonetheless that go far beyond the physical training, gadgets, data, and gear. We're talking about skills to help you to face your fears, push through intense physical discomfort, grow self-belief and confidence, build motivation, and enjoy competition amidst frustration and disappointment. And let's not forget the granddaddy skill of all: keeping it all in perspective. **Whatever the situation, however insurmountable it may appear, the first line of defense is to calm the f*ck down.**

The fundamental building blocks of becoming a brave athlete are represented by the bandaged heart, wings, and a sword. This keeps us from pebble-dashing the page with ideas like "integrated regulation," "ego depletion," and "causality orientation"—silly word combinations that only psychologists could dream up. The issues presented in *The Brave Athlete* certainly don't represent all the mental challenges that athletes face, but in our experience, these are far and away the most common. In your quest to become a badass brave athlete, you're gonna have to learn a few new tricks: develop a humongous heart, grow a pair (of wings, that is), and sharpen a massive tool (a metaphorical sword, obviously). Welcome to Brave Athlete School.

Let's take a peek into the armory and see what elements you're missing.

Heart. This is the passion and motivation that identify you as an athlete. It's why you do what you do. Brave athletes aren't perfect, but they know their "why," believe in their ability, and know how to turn intentions into action.

Wings. This is the ability to rise above obstacles, setbacks, and conflict. Brave athletes keep perspective whatever the circumstances, leverage a healthy attitude to make good choices, and manage the internal conflict that comes with challenge, social comparison, and judgment.

Fight. This is the ability to always give your best when it counts. Brave athletes engage in the internal battle of managing stress and anxiety, feeling competitive, staying focused under pressure, and being able to push through physical discomfort without giving up.

When you acquire these skills you will be better equipped to get stuck in with enjoyment, abandon, and fight. If you are looking for allegorical tales of athletic toughness or inspirational zero-to-hero anecdotes, you won't find them here. In the real world they don't actually help that much (we've tried most of them). Sure, they get you fired up turning the page, but you need more than a one-for-the-Gipper speech. You need long-lasting practical skills. Consider this book your Swiss Army knife. You will find an array of practical strategies grounded in brain science to help you become faster and happier. The onus is on you to do the work—identify your weaknesses, and choose and apply specific techniques in your own training and racing.

THE BASICS

1

HELLO, BRAIN!

A PEEK INSIDE YOUR 3-POUND LUMP OF CRAZY

I don't trust anybody who isn't a little bit neurotic. —MOHADESA NAJUMI

We are about to embark on a Tour de Brain to understand why that 3-pound lump on your shoulders is not only your best friend but also your worst enemy when it comes to being an athlete. If you have the attention span of a flea, here's the executive summary: Over millions of years, the human brain has become wired to protect you from harm. It will kick and scream to warn you that the shit is about to hit the fan, and it has been given ancient powers to ensure that you listen. However, what the ancient parts of your brain don't know is that you live a mostly mundane life. You're not stalked by saber-toothed cats anymore, and there's no risk of being crushed in your sleep by a woolly mammoth. The reality is that modern life in the burbs brings us the daily fear-equivalent of a nipple tweak—annoying, yes, but certainly not genuine pant-crapping danger. The problem is that no one bothered to tell your brain this fact, and so it over-reacts. Aw, bless it. Evolution has enabled you to walk upright and open jars of peanut butter, all while talking about how hard it is to qualify for the Boston marathon, but it has also quietly screwed you at the same time. You often show up to light birthday candles with a flame thrower. Before we learn what we can do about it, let's dig into some juicy evolutionary biology and neuroscience to know why we're in this mess in the first place.

You're a fish out of water.

Our ancestors were all professional swimmers. Okay, that's a little stretch of terminology and evolutionary biology, but scientists agree that we descended from fish. Technically speaking, we evolved from single-cell bacteria before water appeared on earth, but that's getting picky. We arrived via fish. (If you're a panicky triathlete, then there's a cruel irony at work.) Over 350 million years ago, armed with floppy fins and some strange type of gill-lung hybrid things, early amphibians flapped and flopped their way on to the muddy shores. They had a poke about. No one knows exactly why they did this. Perhaps they were just bored with swimming (I can relate) or wanted to try food that wasn't always soggy. Either way, let's be thankful they did. We still carry around remnants of our fishy past, like hiccups and that little groove on your top lip. Get your Google on to find out why.

As our fishy family dragged ass up the muddy shores, they soon realized that they were terribly ill equipped to cope with dry land. Something had to change. Thanks to Chuck Darwin, we now know why and how this happened. Mind you, this was no speedy transition. It took 30 million years to develop a body shape that could crawl properly. Tadpoles now do in it six months. Pah. Kids these days. It wasn't just lungs and mobility we were lacking back then; we also needed more brain power to cope with the new world. The brain we did have was little more than a brain stem and a few basic parts, like a cerebellum—a sort of mini-brain that pulled the puppet strings of our slippery nerves and muscles. We still have a cerebellum, albeit a newer model. Your cerebellum helps coordinate your physical movements and allows you to learn new ones. Tucked underneath your modern brain, it's still perched atop your brain stem, where it has been for millions of years. It looks like it's been sent to the brain's naughty step. (For a sneak peek, see the diagram on p. 7.)

Fast forward another few hundred million years to what we now recognize as the human brain. We've still got lots of other ancient brain parts, like the limbic system. These ancient brain regions are still with us because they've proved to be invaluable for keeping us alive and enjoying life. More on that later. Because evolution never stops, the human brain has tripled in size over the past 7 million years. Most of this growth has occurred over the past 2 million years. Think about that for a moment. It took us 4 billion years to evolve a human brain (we only picked up the trail when we exited the water, a mere 350 million years ago), yet most of the growth and development occurred over the past 2 million years. The sheer speed of this growth had even scientists stumped until recently.[1] That said, the human brain is shrinking again. We've lost the size of a tennis ball over the past 10,000 to 20,000 years, probably because humans have become domesticated and the brain has become more efficient. Your brain is also scaled to body size, which is also shrinking. This is hard to believe unless you looked at trends in skeletal size over thousands of years, rather than body blubber over the last 50 years. If you're not giddy with excitement about what's coming over the next 2 million years, then you need to get your nerd on.

New science has helped us unlock the secrets of the brain.

Your 3-pound lump is a pretty impressive piece of kit. The modern human brain has baffled scientists for years because of its sheer complexity in structure and function and because it's so hard to prod and poke around without dire consequences for the owner. In recent years, new methods of measuring how the brain works have given neuroscientists a much clearer idea of not just what the brain does, but when, where, and how. For example, functional magnetic resonance imaging (fMRI) has enabled us to watch, in real time, where the blood flows in the brain in response to different thoughts, mental tasks, or situations. When you follow blood flow, you follow oxygen and glucose (brain food). Oxygen and glucose supply is a sign of energy demand, which is a sign of neural activity, so brain blood flow shows us the parts that are working hard. FMRI studies have helped us debunk popular myths, such as the notion that there are

---

1 Alok Jha, "Human Brain Result of 'Extraordinarily Fast' Evolution," *The Guardian*, December 28, 2004, http://www.theguardian.com/science/2004/dec/29/evolution.science.

right-brained and left-brained people, or that you only use 10 percent of your brainpower. These are now both proven by science to be utter nonsense.[2]

We need to fudge the science a little to make a point.

What follows is a gross oversimplification of how the brain functions. We've oversimplified the science not because we want to deliberately mislead you or insult your intelligence, but because we need a way of thinking about the brain (and the tricks it plays on us) that makes it easier for us to solve the problems that it gives us in real life. One of the biggest simplifications is that we've conflated anatomy with function. Modern neuroscience has revealed that studying the anatomy of the brain (the physical structures and their location) doesn't accurately reflect the complexity of what the brain actually does (its function). Tasks of the brain don't live exclusively in certain areas. However, we need a "working model" that is at least consistent with the science and, importantly, doesn't fight the biological reality. Practical utility is our goal—we want you to have more thoughts and feelings that are helpful and productive and have fewer psychological and emotional experiences that make you want to crap your pants, tear your hair out, wimp out, shy away, or otherwise mentally self-flagellate. Our working model of the brain relies almost exclusively on metaphors and analogies, many of which aren't even ours. The use of metaphor and analogy to communicate sciencey-things really irritates some people with science backgrounds, because of the oversimplification problem. We stick to our guns on this one (see?) because it is an integral part of science communication, and we've learned that it works.[3] It's also more fun.

2 Christopher Wanjek, "Left Brain vs. Right: It's a Myth, Research Finds," *Live Science*, September 3, 2013, http://www.livescience.com/39373-left-brain-right-brain-myth.html.

3 Caleb A. Scharf, "In Defense of Metaphors in Science Writing," *Scientific American*, July 9, 2013, https://blogs.scientificamerican.com/life-unbounded/in-defense-of-metaphors-in-science-writing/.

Let's take a look inside your second favorite organ.

If you recall from your high school biology class (oh, never mind), your brain has three distinct regions:

The **brain stem** connects your cerebrum and cerebellum to your spinal cord and is responsible for involuntary functions like breathing, heart rate, digestion, swallowing, and sleep-wake cycles, among other things. Your brain stem is not very trainable.

The **cerebellum**, or "little brain," sits on big brain's naughty step and is responsible for coordinating physical movements and aspects of language and memory. Your cerebellum is somewhat trainable.

The **cerebrum** is the biggest part of your brain and comprises left and right hemispheres. In fact, it's so big that it has to be folded up and squished (which is why it looks so wrinkled) in order to fit into that tiny skull of yours. Your cerebrum is responsible for all voluntary movements and for interpreting incoming sensory data, plus all the "higher" functions that make us human, such as reasoning, emotion, capacity for abstract thought, learning, and so on. It does lots of other things too. Each hemisphere of your cerebrum has four regions or lobes: the frontal lobe, the temporal lobe, the parietal lobe, and the occipital lobe. Although each lobe of the brain has a job to do, they never really work in isolation. There's no "I" in lobe.

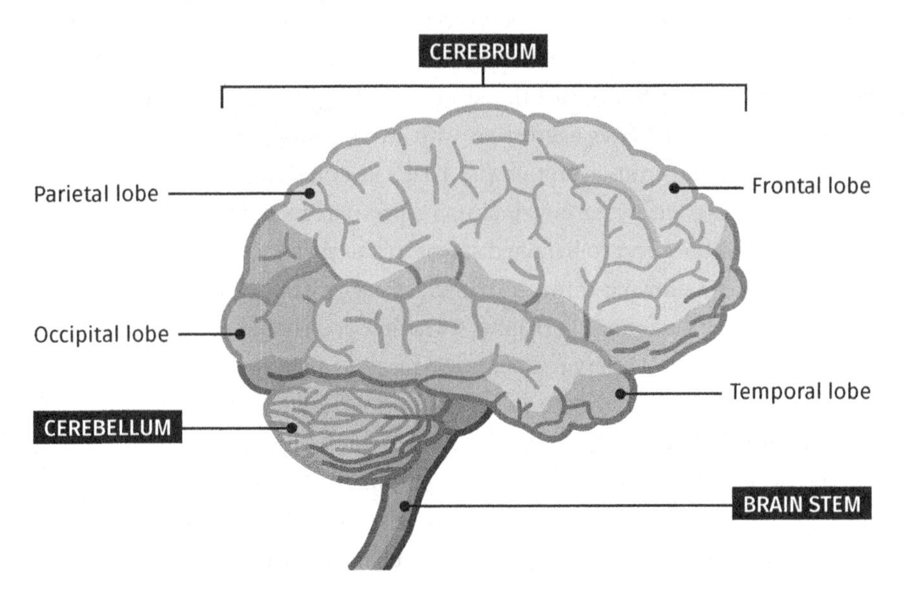

Your cerebrum is very trainable. In fact, your cerebrum loves training so much it will look for things to learn even when you can't be bothered to train it.

Let's start digging a little deeper. Our brains are made up of a mix of old and new parts. Your ancient brain focuses on keeping you alive and convincing you to create mini-me's (among other things), whereas your new brain helps you think and be smart. Your new brain also enables you to think about your thinking. This is called *metacognition*, and it turns out that not many species can actually do it. Later, we will learn why this is a key strategy for unblocking your mental toilet. Some of your old and new brain regions are shown in the diagram on p. 12.

Don't get hung up on the unpronounceable medical names, but do take a look at what the different parts do. This is important because when you're standing on the pool deck worrying that you look fat in your swimmies, or you crap yourself at the mere thought of doing your first marathon, this diagram begins to explain why. Even if you feel none of these things, bar the occasional "I don't want to look like a complete tool," this diagram holds clues as to how you can have more of the thoughts and feelings that you want.

Why can't my brain get along with itself?

Your ancient brain and your new brain argue a lot. Imagine that you had a bodyguard 24/7. What kinds of things do you think you'd argue about? Places you want to go but your bodyguard thinks are too dangerous for you? Your bodyguard getting slightly too aggressive with other people? Getting constantly reminded how dangerous everything is? That's just one of many arguments your ancient brain has with your new brain on a pretty regular basis. Another argument might be how best to handle discomfort during a race, or whether or not you should keep plowing through that jar of cashew butter in a single sitting (yes, you, Lesley Paterson). Perhaps it's whether you should spend $8,000 on a new bike or a month's salary to do a single race. It might not be about sports at all. You might always fall for the wrong guy or girl, or you get taken advantage of by other people. Your brain has a lot to answer for.

Because brain arguments happen at lightning speed (thanks in part to your uncinate fasciculus), you're not even aware of them most of the time. You often end up just being "forced" to implement the decision that gets handed down to you. For example, you stay in a comfort zone; you shy away from pressure-filled situations; you buy something you can't afford; you quit when it gets hard; you gorge on sugar at night, or whatever. Sometimes you're very aware of the back-and-forth but still feel powerless to take charge. Let's explore a brain battle that triathletes know well—coping with an open water swim start.

Inside the head of a triathlete during an open water swim start.

The first event in a triathlon is swimming, and in 99.9 percent of races, this happens in a lake, ocean, or river (hence "open" water). In a triathlon, everyone starts together. If the race is really big, athletes start with others in their age group or gender, but this can still amount to hundreds of people all rushing into the water at once. The first few minutes of any triathlon feels like you've been dumped into a washing machine. It's hard to see anything, arms and elbows are flying, you're swallowing more water than is probably healthy, and all your technique and breathing rhythm are long gone. Just at that moment, someone grabs your ankle. Then they grab your leg. Then you get punched twice and pushed under. Here's the running dialog between the regions of ancient brain and new brain:[4]

Amygdala *(which is emotion central)* [shouting]: You do that once more and I will f*cking drown you!

Orbitofrontal cortex *(which helps us see what we can get away with—the reward-punishment tradeoff)*: Wait, wait! Don't drown him. You'll never get away with that!

Uncinate fasciculus *(which is trying to arbitrate being sensible versus being stupid)*: Hang on, we need to find a compromise here. You can't just drown someone because you're in a race. You won't be able to live with yourself. What about just a swift kick in the teeth?

Dorsolateral prefrontal cortex *(which deals only with facts and logic)*: Stop getting emotional. Is it even the same person? How hurt are you? Is there blood? Are we in danger of drowning? Give me the evidence. I'll stay calm and logical and let you all know what we're going to do.

---

4 We thank Dr. Steve Peters for providing the template of this brain fight. "Optimising the Performance of the Human Mind: Steve Peters at TEDxYouth@Manchester 2012," https://www.youtube.com/watch?v=R-KI1D5NPJs.

Ventromedial prefrontal cortex *(which helps us think about another person's feelings)*: Stop being so selfish. Where's your compassion? They're probably also going through hell back there, which is making them overly aggressive. They're just trying to survive too!

Hippocampus and cingulate gyrus *(which help regulate emotion, pain, and memory)*: I've consulted the memory banks, and this has happened to you before and you got through it. Besides, you can handle more than that. Our data show that in about 6 minutes the thrashing is predicted to stop. If it still goes on, you can stop swimming for a few seconds and just shout at them. This usually does the trick.

Amygdala *(which is emotion central)*: I don't give a shit. Just hurt them so they stop it.

You now have a whole lot of brains in a fight.

One of them has got to get control. And let's hope it isn't the one who wants to drown or hurt the other swimmer. Sometimes the socially acceptable but devious brain takes charge by saying, "Three strong kicks to the face should do it!" Sometimes the rational frontal cortex brain takes control and says, "Just swim two feet over to the left and all will be fine." Depending on your personality, the brain left holding the reins is likely to vary. Regardless of the outcome, you can see the need to stay calm when utter chaos breaks out in your head. **This internal power struggle is a major cause of mental turmoil for athletes because it creates negative emotion, detracts from the task at hand, and almost always slows you down.** It's also just too damn complicated. Let's make things simpler. The main culprit in the ancient brain is the limbic system. The key player in the new brain and defender of all things sensible is the frontal cortex.

In Brainsville, there are always two sides vying for control.

The different regions of the brain take sides as the battle lines are drawn. On one side we have the limbic system, and on the other the frontal cortex. Before you decide who to root for, keep in mind both sides are needed to keep you alive and healthy. Nevertheless, this dual-brain model is helpful because it provides the basis for understanding much of our inner conflict and decision-making. Let's take a closer look:

The **limbic system** comprises all the ancient brain regions—the amygdala, the cingulate gyrus, the hippocampus, and the hypothalamus. The limbic system is an emotional machine that reacts only to drives and instincts, which you experience as feelings and impressions. If your limbic system ruled the roost, you wouldn't have a problem. You'd be as dumb as a post, but you wouldn't have to answer to anyone. You'd have a reacting brain. Your amygdala and hypothalamus would team up to tell you what to do by feeding you feelings and impressions. Your hippocampus would remind you via memories that it feels good to be the King. You'd steal a lot. You'd hump anything. You'd tell people exactly what you thought of them. You'd probably murder a lot. You'd also end up in prison. Some people do end up in prison because their limbic systems are literally controlling their brains.

The **frontal cortex** comprises the parts of the new brain—dorsolateral prefrontal cortex, uncinate fasciculus, ventromedial prefrontal cortex, and orbitofrontal cortex. It's a lot more considerate than your limbic system. Your frontal cortex deals only with facts and logic, and guides empathy, moral judgment, and social conscience. Your frontal cortex is the only part of you that can think. At least in the way we define thinking: using your mind to consider or reason about something. The rest of your brain is simply a machine. When you think about who you are, your values, beliefs, hopes and dreams—it's your frontal cortex doing the work. In short, your frontal cortex is the real you. We like the frontal cortex because it's like your dad: helpful, supportive, and able to put shelves up. Admittedly, he might not be the first person you turn to for emotional comfort, but he'll probably be able to help you with your taxes and he'll know why your engine rattles from a cold start.

A good metaphor will make it easier to follow and even to "win" the brain fight. Because so many psychologists adopt the dual-brain model, there are plenty of metaphors already available. For example, some refer to our limbic system as a "lizard brain" or a "reptilian brain" because of its primordial intentions. Jonathan Haidt, author of *The Happiness Hypothesis,* refers to the two brain systems as the "Elephant" (limbic system) and the "Rider" (frontal cortex).[5] Daniel Kahneman, the Nobel Prize–winning economist and author of *Thinking, Fast and Slow,* refers to them simply as "System 1" and "System 2."[6] By

5 Jonathan Haidt, *The Happiness Hypothesis* (New York: Basic Books, 2006).

6 Daniel Kahneman, *Thinking, Fast and Slow* (New York: Macmillan, 2011).

HELLO, BRAIN: WHERE OLD MEETS NEW

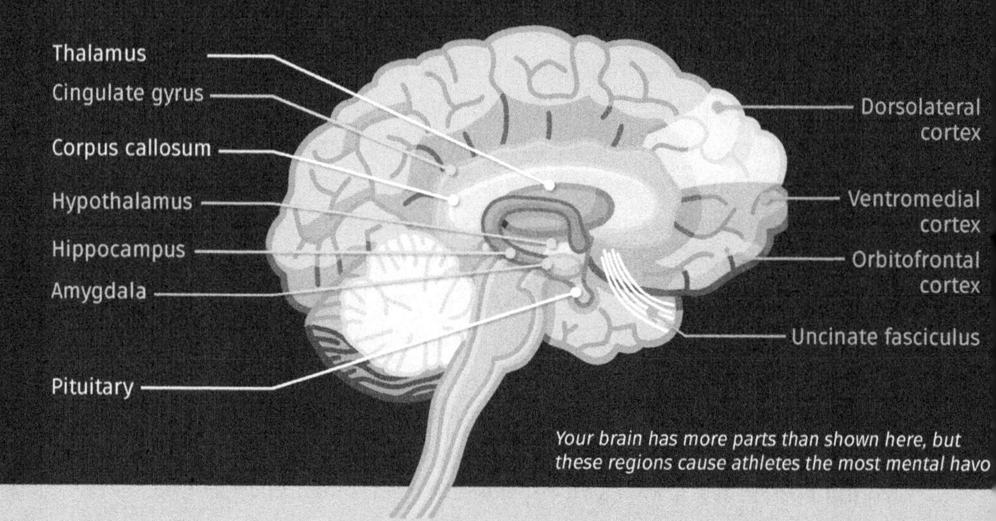

Your brain has more parts than shown here, but these regions cause athletes the most mental havo

LIMBIC SYSTEM [ANCIENT BRAIN]

The **amygdala** is emotion central. It receives information directly from your senses and then speed-dials other brain regions so you can respond quickly. It's the source of your emotions and moods, as well as your survival instincts, like fear. If it was surgically removed, you'd never get nervous or angry again. But then again, you'd not fall in love or have sexy time either. You can't have it both ways.

The **cingulate gyrus** helps regulate emotions and pain. It's also involved in filtering memories. Part of the CG, the anterior cingulate cortex regulates self-control and effort.

The **hypothalamus** helps keep the amygdala in check by making sure bodily functions, instincts, and drives are in balance. It works like a thermostat for the four Fs—food, fun, fever, and fornication—and manages endocrine function (hormone secretion).

The **hippocampus** is the brain's memory maker, good and bad. Damage the hippocampus and you're starring in the sequel to *50 First Dates.*

FRONTAL CORTEX [MODERN BRAIN

The **dorsolateral prefrontal cortex** deals with analysis, rational thought, and logic. This is your mental horsepower. (It's not technically an anatomical structure, but a function.) It doesn't fully mature until you're in your mid-20s. And don't we know it.

The **uncinate fasciculus** is a 4–5 cm "fiber tract" that acts as a hotline between sensible and stupid (and, by extension, between surviv instincts and logic). No one seems to know fo sure what it does, but relaying information at lightning speed between emotion centers an rational centers seems likely.

The **ventromedial prefrontal cortex** helps keep your survival instincts and emotions in check, helps you make morally and socially acceptable decisions, enables you to empathi with other people's feelings, and detects iron and sarcasm. Enlarged in British people.

The **orbitofrontal cortex** also helps you make responsible decisions by controlling impulses and emotions, but is able to weigh up the consequences of reward and punishment. It helps you figure out what you can get away with. One of the reason's you're not currently in jail.

far the best analogy we've come across is from Dr. Steve Peters, a British forensic and sport psychiatrist, who refers to the limbic system as a Chimp. This is a great metaphor for the limbic system because a chimp often acts up, has tantrums, and can be pretty disruptive. But a chimp can also be calm, sleepy, adorable, and cuddly. Most importantly, a chimp doesn't really mean any harm to you because it doesn't know any better. It's just a chimp. We love it, and we have adopted the chimp metaphor as our working model. Thanks, Steve. In contrast to your Chimp, we refer to your frontal cortex as your Professor brain, because it's always logical and only deals in facts and truth.

If there's one book that every athlete should have on their bookshelf, it's Dr. Peters's book, *The Chimp Paradox.*[7] It's not a sports-specific book, but it will help you understand and better manage your Chimp in all aspects of your life.

Chimp versus Professor: Where the shit hits the fan.

In an ideal world, your Chimp brain and your Professor brain would be nice neighbors. Like when your neighbor leans over the fence and asks to borrow something. Polite and considerate. Here's the ideal scenario:

- Your Chimp experiences an urge to [insert instinct of choice here . . . eat, hide, run, have sex].
- Your Chimp asks the Professor brain for permission to get the urge met.
- Your Professor brain carefully considers the request by thinking it through using only facts and logic.
- You make a decision that is in the best interests of both your Chimp and your Professor brains.
- Everyone is pleased and you live happily ever after.

If only things were that simple! But they're not. In fact, we have a major problem. Your Chimp is a bully. And this bully has lightning-fast reflexes and superhuman powers of persuasion.

---

7 Steve Peters, *The Chimp Paradox: The Mind Management Program to Help You Achieve Success, Confidence, and Happiness* (New York: TarcherPerigee, 2013).

Meet your inner primate—your Chimp brain

Scientific studies in neuroscience and cognitive psychology have proven that your Chimp brain is a tough wee bastard. Your Chimp was bestowed with biochemical powers (called neurotransmitters) that enable it to bully your Professor brain into submission. Instead of being a polite and respectful neighbor, your Chimp sets up camp in your basement and just starts using your shit at will. Here are more facts about your Chimp:

- Controls the fight, flight, or freeze response, a powerful response to danger.
- Is first responder for all sensory information. Research shows that your Chimp brain processes and reacts to sensory input data up to five times quicker than your Professor brain.
- Maintains very strong drives for food, power, sex, ego, being accepted by others, security, inquisitiveness, and so on. Your Chimp is motivated to protect these drives at all times.
- Uses powerful neurotransmitters like dopamine, serotonin, oxytocin, acetylcholine, and noradrenaline to get your attention and move you to act.
- Thinks in black and white, there is no gray. Only right or wrong.
- Is paranoid as a result of a deep-seated need for safety. Is hypervigilant about protecting you.
- Elevates threats to catastrophic—they are always a matter of life or death.
- Acts irrationally; never mind if it's reasonable or feasible.
- Is infallible, final, and merciless.

So, you're stuck with this overemotional roommate that is fixated on preserving basic drives or instincts using feelings and impressions, even though you never asked for help. Your Chimp screams at you to make sure you hear, and worry and anxiety are usually the end result. Here are just a few examples of the havoc that your Chimp creates around your athletic performance: *What if I get dropped? I have to race well for my coach. If I don't get on the podium, this race will be for nothing. I look like an overstuffed sausage in this cycling kit. If I have a bad race, my sponsors will write me off.* . . . or the gazillions of other things that make us feel miserable.

5
30%
1.075
2.000
1.950

But your Chimp brain isn't all bad. If your life is truly at risk, it will help you perform amazing acts of bravery, force you to eat grubs when you're close to starvation, and help you fall in love and want to shag like a rabbit. Don't get the impression that all your problems will be solved if you could just be rid of your Chimp. You need your Chimp. We've just got to make sure it's well trained.

Meet your voice of reason—your Professor brain

Your Professor brain is the only part of you that can actually *think* (in the sense that it can be conscious of itself, reason, think abstractly, and so on). Your Professor brain helps you manage money, purchase a house, select a partner, bake a cake, visit a doctor, plan your training program, and ponder moral and ethical conundrums. Your Professor brain got you through school and college. Driven by facts and logic, it's motivated by honesty, compassion, and self-control, and it acts with a conscience, searches for purpose in life, and works for a sense of achievement. It does the intellectual heavy lifting required of good decisions. However, here's the most important point to remember about your Professor brain: **It deals only with facts, truth, and logic**. If your Professor brain was in charge, you'd make smart, rational decisions all the time. However, because it takes time to weigh up pros and cons, consider alternatives, and think through rules and regulations, your Professor brain is notoriously slow. When the Chimp releases powerful neurotransmitters during the decision-making process, your Professor brain gets pushed aside or tricked. In fact, studies in cognitive science and behavioral economics have shown that your Professor brain is pushed, bullied, and tricked most of the time. Why else would you plow through a half-pound bag of Red Vines after 8 p.m., have orange skinny jeans in your closet, or buy yet another training kit that costs more than some families spend on groceries in a month?

Meet your operating system—your Computer brain

We're now going to add in a third brain to the mix. Wait, what? It's not technically a brain on its own, but more a function of many different regions that help you run automatic programs like habits and routines. It also uses your memory banks to shape expectations you have of people and situations. It is akin to a computer's operating system because it runs in the background, it's extremely fast, and it helps you launch programs to deal with different situations. To borrow another metaphor from Dr. Steve Peters, it's like a Computer brain.[8]

The neuroanatomy of your brain's operating system is very complex, and its functions occur in many different brain structures. Most important, your Computer brain helps you act automatically using preprogrammed thoughts and actions. Like a computer, it stores memories. Like a reference book, it stores information about your beliefs and values. We need a Computer brain because much of what we think and do must be automated in order to cope with the sheer number of decisions that need to be made every day (estimated at approximately 35,000!). When we learn skills well, we turn them over to the Computer brain to manage.

When you are born, the hard drive of your Computer brain is blank. As you grow up, it fills with information based on your education and experience. All information on the computer comes from what the Chimp and the Professor have given it. When the Chimp stores information on the computer, it is based on Chimp logic (paranoid, catastrophic, fear-based). When the Professor stores information on the computer, it is based on Professor logic (facts and reasoning). Your Computer brain has a limitless capacity for storage, but things that are associated with strong emotion get special treatment. This is more evidence that your Chimp brain stacks the deck in its favor. Your Chimp puts a lot of crap on your computer to promote its own agenda of staying alive and rewarding your instincts and drives for food, sex, ego, security, territory, inquisitiveness, and so on. Often we don't focus on facts and logic but instead recall only emotionally charged experiences to help us determine how we feel about something. In some instances, this creates an extreme pattern of behavior that defies logic and reason but persists anyway. This is what causes phobias or irrational fears.

We're all plagued by bugs in our operating systems.

Your Computer brain is much quicker than either your Chimp brain or your Professor brain. In fact, it's the quickest brain of all. If you have painful, fearful, or embarrassing memories, then those are brought to your attention with such

8 Peters, *The Chimp Paradox.*

lightning speed that the ensuing emotional reactions often occur before you're even consciously aware of them. When the feelings are not in proportion to the actual danger present, or you tend to react in a certain way despite not wanting to, it's the equivalent of having a bug in your Operating System. We call that a Computer brain virus. For example, worrying all the time about crashing on your bike or not drowning in the swim are Computer brain viruses. If you never train in the open water because you're scared of sharks—yup, it's a Computer brain virus. If you enjoy training but become terrified at the thought of competing, you're infected with a Computer brain virus. If you downplay your triathlon exploits by saying things like "I'm *just* a . . ." then you have a Computer brain virus. And that habit of hitting the pantry because you're bored? Yup, another Computer brain virus. For the record, no one is virus free. Yes, that includes you. It's part of the human condition. We all come with some level of emotional baggage or strange reactions to silly things. **The solutions to many of the psychological and emotional roadblocks presented in this book are attempts to clean up your operating system and install some virus protection software.**

Now that we've learned some of the functional anatomy of your brain, it's time to focus on how it screws up your thinking and performance in sports. Remember, it is in constant conflict. As an example, let's look at how your Chimp, Professor, and Computer brains respond to race anxiety caused by the pressure of high expectations (see the sidebar "It's Race Day . . . Yay! Or Not").

IT'S RACE DAY . . . YAY! OR NOT

IT'S YOUR LOCAL HALF-MARATHON. You arrive at the race site early in the morning and you are figuratively, and sometimes literally, crapping yourself. You've had a series of great results (a PR, a podium, beating an archrival, etc.), but this morning you don't feel all that good. Your legs feel a bit heavy, and for some unknown reason you don't feel that motivated. You then see two athletes in your age group who are your archrivals. They both look exceptionally fit, strong, and confident. Your thalamus (a structure in your Chimp brain) gets this information from your visual system first. Your amygdala (another structure in your Chimp brain) floods your brain with neurotransmitters that cause feelings of anxiety, nervousness, and mild nausea. You start to have worries about losing your "streak," you worry about what others will think of your upcoming subpar performance and why you should not be racing because you've had a sore throat.

Your Computer brain quickly determines that you never race well when slightly sick and unmotivated and all your rivals are there. You feel a bit of a fraud anyway. Your Chimp is now firmly in charge. As a double blow, your Chimp then hits you with a chemical brick. It floods you with neurotransmitters to ensure you don't interfere with your Chimp reaction. Your Chimp is convinced that lives are at stake. It's now at DEFCON 3 preparing for a battle of life or death. Your Professor brain tries to take over, saying, "Everything's fine; it's only a race," but it's no match for the Chimp.

As you walk to the start line, you need the bathroom for the fourth time. As the race starts, you go off too hard and go into massive oxygen debt within two minutes. You have to ease off and get dropped by the group that you're running with. You realize this is happening, and your Professor brains starts telling you off for beginning too fast.

You go through the 5-mile marker way behind your target pace, and you start thinking that your race is already pretty much over. Your rivals are already two minutes up the road, and even though you can turn it up a notch, you are usually outkicked in the final stretch. You get mad at yourself. Needless to say, you confirm your expectations. You finish 8th in your age group, four minutes down on people you should be beating. After the race is over, you see your family.

Your Professor brain is now back in charge and starts to apologize to your family for wasting their time and making them come out so early to see you have a horrible race. Your Computer brain gets sent more information to make the virus even bigger: You don't race well when the pressure is on. And so the cycle continues. Sound familiar?

So, in a nutshell.

Your Professor brain deals with facts, truth, and logic. Your Chimp brain deals with feelings, impressions, and emotions, based on instincts and drives. Your Computer brain acts like a machine that takes orders from the Chimp or Professor and runs stored programs based on your experiences and memories so you don't have to think too much. These brain systems all fight for control.

> Learning how to calm the f*ck down and rise to the occasion is about recognizing which brain is in charge and then doing some BRAIN WRANGLING to get the right brain for the job back in control.

How do I know which brain is in charge?

Aside from the fMRI method we described earlier, there is a really simple way of figuring out which brain is in charge at any given moment. As Dr. Steve Peters recommends, you can simply ask yourself this question: *Do I want to think or feel like this?* If your answer is no, your Chimp is in charge. If your answer is yes, your Professor is in charge. It's really that simple.

Research has revealed that some of us spend as much as 95 percent of our day wishing that we thought or felt something else. So, in essence, many of us have a Chimp problem. Our brains are always getting hijacked by our Chimp, who takes over with things we don't want to think and feel. Because your Chimp is enlisted in Operation Save You, it will react to every perceived threat. Incoming sensory information goes straight to a switchboard in your limbic system (the thalamus) that raises the alarm. Your amygdala hears the alarm and freaks out. Your Chimp is screaming, "Help, Help! Do something!!" But you can't be mad at it; it's just a Chimp! Would you get mad at a dog or a small child? Well, maybe. It's just that you can't blame your Chimp. It's acting out of a desire to save you. It's hardwired that way and there's nothing you can do about it, even when you don't need saving.

Your Professor brain knows your Chimp reaction is ridiculous. After all, it's only a training session or race. No one's going to die. But here's the kicker: Your Chimp is not easily contained. Remember, our brains are wired to send all incoming info to the Chimp first. It thinks five times quicker than your Professor brain and has five times more willpower. In short, it will not shut the f*ck up and get back in its cage. That's actually a good thing. Remember, your Chimp is there to protect you. But from real harm. Because it's a Chimp, it doesn't have the intellect to know what's real and what's fake. For all it knows, trying to PR at the Turkey Trot 10K is akin to going over the top of a trench in WWI. We just need to make sure your Chimp feels safe and secure before we can move on with the rather dull and nonthreatening world of running, cycling, or swimming.

A plan of attack for your Chimp problem.

First you need to get to know your Chimp, and this starts with understanding our mental model (i.e., reading this book). That leads to a golden rule of Chimp training: **Never ever, ever, try to control your Chimp with brute force. You will lose. Every time.** Your Chimp is much stronger than you and can act many times quicker.

You need to be more cunning. You need to learn how to nurture your Chimp by first figuring out what is getting its knickers in a twist. This means making sure your fundamental Chimp needs are met (instincts and drives). If you have been described as a hypercompetitive person (i.e., someone who loves the head-to-head challenge, hates losing, and makes everything a competition), it's often because a fundamental Chimp need for recognition and acceptance has been thwarted somewhere along the line. Part of sport psychology is identifying the Chimp needs that must be met so you can train and race with a happy Chimp. From there, you will need to manage its outbursts and install some virus protection software. The one thing you have going for you is that your Chimp cannot act alone. It must get your permission. In fact, the Chimp simply offers up a course of action for you. Yes, you're often waterboarded into submission by chemical messengers (neurotransmitters), but it's still a choice. Getting your Professor brain back in charge is akin to getting a drunk CEO out from under the desk, sobered up, and back to running the company.

And that's where our journey begins.

HEART

HONE YOUR PASSION, MOTIVATION, AND IDENTITY

2

I WISH I FELT MORE LIKE AN ATHLETE

TACKLING THE FLAWED THINKING AROUND YOUR ATHLETIC IDENTITY

We don't see things as they are, we see them as we are. —ANAÏS NIN

"Tell me about yourself as an athlete." You would be amazed at how athletes respond to this simple question. On the face of it, it's an invitation to talk about routine and quantifiable aspects of athletic life: the event an athlete competes in, the type and amount of training she does, recent results, PRs, and so on. However, far more revealing is how athletes talk about themselves—the words they use, what they choose to focus on first and second and, sometimes more importantly, what they don't mention at all. Consider these responses from three athletes.

> Sure. I'm pretty good. I'll probably turn pro soon. I started off as a mountain biker and was racing elite for a few years. I smashed it. A guy I used to race with—and beat pretty consistently—switched to XTERRA and started doing really well—you might know him [names a top XTERRA pro]—yeah, I know him pretty well. Anyway, so I gave XTERRA a go and got some success pretty quick. I won my age group at [Race X] and was third at Nationals. I qualified for Worlds in my first season. I don't know who else has done that. —DAVE, 27, OFF-ROAD TRIATHLETE

> I do Olympic [distance] and a few 70.3s. I'm looking to step up to the longer stuff over the next few years because I feel I can be really competitive there. I think I lack the pure speed for the short-course stuff. Of course I'm totally realistic about how long it takes to get good at Ironman distance but would like to take it to the next level. I'm really disciplined and pretty driven. My family thinks I'm a bit crazy but they see how much I love it and they come to all my races. That means a lot to me.
>
> —STEPHEN, 44, TRIATHLETE

> I'm not sure I'd call myself an athlete. I mean, I'm trying to become one. I'm just super slow. I'm probably the gal that just gets in your way. I think I lack a bit of confidence. I really enjoy it but . . . [long pause] . . . well, take my group runs for example. I hate getting left behind, not just because I'm slow but because the thought that other people are waiting for me makes me feel like shit. I'm sure they're all thinking, "Oh great, we have to wait for her again." D'you think I'm a lost cause? Do you only work with fast people?
>
> —KATHERINE, 46, RUNNER

Of course, these are not the full responses from Dave, Stephen, and Katherine, but you can get a sense of how differently they talk about themselves as athletes. You might even personally identify with one of them. Even more revealing was the fact that they projected a consistent self-perception in virtually every conversation we had with them. Dave was always telling us how great he is, Stephen was reflective and realistic, and Katherine was constantly criticizing herself. Now we're not suggesting that it's necessary to pore over every word that people use when they talk about their athleticism or even to read too deeply into what could be considered athletic small talk. What we are suggesting is that how you talk about your sport and your place in it is almost always a window to your inner world of beliefs, expectations, and experiences. Of course, these conversations can also be cloaked in hidden meaning and/or full of outright lies. See the nerd alert for why some of us do this.

One aspect of your inner world is your athletic identity, which is the degree to which you identify as being an "athlete" and how you look to others to confirm or validate your beliefs about your athleticism. **Athletic identity is all about thinking and feeling like an athlete. Athletic identity has nothing to do with how fast you are, how much racing you do, or how much you train.** Although

NERD ALERT!

Cognitive distortion, impression management, and the science of self-deceit

"I WISH MY ATHLETE would just be honest with me," said every coach, ever, at least once. Incidentally, many athletes also say the same thing about their coaches. And FYI, if you're a coach or an athlete and find yourself saying, "Nonsense, my athlete/coach is always honest with me," then here's a newsflash: You're delusional. Well, technically speaking, you're suffering from confirmatory bias with a sprinkle of illusion transparency, but that's for another time. When it comes to telling it like it is, the science has spoken: We're all liars and manipulators. This statement needs some clarification. The kind of deceit we're talking about here isn't the deliberate and capricious kind associated with used car salesmen, cheating spouses, or subprime mortgage creeps, although that's certainly a form of it. The kind we're referring to here is far more benign, self-directed, and effortless. Welcome to the heady science of cognitive distortion.

When you convince yourself that you really need a $10,000 TT superbike to be a competitive age-group triathlete, you've got a big receipt for self-deceit coming. When you blame your coach for not getting faster despite only completing 60 percent of the sessions (*shh*), you're being, ahem, selective with the facts. Psychologists call these little self-delusions "cognitive biases," and they're as natural as breathing. They are systematic errors in thinking that predispose us to think or act one way over another, when pure logic would suggest a different thought or action.

The human brain is so prone to self-deception that many scientists now think it must serve a very useful purpose for survival. Why else would we constantly lie to ourselves in 70 different ways?* Scientific studies tell us that you deceive your own brain far more often than you deceive others, you rarely know you're doing it, it's mostly harmless and probably even "natural," but you should probably do the occasional self-check to stop it from getting out of hand (e.g., buying crap you can't afford).

>

* "List of Cognitive Biases," Rational Wiki, http://rationalwiki.org/wiki/List_of_cognitive_biases.

Continued

When it comes to managing our outer athletic identity, one kind of distortion tops the chart: social desirability bias. It's a fancy way of saying that we have a tendency to tell people things that help us be seen in a favorable light. As any good coach knows, when athletes say they are "really disciplined," it's best to wait for evidence of this rather than assume you're using the same dictionary. Social desirability bias is one strategy in a family of cognitive distortions that try to control how the world sees us. Shrinks call this "impression management." Almost all of us are naturally motivated to engage in impression management because our external identity is at stake (in everyday speak, our reputation or character). Imagine if someone invented special software to continuously pump out data to the world that expertly managed the public impression of you. They'd be a billionaire! Oh wait, it's called Facebook—a.k.a. impression management software. Remember that the next time someone posts a screen capture of their workout stats. In Chapter 5, we discuss impression management in more detail and the shenanigans people play on Facebook.

these details can all be signs of having a mature athletic identity, they're certainly not required. If you really want to nerd out, you should read one of the scientific articles that started it all.[1] So what constitutes a mature athletic identity?

1. You currently participate in sports or exercise.
2. You are comfortable calling yourself an athlete.
3. You are comfortable being called an athlete by others.
4. You "own" your athletic ability. You're neither embarrassed by it, nor do you feel the need to prove your athletic ability to others.
5. You don't engage in excessive self-criticism or self-aggrandizement (telling people how awesome you are) when talking about your ability or performance.

1 B. W. Brewer, J. L. Van Raalte, and D. E. Linder, "Athletic Identity: Hercules' Muscles or Achilles Heel?" *International Journal of Sport Psychology* 24 (1993): 237–254.

6. You maintain a healthy balance between your sport and other interests. Your ability and/or performance in sports is not the sole contributor to your self-worth. You have friends who are not athletes, and you frequently talk about non-sport-related topics in social situations.
7. You have emotional reactions that most people would consider reasonable when shit goes wrong (e.g., losing, failing, getting penalized, getting injured, etc.).

The fact that you are reading this book is a sign that you already possess some level of athletic identity. You will notice from our definition that there are two elements to athletic identity: your inner thoughts and feelings about being an athlete, and the extent to which others see you as an athlete (or more correctly, how you perceive that they see you).[2] We develop our inner and outer athletic identities when we do endurance sport—we learn skills and techniques, we develop fitness, and we interact with fellow athletes. A sign that our internal athletic identity is maturing is our use of the sport to define our athleticism. *I'm a triathlete. I'm a CrossFit® athlete. I'm a runner.* A sign that our outer athletic identity is getting stronger comes when we notice others are calling us that too.

The nuts and bolts of building a mature athletic identity.

Having a mature athletic identity is crucial to becoming a brave athlete. Notice that we use the word "mature" instead of "strong" when describing the ideal athletic identity. A mature identity is fully grown and has not developed at the expense of all other identities (e.g., a partner, a worker, a friend, and so on). A mature athletic identity fuels confidence, grit, contentment, and a sense of healthy competitiveness. Although a strong athletic identity also fuels these qualities, it often comes with a giant dollop of negative consequence. For example, people with a very strong athletic identity often struggle to cope with injury and suffer excessive emotional distress when they are not able to train.

2 S. A. Nasco, and W. M. Webb, "Towards an Expanded Measure of Athletic Identity: The Inclusion of Public and Private Dimensions," *Journal of Sport and Exercise Psychology* 28 (2006): 434–453.

To understand how to build athletic identity, we need to dig a little deeper into its psychological roots—the awkward-sounding "**self-schema.**" That refers to the thoughts people have about themselves in different areas of life—a sort of mental blueprint of who they are, what they can do, and how they think others perceive them. Think of a self-schema as cognitive scaffolding or a self-stereotype—how your thoughts are assembled about aspects of yourself. *Oh, I'm not that competitive* or *I'm a pretty outgoing person* are types of self-schema statements. You have self-schema about many different spheres of your life—your identity as a romantic partner, as an employee or student, as a parent, a friend, an athlete, or whatever. All these identities feed into your broader "self-concept," an overall sense of who you are, what your attributes are, and what and why certain things are important to you. The strength of your overall self-concept is determined by the relative importance you give to each of your identities. For example, if you consider that being a good parent (your parent identity) is more important than being a good athlete (your athletic identity), then your parent identity contributes more to your overall self-concept than your athletic identity. Predictably, your individual self-schemas are interconnected—they talk to one another. After all, thoughts and feelings don't exist in a vacuum. Feeling crappy or amazing about one aspect of your life can contaminate your other identities. It's quite unusual to find athletes who suffer from self-schema knots in only one aspect of their lives. This is actually good news because it means that improving the way you think and feel about yourself as an athlete can have a positive knock-on effect in other areas of your life too.

Your athletic self-schema develops from memories of your experiences but is also influenced by expectations of what you think your future self will be like in certain situations. For example, your self-schema as a runner would likely be strong if you ran track and cross-country in college, but you might also have a basic self-schema of being a triathlete even if you've never been one. Why? Because you know the discipline and commitment needed to be an athlete and you currently swim and bike to keep fit. In areas where you have little or no experience or you're simply indifferent, you might have no schema at all. In these cases, you're said to be aschematic in that area. For example, I'm aschematic about being a farmer. Lesley is aschematic about being a neat and tidy person. Ahem.

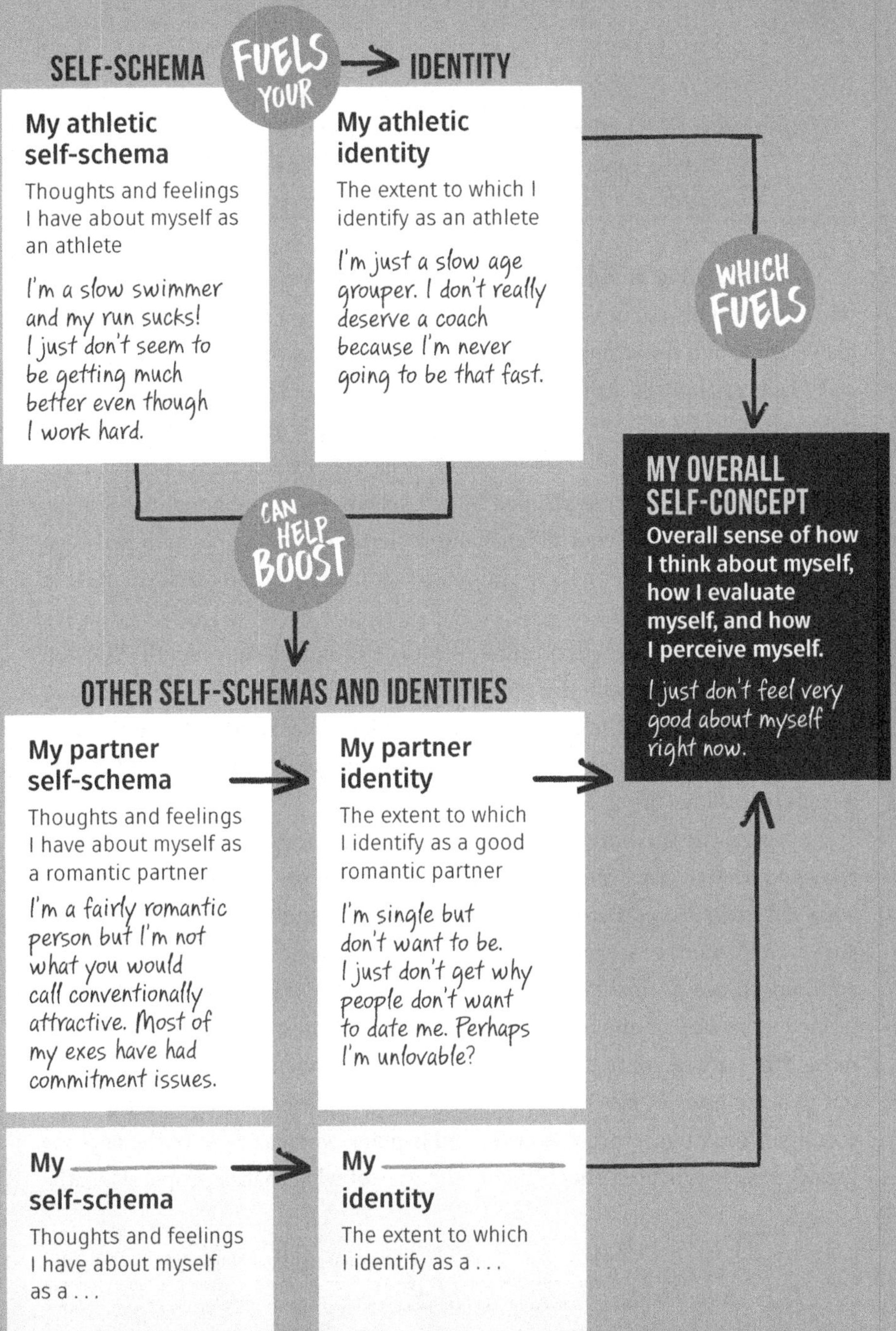

SELF-SCHEMA FUELS YOUR → **IDENTITY**

My athletic self-schema

Thoughts and feelings I have about myself as an athlete

I'm a slow swimmer and my run sucks! I just don't seem to be getting much better even though I work hard.

My athletic identity

The extent to which I identify as an athlete

I'm just a slow age grouper. I don't really deserve a coach because I'm never going to be that fast.

WHICH FUELS ↓

MY OVERALL SELF-CONCEPT

Overall sense of how I think about myself, how I evaluate myself, and how I perceive myself.

I just don't feel very good about myself right now.

CAN HELP BOOST ↓

OTHER SELF-SCHEMAS AND IDENTITIES

My partner self-schema →

Thoughts and feelings I have about myself as a romantic partner

I'm a fairly romantic person but I'm not what you would call conventionally attractive. Most of my exes have had commitment issues.

My partner identity →

The extent to which I identify as a good romantic partner

I'm single but don't want to be. I just don't get why people don't want to date me. Perhaps I'm unlovable?

My ______ self-schema →

Thoughts and feelings I have about myself as a . . .

My ______ identity →

The extent to which I identify as a . . .

Your SELF-SCHEMA shapes your expectations of what you *think* you can do, what you attempt and persist at, how you explain your success and failure, and how you want others to see you in certain areas of life.

Understanding an athlete's self-schema is important because it helps us make predictions about the sorts of situations that are likely to feel stressful, challenging, and rewarding to you and, critically, what things we need to focus on to help you improve confidence and grit, take responsibility, and learn acceptance skills ("owning it"). This means that building a mature athletic identity requires that your athletic self-schema is relatively free of bugs and gremlins. How do we know if you're plagued by self-schema bugs and gremlins? Simple. We ask you to describe yourself and your athleticism, and we listen to what you say and how you say it. We'll ask you to do that later and then teach you how to become your own shrink.

In this chapter, we focus on athletes who need their athletic identity boosted or strengthened, like Katherine. We devote other chapters of this book to helping athletes cope with the exact opposite problem—an overdeveloped sense of athletic identity and the shit balls that come down the pike when you've become a one-dimensional bore.

It's important to note that there's really no science to back up a claim that someone needs to have his or her athletic identity grown and matured (or bushwhacked back). Sure, there are plenty of published studies about how to measure athletic identity as well as how to classify people according to the strength and importance of this identification, but they have virtually no practical relevance to you as an endurance athlete because it doesn't tell you what to do next.[3] This isn't meant to denigrate the utility of the science, but simply to point out that the goals of psychological research and the endurance athlete are not the same. You want to become faster and happier, whereas most of the psychological research focuses on advancing theories of what makes people tick, ath-

3 B. W. Brewer, and A. E. Cornelius, "Norms and Factorial Invariance of the Athletic Identity Measurement Scale (AIMS)," *Academic Athletic Journal* (Fall 2002): 103–113; T. J. Curry and J. S. Weaner, "Sport Identity Salience, Commitment, and the Involvement of Self in Role: Measurement Issues," *Sociology of Sport Journal* 4 (1987): 280–288.

letically speaking. There are plenty of reasons why both are noble causes, but to figure out what we *can* do, let's get back to Katherine.

Katherine doesn't see herself as an athlete. So what, you might ask? If she's getting out there, enjoying most of her experiences in sport, and doing her best, is deeper analysis really needed? Well, this is really up to Katherine. Our litmus test for helping Katherine decide whether it's worth exploring further is usually a conversation that goes something like this:

Simon: Katherine, are you interested in working on how you think and feel about yourself as an athlete?

Katherine: What do you mean?

Simon: Well, we've noticed that when you talk about yourself, you often say things that suggest you don't feel worthy of being called an athlete.

Katherine: Well, that's because I'm not. I mean, that's why I'm looking for a coach. I want to become an athlete.

Simon: That's my point. You already train and compete as a runner but don't see yourself as an athlete.

Katherine: You mean the mindset?

Simon: Yeah, sort of. More like how you think of yourself. You want to look in the mirror and see an athlete, inside and out, right?

Katherine: Yes!

Because we know that one self-schema can influence another, it should come as no surprise that Katherine was pretty self-critical of a few of her other identities too. We might expect to see some trickle-down effects in other areas of her life simply by targeting her athletic world.

Common athletic identity issues.

Katherine has what we call an immature athletic identity—both her internal and external senses of being an athlete need booster seats. Before we focus on how to help athletes like Katherine, let's look at a few other athletic identity issues we've come across in our work with athletes. These types are entirely our own creation. They've certainly not been subject to rigorous scientific analysis, but they reflect some of the common themes we've noticed, and grouping them in this way illustrates the underlying psychology of identity formation. There are plenty of other reasons why athletic identity and the precursory self-schema can be a tad wobbly. It's worth pointing out that these different types of identity issues don't necessarily have unique solutions. You'll find some quick tips to help you begin to reshape your thinking, but the real fixes come with the exercises later in this chapter. The goal is to help you to recognize some of the thoughts and feelings you experience.

Problems with identity mismatch

Sometimes there's a big mismatch between the inner and outer worlds of your athletic identity. For example, if others see you as an athlete but you don't feel like one, there's a mismatch. Conversely, if you feel like an athlete but some people constantly tell you that you're not really one, there's a mismatch. Identity mismatch can also develop in subtle ways. For example, in the United States, there's a growing perception that you're not a real triathlete until you've done an Ironman. Just ask any short-course athlete how many times they've been asked when they will do an Ironman-distance race. It can get pretty irritating.

Our internal and external athletic identities can also diverge because of the people we spend time around. For example, I'm a mid-pack age-group triathlete (Simon) who married a professional world champion (Lesley). My internal athletic identity initially took a beating because I moved in with someone who had an external athletic identity forged in steel. When you're constantly surrounded by reminders of what it's like to be a "real athlete"—how they train, how they recover, how they eat—your internal athletic identity starts to backtrack a little. My epic three-hour rides no longer felt that epic anymore. If you want to fast-track your way to a case of the *Justas* (as in, "Oh, I'm just a . . ."), then date a professional triathlete. It can be painfully demoralizing until your self-schema finally recalibrates.

★ **Quick tips to help.** Make sure that you stretch your own self-schema by training with people of different experience levels and athletic ability. When you train only with people who are much faster or much slower, it can affect the way you think about your own ability. It's hard to feel great when you're constantly getting dropped by others, and there's the danger of false comfort that comes with always being the top dog. A good strategy is to "periodize" your training partners. By matching your training partners to your particular session or phase of training (e.g., avoiding the hammerheads on your easy days) you can make sure your training goals are met and your self-schema isn't always getting aggravated.

Problems with a volatile identity

If your thoughts of "I'm an athlete" fluctuate wildly, then your athletic identity is said to be "volatile." One week you might feel like a total stud, but another week you feel like a total dud. This is not to be confused with changes in confidence, which fluctuates normally for all athletes. For those with a volatile identity, "feeling like an athlete" is strongly influenced by training habits. Do less training and you'll feel less like an athlete. Because consistent training is the behavioral demonstration of athletic identity, establishing rock-solid training habits will help you ride out the bumps in the road and contribute to you feeling like an athlete. This is one reason why chronic injury can be so emotionally challenging. It's as if someone is using an eraser on your athleticism.

★ **Quick tips to help.** Consistency and successful completion of training are key to helping you stabilize your athletic identity. Set attainable goals and patterns that you can sustain for weeks and months, not just a weekend. Smashing yourself after a break in order to kick-start your sense of "feeling like an athlete" again may work for a few days, but it's not sustainable and often proves to be a recipe for injury.

Problems with chasing a former identity

If you have prior experience being a "good" athlete, but various life events and decisions have turned you into an inactive and unfit version of yourself, returning to sport can spawn an identity crisis because comebacks tend to get emotionally calibrated to your former self. Perhaps you used to be one of the top dogs on the local tri scene. Everyone knew you as the guy because you'd crush the local group ride or be one of the fastest at your club run sessions. After a two-year hiatus due to injury, work, or family stuff, you come back to the sport. You're still feisty and competitive, except you're now as slow as molasses (at least in your eyes). Guys you used to beat with ease seemed to have gotten a lot better and are now passing you effortlessly. Perhaps you just get really demoralized at seeing your mile pace slower than you've ever seen it before. This can be extremely frustrating and, in some instances, emotionally challenging enough to undermine motivation and make you question whether it's even worth it anymore. The solution here is to focus on building a new identity in the sport, a revised sense of what's important and how you measure success—your new normal.

★ **Quick tips to help.** Think about your new identity as the beginning phase of a makeover, or the start of a 2.0 version of your former athletic self. Instead of recalling the past with rosy retrospection, focus on what you didn't like about your training habits back then and what you plan to do differently this time around. Perhaps you neglected stretching, or didn't do any analysis of your run biomechanics to reduce risk of injury. Perhaps you overtrained. During training sessions, spend more time on process goals such as technique and form instead of outcome goals like overall time or average pace for a set distance.

Problems with identity foreclosure

When people settle on a sense of self too soon, psychologists call it identity foreclosure. It's the premature termination of identity growth because they think they already know who they are. In essence they stop critically evaluating the belief system that comes with their identity. Think of teens who grow up with a very firm belief system without ever really questioning it. It's not a mature identity because it never really got a chance to develop in the first place. However, once they get older they may start to question their belief system and even revisit an identity previously discounted. In endurance sports, identity foreclosure can occur at any time, whether it's the clumsy kids who quickly decide they are "not the sporty type" or the top pros who retire prematurely because they have become disillusioned with the sport or have become reliant on external factors to motivate them.

Feeling as though you've lost sight of what's important in life or your sport is one signal that you are at risk of identity foreclosure. For example, no longer enjoying the sport the way you used to or feeling trapped by circumstances can be signs that you're losing touch with an identity that got you there in the first place.

Identity foreclosure is especially common during childhood because that's when we're quite vulnerable to adopting the belief system of others or we have experiences that turn us off from something altogether. For example, you might have been repeatedly chosen last in PE when it was time to pick teams. You may have even been rather good at sports, but your parents didn't encourage your participation or your friends made fun of you. These can all lead to athletic identity foreclosure. Dealing with it can be especially necessary when trying to move someone off the couch. The case study at the end of the chapter is proof that you can reverse identity foreclosure in yourself or someone close to you.

★ **Quick tips to help.** For the newbie: Seek the guidance of other athletes to help you get started and try to avoid training on your own. Most local clubs have sessions designed for beginners. Begin by simply going to watch. Another strategy is to find a buddy who is willing to go on the transformational journey with you. For the experienced athlete: Focus on your original motives and try to connect your training with your value system.

FIXING ATHLETIC IDENTITY ISSUES

There are two types of solutions to help boost athletic identity. Either you can change the underlying beliefs that you hold about yourself as an athlete (your athletic self-schema), or you simply pretend to be an identity that you're not. Yup, you can fake it. It's called acting. Changing your self-schema is an inside-to-out strategy (targeting thoughts to change feelings to change actions), whereas *faking it* is an outside-to-in strategy (targeting actions to influence feelings to change thoughts). Both strategies are grounded in good scientific evidence. The former works by addressing the fundamental root causes but takes time, effort, and more motivation on your part. The latter is a quicker fix but doesn't directly address the underlying problem. We recommend using both techniques because they help you to develop a mature athletic identity quicker than if each one was used in isolation.

Build your athletic identity by fixing your self-schema.

Regardless of the type of identity conundrum you are experiencing, the most direct solution is to change the underlying source code, your athletic self-schema.

Remember, athletic self-schema is the cognitive scaffolding of thinking and feeling like an athlete. Yeah, so we need to change that. *Gulp.* How realistic is it to expect to change your fundamental belief system as an athlete and recalibrate the expectations you have of yourself in the sport? It turns out that it's entirely realistic. It just takes a bit of work.

Grit your teeth; we're going deep

We need to get a bit metaphysical for a moment. You're now familiar with the concepts of athletic self-schema, athletic identity, and self-concept. We're going to introduce another concept, the Definable You.

The Definable You refers to your characteristics, attributes, and experiences that can be measured objectively. So, whether you like it or not, the Definable You is just there. Tough shit. For example, you weigh 163 pounds, you have 28 percent body fat, you have a measured functional threshold power (FTP) of 245 watts, you've lived in 7 different houses, you have 2 kids, you've held 9 jobs, you have finished 4 half-marathons, you have no appendix, and you've had 2 speeding tickets. The Definable You is what it is. You can't change the past. It's like an encyclopedia-size resume of yourself, but with less lying.

The Definable You	**Athletic self-schema**	**Athletic identity** →	**SELF-CONCEPT**
Measurable things about yourself and your athletic history	The thoughts and feelings you have about yourself as an athlete	The extent to which you identify as an athlete	Your overall judgment of yourself as a person

Knowing the difference between the various aspects of "self" is the critical first step to fixing the cluster f*ck you've created about yourself in your own head. To show you why it's such a cluster f*ck, we need an analogy.

The chess game analogy

Think of the Definable You as a chessboard. It's an objective thing at any particular point in time. It exists regardless of whether a game is being played or not. Just as it isn't up for debate whether a chessboard contains squares or circles, it isn't up for debate that you've run a 44:55 for a 10K (or whatever your PR is), that you weigh 170 pounds, that you got top 10 in your age group at Nationals, that you can hold 215 watts on the bike for an hour, that you've never done an Ironman, and that you pulled out of your first 70.3 last year because you had an asthma attack during the swim. You can't change these facts. They just are. That is your chessboard.

In contrast, the thoughts and feelings you have about yourself are your chess pieces. They are the mental representations of the Definable You, plus the thoughts about the thoughts (called metacognition, as in *I wish I didn't feel like this!* or *Why do I think this way?*). Each chess piece is a different thought or emotion. Some are pleasant thoughts, some unpleasant; some are negative emotions, some positive. "Feeling fat" is a chess piece because it's a thought, whereas your actual measured body composition is part of your chessboard. Not feeling like an athlete is a chess piece; being an athlete is part of your chessboard (if you train and compete in sport, you're an athlete, whether you like it or not!). Thinking *I could never do that* is a chess piece based on aspects of the Definable You—what you've done in the past, your fitness or skill level, and so on. It's irrelevant whether you could do it or not, because it's a subjective representation and evaluation of yourself and what you think you can do.

Sometimes your chess pieces attack other pieces, and sometimes they defend. Sometimes they are quiet and just sit there. For example, on some days you might feel very much like an athlete, but on other days you don't. Some days you have lots of confidence in your athletic ability; other days you don't. The pieces move, but the board doesn't. When we flood the board with chess pieces, it can feel overwhelming because they compete for our attention and can trick us into thinking that their evaluation is reality. When you spend time worrying about the worry (metacognition), you are piling on yet more chess pieces. When your head turns into a bloody battle between thoughts of not being good enough or worthy enough (a chess piece) but desperately wishing you were (another chess piece), all you can think and feel is struggle and conflict (more chess pieces), perhaps caught up in the thinking that one side must win in order for you to be happy (oh God, yet another chess piece). Before you know it, it can look more like a game of Jenga, and that's bloody exhausting. The good news is there is a critical element missing from our analogy: the chess player. So here's

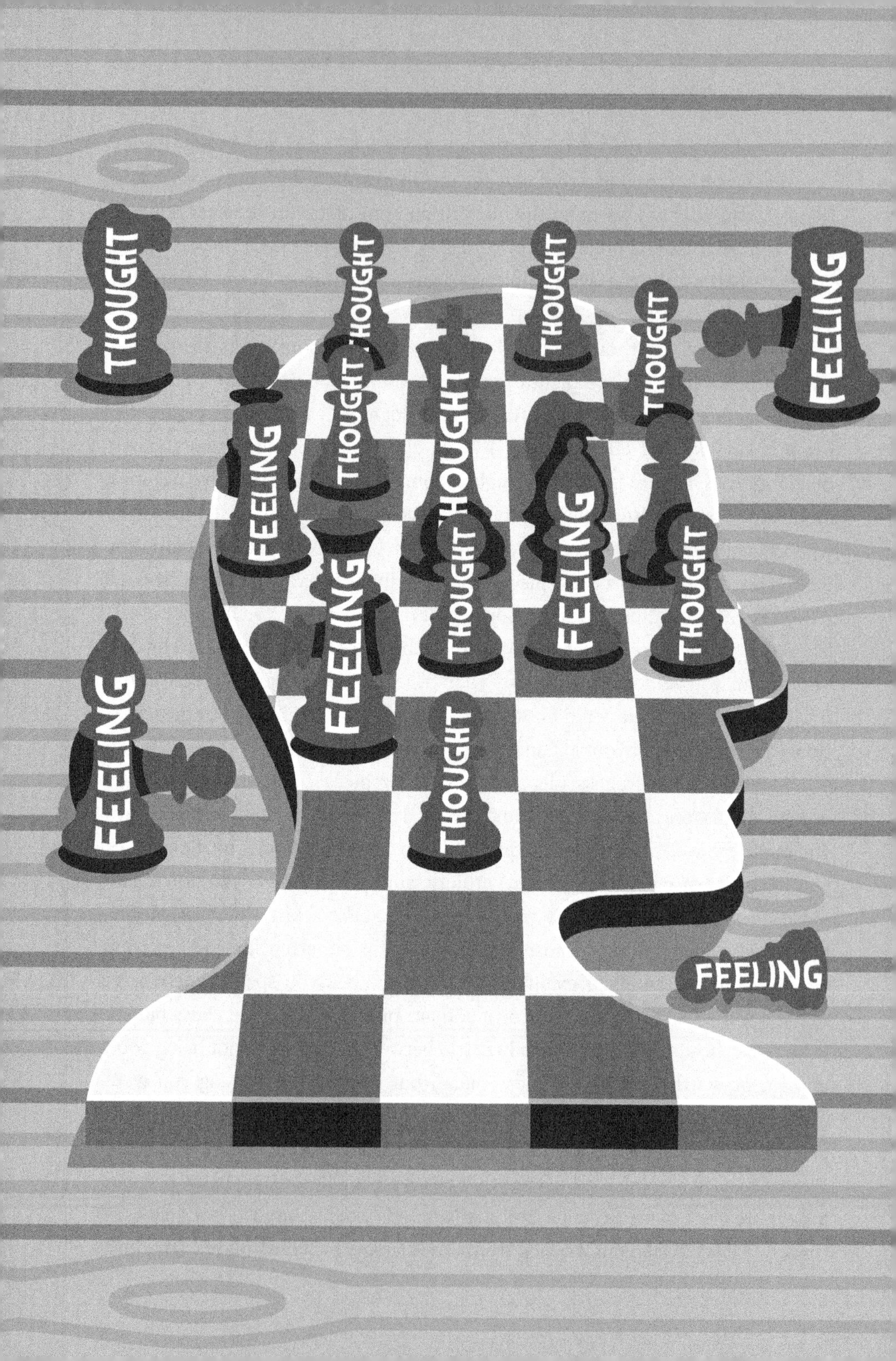

THOUGHT
THOUGHT
THOUGHT
THOUGHT
FEELING
THOUGHT
FEELING
THOUGHT
THOUGHT
FEELING
THOUGHT
FEELING
THOUGHT
FEELING
THOUGHT
FEELING

the big take-home lesson: **The thoughts and feelings you experience are not actually you at all because you are a chess player, not a chess piece. You experience your thoughts but you are not actually them. You are the carrying container of the experience; you are not the experience itself.** If you're ever going to free yourself from thoughts and feelings you don't want, then the first step is practicing a strategy called detachment. Detachment is a technique designed to unglue you from the way you experience you. Wait, what? Let's demonstrate this existential brain-twister with Exercise 1 (p. 42).

Changing the narrative about yourself

Athletes who struggle with identity conflicts have usually convinced themselves that they are their thoughts and emotions. Telling yourself that you will *never be a real athlete* or that you're *just a slow age grouper* is to make the mistake of thinking thoughts and feelings are the same thing as you. Yeah, stop doing that.

You can decide which of your athlete-related thoughts and feelings you want to ignore and which you want to listen to. What you currently listen to is equivalent to your athletic identity. This is why athletic identity is not about your speed, placings, leanness, or amount of training. A mature athletic identity is simply a special configuration of thoughts about emotions. For chess nerds, think of the Stonewall Attack or the King's Indian attack: the perfect balance of confidence and risk. Even if you don't always feel in control of what those thoughts and feelings are, you are always in control of what you choose to do with them. This is a critical distinction: we can't make certain thoughts and feelings magically disappear, but we can control which of them we listen to, and we can use actions to help shape them. But first we need to know more about you.

Take a minute to describe yourself as an athlete in Exercise 2 (p. 43). Once you have labeled your self-description, you can begin to spot possible mismatches between the facts about yourself and your thoughts. Don't get bogged down with exact words or phrases, but instead focus on general themes. For example, "I doubt my ability, but I've actually accomplished quite a lot."

EXERCISE 1

WATCHING THE SUCK

Do this exercise while sitting comfortably and in a quiet environment.

Recall a recent experience that you've had in sport that felt less than stellar, preferably one that totally sucked. It could have been a race that didn't go well, a training session that went sideways, or some other thing that felt awful.

Recreate that experience in your head—the sights, sounds, and smells, everything that makes it come back to life. Don't worry if you find this difficult. It is. Once you've got the movie playing, leave your body and hover above it, as if you were a human drone, following yourself around, watching yourself go through the suck. You can see yourself, but you are not you in the moment. I know, it sounds bananas.

Pick out the thoughts and feelings the "you" down on the ground is experiencing. Try to be aware enough to label the experience but not actually have it (a bit like watching a friend grimace in a race and just knowing what's going through their mind). If it helps, see thought bubbles appear with the stuff that was going through your head. Now start describing and labeling what you see and the thoughts and feelings you remember yourself having: *Oh yes, that's the part when Judith caught me. She's coming up on the inside. And now she's passing me. There's the first thought: "Judith is passing me? I mean, really? F*cking Judith?" And there goes the second thought: "I must be having a bad day if she's caught me. See how my whole body starts to tense because I'm so pissed at myself?"* And so on. If you find yourself wandering down and into the body of the you below, get back up to your drone!

Continue to label the thought bubbles for another few minutes.

Congratulations! You've just managed to detach yourself from a cognitive and emotional experience! The real you (the chess player) was up in the drone, while your thoughts and feelings (your chess pieces) were busy down below making your life hell. The next time you get overwhelmed by feelings of not being good enough or worthy enough as an athlete, use this exercise to separate the real you from the painful self-schema that's causing you problems. This technique is also used extensively in the practice of meditation because it helps us to avoid getting bogged down or overwhelmed by negative thoughts and feelings.

TELL ME ABOUT YOURSELF AS AN ATHLETE

In the space below, describe yourself as an athlete. No one else is going to read this, so try to be as honest as you can. Know that there isn't a right or wrong answer—this is just a chance for you to write about your athleticism. Write whatever you want in the way that feels most natural.

Now reread your self-description and circle all the words or statements that relate to the Definable You (things that are factually accurate). Read it through a second time and underline all of the words or statements that reflect thoughts or feelings about yourself as an athlete.

Here's an example of self-description, coded for facts, thoughts, and feelings:

I'm Isaac, an age-group triathlete and mountain biker. I'm 34 and have been racing for about 6 years. It's hard to train as much as I want because I have a new baby and demanding job! I enjoy racing but love the training most of all. I'm a pretty decent athlete—I ran track and cross country in high school and was headed to UNC on a scholarship but injured my ACL in my senior year. In triathlon, I do sprint- and Olympic-distance racing. My run is my fastest sport but my swimming sucks! I didn't grow up as a swimmer, so I'm never going to be that good at it. I really want to improve, but I think that I lack a bit of confidence to really lay it all out there. When it starts to get hard, I mentally back down. Perhaps I just don't want to hurt that much. Etc., etc.

Getting your self-schema ducks in a row

To realign our self-schema, we need to revisit the hallmarks of a mature athletic identity. Why? To (1) identify which of our current thoughts and feeling are compatible with it, (2) highlight the thoughts we need to pay more attention to in order to improve athletic identity, and (3) identify concrete actions we can take on a regular basis to help the good thoughts "stick." Let's look at some examples:

ATTRIBUTE #2: *I call myself an athlete.*

Current thoughts and actions	What I will say to myself / Actions I will take
Current thoughts and actions: *Yes, I train my ass off and compete for a local XC team. I'm always reading trail-running mags. Work colleagues call me Forrest Gump!* *I secretly love that they think of me as a badass athlete.*	**What I will say to myself:** *When at the bigger races or around the top guys, tell myself that I've put the work in, and that I belong there.* **Actions I will take:** *Be more proactive about the marginal gains. Get a biomechanical analysis (finally!) and use foam roller six nights a week!*

ATTRIBUTE #4: *I don't feel the need to prove it to others.*

Current thoughts and actions	What I will say to myself / Actions I will take
Current thoughts and actions: *Yup, I'm guilty of posting my workout stats on social media to show that I'm a badass. Want people to see how hard I work and love seeing people comment on it.*	**What I will say to myself:** *I will ask myself, why am I posting this? To show off? To encourage others? Does it really do that?* **Actions I will take:** *Stop posting screen captures of my workouts on social media that are solely to fish for likes. Try to add posts about sessions in which I struggled or learned a valuable lesson.*

Actions are a great way to help realign thoughts and feelings because they become part of the Definable You (observable facts about yourself). Your brain is forced to listen to factually accurate things about yourself when it tries to make sense of situations. It doesn't always interpret them correctly, but it is forced to pay attention to them. In essence, we are making your chessboard bigger by adding new squares that exemplify a mature athletic identity. Try it in Exercise 3.

GETTING YOUR SELF-SCHEMA DUCKS IN A ROW

Let's take a look at how your current thoughts and actions match up with the self-schema of a mature athletic identity. The statements that follow are what we are striving toward. It doesn't matter if this isn't you now. In the space below each statement, describe how your current actions and thoughts do or don't match up. Then think through how you can modify them to better align with a mature athletic identity. In other words, going forward what things will you say to yourself to help nurture maturity, and what actions will you take to reinforce this thinking?

I currently participate in sports or exercise.

Current thoughts and actions:

What I will say to myself:

Actions I will take:

I call myself an athlete.

Current thoughts and actions:

What I will say to myself:

Actions I will take:

Others call me an athlete.

Current thoughts and actions:

What I will say to myself:

Actions I will take:

Continued

I am not embarrassed about my athletic ability or performance. I don't feel the need to prove it to others.

Current thoughts and actions:

What I will say to myself:

Actions I will take:

I don't engage in excessive self-criticism or self-aggrandizement about my ability or performance.

Current thoughts and actions:

What I will say to myself:

Actions I will take:

I have pastimes or hobbies outside of sport. I have non-athlete friends and/or I enjoy talking about non-sports-related topics in social situations.

Current thoughts and actions:

What I will say to myself:

Actions I will take:

I have emotional reactions that most people would consider reasonable when shit goes wrong.

Current thoughts and actions:

What I will say to myself:

Actions I will take:

Build your athletic identity by faking it.

It turns out that following advice to "just be yourself" is often the worst thing you can do. Scientific evidence increasingly suggests that pretending to be someone else can be a powerful strategy to instantly transform into an aspirational version of yourself. Your true self might be shy, self-critical, and easily intimidated by the competition, but what if for just a few hours you could try on a new athletic identity—someone who thrives in competition, has tons of confidence, refuses to quit, and doesn't care what others think? Anecdotally, we know that many top performers already do this. For years, Beyoncé performed as Sasha Fierce until her true identity caught up. Lesley competes as the gritty boxer, Paddy McGinty. We call these temporary identities "alter egos" and they aren't just for superhero movies or people with dissociative identity disorders. Using an alternative identity can play a strong therapeutic role in psychotherapy, and new evidence suggests that pretending can favorably alter your biochemistry and improve performance.[4] Yes, "fake it 'til you make it" is now backed by science.

Regardless of the scientific basis for forming an alter ego, we find that many athletes are relieved to know that they don't have to undergo a complete personality makeover to develop the athletic identity they want. It's far less intimidating to simply suit up as a new character rather than tackle years of entrenched thinking. Until the true identity has a chance to catch up (through fixing self-schema and experience), stepping into some new shoes is a great way to start.

We've created an alter ego development kit (Exercise 4, p. 50) to help you flesh out your character. The first step in creating your athletic alter ego is to think of the attributes you want your new identity to have. It sometimes helps to think of actual people or fictional characters that embody the identity you're seeking. Perhaps you're looking for a sleek ninja or a bare-knuckle boxer? Perhaps you want to think and act like an actual athlete you admire for his or her

---

4 E. Berne, *Transactional Analysis in Psychotherapy* (New York: Ballantine Books, 1986); Dana R. Carney et al., "Review and Summary of Research on the Embodied Effects of Expansive (vs. Contractive) Nonverbal Displays," *Psychological Science* 26, no. 5 (May 2015): 657–663; A. J. Cuddy et al., "Preparatory Power Posing Affects Nonverbal Presence and Job Interview Performance," *Journal of Applied Psychology* 100, no. 4 (July 2015): 1286–1295.

guts and tenacity. If there are people or characters who remind you of this identity, make a note of them to help you get into character. Then choose a name for your alter ego that matches the traits of your character and develop a backstory. How did they develop these traits? What kind of life have they experienced? What have they already endured? The final elements in bringing the character to life involve thinking through the behaviors and self-talk that get you into the mindset of the identity. They include personal mantras, actions, and routines, as well as physical reminders that help you step into that identity. The great advantage of being an athlete is that we already have good triggers for the transition—our race kit can literally become our costume.

Before you get to work, meet Lesley's alter ego, Paddy McGinty. Those of you who know Lesley also know Paddy! Lesley is a really sweet girl, but when Paddy shows up, you get the f*ck out of the way.

LESLEY PATERSON'S ALTER EGO

Name: Paddy McGinty

Characteristics: An old-school boxer. Not graceful or pretty but a rough-around-the-edges fighter. Thrives on being the underdog. Loves tough conditions. Turns feral when backed into a corner. Will out-suffer anyone. Gets knocked down five times, will get up six. When in pain or discomfort, raises the stakes by asking, "Is that all you've got?"

INSPIRATION

My alter ego reminds me of . . . Tom Hardy's MMA character in the movie *Warrior*. William Wallace in *Braveheart*.

Their backstory: Started with nothing. Fought against impossible odds to win. People always write him off, but he out-works and out-suffers everyone. Finishes every match beaten and bloody but still standing.

How I will get into character: I become Paddy when I put on my race suit or certain types of training gear for hard sessions.

How I will act: Avoid eye contact with other competitors before the race starts. Wear hoodie and headphones. Walk everywhere with strong body language and real sense of purpose. Shoulders up, chest out. Eyes say "not to be f*cked with."

Things I will say to myself: Always fight. It's never over.

Something I will wear or do: Write "I am Free" and "Be Brave" in big letters on my forearms before a race. Being brave is about having the courage to give it everything. "I am free" reminds me to not care about expectations. On good days and bad days, being free is about just getting lost in the personal struggle.

EXERCISE 4

ALTER EGO DEVELOPMENT KIT

Name: *Give your alter ego a name that fits his or her personality*

Characteristics: *Describe the traits or personality of your alter ego*

INSPIRATION

My alter ego reminds me of . . . *List people or characters whom your alter ego reminds you of*

Their backstory: *Describe the kind of life your alter ego has lived; things already endured*

How I will get into character: *Describe how you will mark the transition*

How I will act: *Describe your posture, how you will walk and talk, or other actions that get you into character*

Things I will say to myself: *Include statements or mantras that are typical of how your alter ego thinks*

Something I will wear or do: *Describe physical reminders you can use that will be noticeable during races*

CASE STUDY

BUT I'M NOT THE SPORTY TYPE!

Remedying athletic identity foreclosure

MEET MY SISTER, Victoria Marshall, a 48-year-old business owner who lives with her hubby and three kids in the center of Paris, France. As a teen, she experienced sports only when forced to by school PE teachers and veered away from almost anything physical and competitive. By 15 years of age, Victoria was unapologetically unathletic. For the next 31 years, she did virtually no exercise, wasn't remotely interested in sports and didn't own a single pair of sneakers. (How is that even possible?) She led an active lifestyle but only because she lived in Paris and had to walk a lot. She certainly never equated any of this with exercise. My sister's athletic self-schema stopped growing at age 15.

Tired of the growing muffin top and feeling exhausted from work, she agreed to let us help her start a fitness regime using the principle of tiny habits. (See Chapter 4 for more information about this motivational baking powder.) Her initial 10-minute training sessions consisted of jogging for 1 minute and then walking for 1 minute. We always talked about her program in terms of "training sessions" to help nurture her athletic identity. When she could sustain 20 minutes of walk/jog, she started doing separate 10-minute walk/jogs on hills (hill interval training) plus the occasional 10-second burst of running as fast as she could (sprint training). After three months, her hubby and I persuaded her to enter a local women's 5K. She finished and was invigorated. Being around thousands of other women who were running, jogging, and walking, she realized she wasn't out of place at all. Then the power of goal setting was introduced—next came a 10K, then a 15K. Energy levels were up, muscle tone was up, and the muffin top was shrinking. She was hooked.

One year after her first 10-minute walk/jog training session, my sister finished an 18-kilometer hilly trail race in which she ran continuously for 2 hours and 20 minutes. She started reading running shoe reviews and asking about hydration packs. Her athletic identity foreclosure was being revisited. A new, healthy part of Victoria's self-concept was born (again).

3

I DON'T THINK I CAN

BUILDING CONFIDENCE AND SELF-BELIEF

Whether you think you can, or you think you can't—you're right. —HENRY FORD

Self-confidence is the psychological wonder drug. Everything improves when an athlete's self-confidence is high. Athletes with high confidence feel less anxious, relish adversity, set higher goals, try harder, tolerate more exertional pain, feel more in control, are more optimistic and enthusiastic, and do better under pressure. They also give less of a shit when things don't go according to plan. And these are just the outcomes that have been studied extensively.

What's the single-most-important psychological skill for an athlete to possess? It isn't motivation, tenacity, optimism, concentration, or attitude—it's **SELF-CONFIDENCE**, the belief that you can succeed.

Self-confidence is the nutrient-dense soil in the veggie patch of mental skills. It has an impact on almost every aspect of your identity and behavior as an athlete. Self-confidence is so fundamental to the brave athlete that when it improves, many other psychological complaints shrink quicker than a testicle in the English

Channel. Some problems disappear altogether. The effects of self-confidence training are remarkable. Many athletes feel a bit awkward talking about a desire to build sky-high levels of confidence, probably because it conjures up characteristics of the quintessential douchebag—arrogant, selfish, and superior. Arrogant athletes talk of their accomplishments, status, and superiority with such ease and conviction that you wonder what planet they're living on. Enjoyable company they do not make. When their self-absorption and lack of empathy become extreme, we call it "grandiose narcissism."[1] So when we talk about sky-high confidence, we're not talking about those peeps. We're talking about the athletes who are willing to put themselves out there, who can handle failure and criticism, take risks, rarely panic, and enjoy the challenge of getting stuck in. Developing self-confidence is an important first step in becoming a brave athlete.

We all know athletes who lack confidence or self-belief. At the extreme, they may engage in obsessive self-criticism, especially when things don't go right for them. A few even consider themselves abject failures. Excessive self-criticizers have been taught from a young age that being hard on yourself is the only way to make things better. In the face of perceived failure, they double down on the criticism and believe that if only they could try harder and be less forgiving of their failures and limitations they will eventually succeed. If that sounds like a perfectly reasonable perspective, then yup, that might be you. Most of us are somewhere in between, but many skew one way or the other. Take Dave and Katherine, whom we met in Chapter 2. When asked to describe themselves as athletes, here's what they said:

> Sure. I'm pretty good. I'll probably turn pro soon. I started off as a mountain biker and was racing elite for a few years. I smashed it. A guy I used to race with—and beat pretty consistently—switched to XTERRA and started doing really well—you

---

1 Contrary to popular belief, grandiose narcissists are not compensating for anything. They've got genuinely high self-esteem because they've been told constantly from an early age that their shit don't stink. Grandiose narcissists lack emotional sensitivity and will often retaliate against others who don't treat them as superior. In contrast, the vulnerable narcissist is much more emotionally sensitive but feels helpless, anxious, and victimized when people don't treat them as superior. Vulnerable narcissists are also self-absorbed but are usually compensating for fear of rejection and abandonment. Vulnerable narcissism often develops as a coping mechanism to deal with neglect, abuse, or a dismissive style of parent-child attachment. For every 100 people you meet, one is most likely a raging narcissist, and there's a 75 percent chance it's a man. If you're a woman, you probably already knew that.

> might know him [names a top XTERRA pro]—yeah, I know him pretty well. Anyway, so I gave XTERRA a go and got some success pretty quick. I won my age group at [Race X] and was third at Nationals. I qualified for Worlds in my first season. I don't know who else has done that. —DAVE, 27, OFF-ROAD TRIATHLETE

> I'm not sure I'd call myself an athlete. I mean, I'm trying to become one, you know. I'm just super slow. I'm probably the gal that just gets in your way. I think I lack a bit of confidence. I really enjoy it but . . . [long pause] . . . well, take my group runs for example. I hate getting left behind, not just because I'm slow but because the thought that other people are waiting for me makes me feel like shit. I'm sure they're all thinking, "Oh great, we have to wait for her again." D'you think I'm a lost cause? Do you only work with fast people? —KATHERINE, 46, RUNNER

When we first met April, a 38-year-old runner and successful physician, every other sentence was self-critical. She was coping with a lot of stressful life events, including a cheating husband, an angry and verbally aggressive former coach, and a chronic injury that prevented her from training. April's interpretation of events focused on self-blame:

> My run group all talk behind my back about how slow and useless I am. I want to get better, but everything I try ends up going badly. [My coach] fired me because I don't try hard enough; my husband wants a divorce because I'm too boring. I can't even be a good wife. I'm obviously worthless to everybody. I feel like a total loser.

When you peek at a person's inner dialogue, you soon get a sense of their self-judgment system. Just spend five minutes listening to the way someone talks about their abilities and you'll get a good look behind their curtain. It's bloody eye-opening.

The spank-hug system.

We often do a decent job of balancing self-criticism with self-congratulation. We call this the spank-hug system, and your brain does it for good reason. If you didn't have the ability to spank or hug yourself, you'd not feel motivated to get shit done, improve, or feel good when you succeed at something. From an evolutionary perspective, laziness and complacency aren't exactly characteristics you want splashing around in the gene pool. We need to be motivated. Our species depends on it. To help us stay this way, evolution has given us very specific brain chemistry and a self-regulation system that manifests as inner chatter of criticism (spanks) and encouragement (hugs). We meet a few of the key neurochemical players in your motivational spank-hug system in Chapters 1 and 4:

Dopamine
makes you want to do stuff and thanks you for it

Adrenaline
helps get your body ready for action

Endorphins
help stress, fear, and pain become more manageable

Oxytocin
helps us feel compassionate, trusting, and intimate

Serotonin
helps us feel significant, important, and less lonely

This neurochemical soup is influenced by genetics (nature), but the judgments we make about success and failure are determined mostly by our experiences (nurture). These experiences shape the type and extent of criticism and encouragement we feed ourselves. This is why two athletes can have the exact same race but interpret the results in very different ways. At an early age we learn from others—mainly parents—about the relationship between effort, ability, and outcome, and this shapes how we interpret success and failure. By the time you reach adulthood, your internal spank-hug system is set in motion, filtering your experiences and churning out judgments of yourself and others. For example, take these real comments from athletes in response to a race:

> That was piss easy. I was one of the strongest out there.
>
> —MALE CYCLIST, AFTER COMING IN 34TH IN A LOCAL ROAD RACE

> I mean, I did okay.
>
> —FEMALE RUNNER, AFTER FINISHING 4TH OVERALL

> I'm super stoked. I left it all out there.
>
> —FEMALE TRIATHLETE, AFTER COMING IN 25TH IN AGE GROUP

> Well, of course I won; the competition was shit.
>
> —MALE TRIATHLETE, AFTER WINNING OVERALL AMATEUR RACE

> My time was embarrassing. I was embarrassing.
>
> —FEMALE RUNNER, AFTER FINISHING 2ND IN AGE GROUP

What's the right balance of self-spanking and hugging if you want to maximize your athletic ability, happiness, and achievement? How do you correct imbalances in how frequently you spank and hug yourself? Of course real people don't think like this. Here's what real athletes say:

> How do I stop feeling so intimidated by [that person, this race, or a certain training session]?
>
> I lack confidence. I wish I had more, but it's hard to feel confident when you're as slow as I am.
>
> People tell me I have the talent but I need to believe in myself more.
>
> I'm a solid runner-biker, but I have zero confidence in the swim.
>
> I want to stop feeling like such a loser.
>
> I avoid the big races because I'm not a huge fan of getting my ass whooped.

The first thing to recognize is that these are just symptoms. Talking to yourself in a critical or demeaning way is simply a sign of a gremlin in your larger self-judgment system. Because most psychological self-help books for athletes focus on treating symptoms and not causes, problems usually come back quickly. If you don't feel worthy as a person, or doubt your ability to swim in the open ocean, no amount of staring into a mirror and repeating "I'm strong, I'm confident, and I'm ready" is going to help. Sorry to break the bad news. You are, however, more likely to notice spinach in your teeth, so it's not a total waste of time. Motivational pep talks are like hot baths. They soon go cold.

Don't get your confidence from the Internet.

Social media is littered with self-affirmation meme-turds that pretend the path to self-confidence is simple. Let's weigh up their usefulness in terms of spanks and hugs.

Never say anything about YOURSELF you do not want to come TRUE.

Wait, what? Dreadful double negatives aside, this pile o' twaddle suggests that the mere whiff of negative self-talk is enough to ensure a destiny filled with shitty disappointment. Great, now I feel guilty too. **USEFULNESS RATING: 1/10.**

Err, no you can't. Anybody with half a brain knows this. This bullshit was born from the (failed) self-esteem movement that spouted advice about "just trying" being all that matters. This is the reason your kid gets a medal just for showing up. As research has shown time and time again: wrong, wrong, wrong. **USEFULNESS RATING: 1/10.**

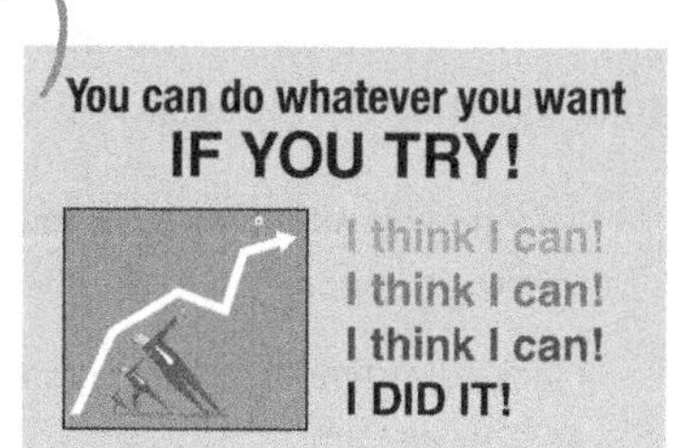

It's not *WHO* you are that holds you back, it's who you think you're *NOT*.

Wait, what? This Cirque du Soleil of bullshit hurts my eyes just reading it. Thinking I'm not Chris Froome isn't the f*cking problem. Trust me. **USEFULNESS RATING: 2/10.**

So if I believe in myself, I will have superior power that causes unexplainable things to happen? Makes total sense. **USEFULNESS RATING: 0/10.**

That's great. BTW, everyone else thinks you're a narcissistic idiot. **USEFULNESS RATING: 0/10.**

Yes, all a little unfair. We know these are just little motivational nuggets o' fun, but it's important to explain why they don't work. As we've now learned, having thoughts and feelings that you do want requires a domesticated Chimp brain, a strong Professor brain, and a Computer brain ready to offer up memories of confidence and success. All three brains must be working in harmony unless you want the offering of one brain to be swatted away like a fly by another brain. A common theme in meme-ville is an apparently sensible Professor brain thought being offered up as the path to happiness—*You can do whatever you want if you just try!* The problem is that if your Computer brain is littered with memories of failure and embarrassment, or your Chimp brain keeps shouting at you to avoid challenge for fear of even more failure and embarrassment, then this Professor-generated suggestion doesn't stand a chance. A second reason that these memes are turds is because they're all hugs, born almost certainly from the shitty self-esteem movement. You can stroke your Professor and Chimp all you like, but motivated behavior and confidence also require that you experience failure and then get the f*ck back up.

Pass the scalpel—we're about to open you up.

We constantly judge and evaluate ourselves. Nothing wrong with that. It helps us stay motivated, get shit done, and feel successful. Psychologists have identified lots of different ways in which we judge ourselves, our abilities, and our actions. Distinguishing between different types of self-judgment is important if we want to know what strategies are likely to work to help us be more accepting of, compassionate toward, and supportive of Team Me. Different forms of excessive self-judgment reflect different viruses in our operating system, a.k.a. our Computer brain. For example, an athlete who feels like a "total loser" needs something quite different from someone who lacks self-belief only as an athlete, who in turn needs something quite different from an otherwise confident athlete who is paralyzed by thoughts of an open swim start or descending on a mountain bike like a rocket. To help us decode this self-judgment system and learn when and how to intervene, we need a metaphor.

The Me Tree

Think of your entire self-judgment system as a tree—your *Me Tree.*[2] Each part of your tree reflects a different kind of judgment that you make about yourself and your abilities. Different parts of the tree support, or "prop up," other parts. Helping athletes identify and correct shitty self-judgments requires that we know how deep in the Me Tree the problem lies. The deeper the problem lies, the more mental firepower is needed to correct it.

Self-worth as deep roots. Your self-worth is based on deeply held feelings about your value and worth as a person. It is not about what you do but *who you are*—your values, morals, passions, and fundamental beliefs about yourself. The extent to which your emotional and psychological needs were met as a kid largely determines your self-worth. From a young age, we start to express psychological and emotional needs that we are highly motivated to meet: the need for love, security, safety, affirmation, belonging, and so on. If these needs are not met, we try to figure out why. Because our young brains are not capable of analyzing the causes logically and exhaustively, our focus often turns inward. We start to blame ourselves, and the conclusions we settle on are pretty damning: We are not good enough, not worthy enough, not competent enough, and so on. After all, why else would we not get attention, get rejected, or not feel encouraged or protected? Couple those ideas with a fixed mindset (see the nerd alert "You see failure, I see feedback" on p. 63), and the end result is usually the same: I must be a bad person of little value. The seeds of low self-worth take root. These biased beliefs grow and infect our adult brain like viruses.

Your root system of self-worth supports every other part of your Me Tree. When we reach adulthood, we hope that our root system of self-worth is healthy. A healthy self-worth means that you know your life is valuable and important and that you are loveable. A healthy self-worth also implies that your roots are not exposed to the air—meaning that your value as a person isn't influenced by the ups and downs of daily life. If you constantly compare yourself to other athletes and if losing makes you feel worthless as a person, it should be clear why

---

2 And like most metaphors, it breaks down under serious scrutiny. But it helps get across the notion that our self-judgment systems are hierarchical. The deeper the problem, the more you're f*cked.

The belief that you can perform a specific task at a certain level

I'm 80 percent confident that I can run a flat 5K in under 20 minutes.

Beliefs about your general abilities

I'm a good athlete.

Generalized emotional judgments about yourself based on what you've experienced in life

I'm a competent person.

Deeply held beliefs about your value and worth as a person

I'm a good person.

this is damaging to your mental health. Because self-worth is a relatively stable characteristic of our personality and it affects virtually every self-perception we have, changing it often requires the help of a mental health professional.

Self-esteem as a sturdy trunk. Many psychologists would consider self-worth and self-esteem to be the same thing, but we differentiate them because we view self-worth as more fundamental than self-esteem to happiness and human life. Self-esteem is the trunk of the tree because it supports everything above it. Just as a bad root system (low self-worth) can't create a healthy tree trunk (self-esteem), strong self-esteem is required to support self-confidence (the tree branches). It's extremely rare to find athletes who are supremely confident but have low self-esteem.

Even though your self-esteem is attached to your self-worth, it's above ground and more influenced by current experience. Self-esteem reflects generalized emotional judgments about yourself based on what you believe you've experienced, achieved, or accomplished. These "achievements" can be real and tangible (e.g., you've done well at school, at work, in sports, etc.) or they can be imagined (e.g., you've been told that you're successful). The curse of low self-esteem has been studied by psychologists and educators for decades, but it wasn't until the early 1970s that we were told to promote and protect the self-esteem of our youth at all costs. It turns out that this was a terrible idea and has since been widely debunked as a strategy for raising confident, skilled, and self-reflective youth. You can read about how the self-esteem movement failed one athlete in particular, Andy, in the case study at the end of this chapter.

Self-confidence as thick branches. Because self-confidence is defined by your perception of your ability, it has a future orientation and predicts what things people will attempt. When people use the term "self-belief" they are usually referring to self-confidence. Self-confidence is the first area in which your self-judgment system can appear differentiated, meaning that you can have strong and weak branches on the same tree. You can have high self-confidence in one area of your life but low self-confidence in another area. For example, you might be extremely confident as a marketing manager but lack confidence as an athlete. Even though low confidence can affect other aspects of your life, it rarely affects everything if your underlying self-esteem (tree trunk) is healthy. When you lack self-confidence across the board, the problem is most likely low self-esteem.

Self-efficacy as leaves. Self-efficacy is a task-specific form of confidence. Technically speaking, self-efficacy refers to your beliefs about your capability of producing a very specific level of performance.[3] For example, if we asked you to rate your confidence on a scale of 1 to 10 about your ability to run one mile in under six minutes tomorrow morning, this would be a self-efficacy rating. Self-efficacy is so critical to athletes because it predicts motivation, effort, and

3 A. Bandura, *Self-Efficacy: The Exercise of Control* (New York: Freeman, 1997).

You see failure, I see feedback

NERD ALERT!

DR. CAROL DWECK, a psychologist at Stanford University and a leading authority on self-belief systems, discovered that students' perceptions of their abilities played a pivotal role in their motivation and achievement. Dweck called these perceptions "mindsets."* A person with a **fixed mindset** assumes that talent, intelligence, and creative ability are static—they can't change in any fundamental way. A fixed mindset assumes there are limits to personal assets like talent, intelligence, and creativity, and that you constantly compare yourself against an equally fixed standard of "what it takes" to be successful, smart, or fast.

In sports, a fixed mindset is embodied in athletes who always need to prove how fast, fit, or accomplished they are but who often point fingers at everyone and everything except themselves when things go wrong. After all, the failure can't possibly result from things they did wrong, right? This often results in such a strong need to avoid failure that competition can bring incredible anxiety. Because anything other than a win is considered a failure, fixed-mindset athletes are likely to give up in the face of adversity, ease up when a win is out of reach, or drop out of a race entirely. Some prefer to avoid competition altogether to help maintain their belief that their true talent is simply untapped (to avoid their ability ever being contested).

In contrast, a **growth mindset** thrives on challenge and interprets failure not as evidence of lack of ability but as valuable feedback for improvement and growth. It's seen as a challenge. In our experience, the vast majority of endurance athletes do have a growth mindset (phew). After all, competing in running, cycling, and triathlon requires that you try hard, and there are very objective criteria that force you to compare your skills and speed to others—hardly a great environment for people with a fixed mindset. However, we do come across fixed-mindset athletes in endurance sport who seem to conceptualize talent as static and immutable. We notice that they often struggle with taking responsibility for poor races, often bounce between coaches, and are overly concerned with being and looking talented.

---

* C. Dweck, *Mindset: The New Psychology of Success* (New York: Ballantine Books, 2006).

"stickability" during adversity.[4] It's important to note that self-efficacy beliefs don't have to be grounded in reality—self-efficacy is about what you *think* you can do in very specific tasks, not what you can *actually* do. We all know athletes who consistently under- or overestimate their own capabilities—a self-efficacy problem that is "fed" by their confidence. Because humans have the capacity to perform thousands of tasks, your tree has thousands of leaves, and you've subconsciously given each a self-efficacy rating. Perhaps you have a 9/10 self-efficacy rating for cornering around left-hand turns at speed on a road bike, but you have only 3/10 self-efficacy on right handers at the same speed. It's perfectly normal to have high self-efficacy for some tasks and zero self-efficacy for others, with most falling somewhere in between. It should be clear why self-confidence and self-efficacy are not the same thing. For example, you might have high self-confidence as a triathlete but low self-efficacy for ocean swim starts. Because self-efficacy is situation specific, your confidence to execute a given task may vary depending on the circumstances. For example, you might have high self-efficacy to keep pushing (i.e., to maximize effort) during a 10K run when you're in podium contention, but have low self-efficacy to maximize effort when you're not feeling good or you're out of contention in an identical race. As we will learn later, the fact that self-efficacy is so changeable is both good and bad news for the competitive athlete.

---

4 D. Feltz, S. Short, and P. Sullivan, *Self-Efficacy in Sport: Research and Strategies for Working with Athletes, Teams, and Coaches* (Champaign-Urbana, IL: Human Kinetics, 2008).

FIXING SELF-JUDGMENT PROBLEMS

To help athletes with self-judgment problems (worth, esteem, confidence, or efficacy), we first need to know how deep on the Me Tree the problem goes. If athletes come to us asking for help with their confidence to really push themselves into the hurt locker or to increase their confidence for triathlon swim starts (i.e., it presents as a self-efficacy problem), strategies that target self-efficacy are likely to be ineffective in the long term if the underlying problem is low self-esteem. Conversely, trying to help someone with low self-worth by giving them easier and easier challenges so they can feel successful is pretty pointless because they are likely to interpret this as yet more evidence that they are useless at even the most basic things. It's no easy task to accurately diagnose and pinpoint causes of a wonky self-judgment system. If it takes skilled therapists countless hours to do it in person, a few pages in our little book of self-help ain't gonna cut it. However, we can point you in the general direction—a sort of "this-should-help-and-it's-certainly-better-than-the-moronic-claptrap-likely-to-appear-at-*memes-r-us*" approach.

One of the reasons we have such difficulty diagnosing self-judgment problems is that our brains are wired to be biased from the outset. Psychologists call this fault wiring *cognitive bias.* One form of cognitive bias that affects our self-perceptions is called "illusory superiority," or the "above-average" effect. Studies show that people (and men in particular) tend to rate themselves as better than average on a whole host of things, including popularity, happiness, driving ability, health, and, in a wonderfully ironic twist, being less susceptible to bias. Of course, low self-worth and low self-esteem are also forms of cognitive bias, but in the opposite direction. What this tells us is that we can't always rely on our self-assessments to reveal our personal strengths and weaknesses. As the fictional doctor in TV's *House M.D.* put it: "If you want to know the truth about someone, that someone is the last person you should ask."

Because of our tendency to be biased thinkers, we recommend that you look for additional sources to corroborate your self-assessment. For example, you could ask your spouse/partner or a trusted friend to rate you on the dimensions in Exercise 1 (pp. 67–8), and you could identify concrete actions you've taken that support your responses as validation.

Even though we can't diagnose your self-judgment problem, we can offer a big foam finger that points you in the general direction. In the exercise that follows, you'll find examples of the types of questions that psychologists use to help determine what your self-judgment system is like.[5] Again, these are just sample questions. This isn't a psychometric test, and you can't get a "score" from this. In reality, we often use 30–50 questions for each area, plus a clinical interview. However, if you find yourself thinking *Yes, this is completely true or mostly true of me* to certain clusters of questions, it's probably smoke from a fire. Or a pointy foam finger.

Dealing with low self-efficacy.

Low self-efficacy is the easiest of the self-judgment systems to correct because it changes in response to your experiences. This of course, brings good and bad news. For some tasks, self-efficacy changes while you're doing it. For example, Vince is an established roadie but relatively new to mountain biking at age 49. Listen to him talk about descending a fast technical trail on a mountain bike:

> As I get into a groove I'm feeling more and more relaxed. I take things faster, ride closer to my limit. When it's going well, it's like a dance. You take great lines and you're killing it. Your confidence is going up and up with every second. Then suddenly you overcook a corner, or your front wheel gets caught in a rut, or whatever. . . . You almost stack it. You need to clip out or you get spat off the trail. The surge in adrenaline hits you because you know it could have been much worse. It's like hitting reset on your confidence. You start back a bit timidly as your confidence builds again. Before long you're cranking it and then it happens again. My confidence is like the trail itself, up down, up down, all within the space of 5 minutes!

Research has revealed four essential strategies for increasing self-efficacy, which we will present to you in decreasing order of potency.

---

5 "Self Tests," *Psychology Today*, http://psychologytoday.tests.psychtests.com/.

EXERCISE 1

A CHECKUP FOR YOUR SELF-JUDGMENT SYSTEM

In each category, we've included a sample of the questions that tap into different aspects of your self-judgment system. Remember to get a second opinion from someone who knows you well.

SELF-WORTH	COMPLETELY TRUE	MOSTLY TRUE	SOMEWHAT TRUE/FALSE	MOSTLY FALSE	COMPLETELY FALSE
1. I could disappear from the surface of the earth and nobody would notice or care.	☐	☐	☐	☐	☐
2. I feel worthless and useless.	☐	☐	☐	☐	☐
3. I will never amount to anything or anyone significant.	☐	☐	☐	☐	☐
4. I don't deserve to be loved and respected.	☐	☐	☐	☐	☐
5. I constantly ask those I care about whether they love me.	☐	☐	☐	☐	☐
6. I think I'm a failure.	☐	☐	☐	☐	☐
SELF-ESTEEM					
1. I think that overall, people find me boring to talk to.	☐	☐	☐	☐	☐
2. I mess up everything I touch.	☐	☐	☐	☐	☐
3. I feel as though I let down those I care about.	☐	☐	☐	☐	☐
4. When someone criticizes me, I can't help but feel that I really am incompetent.	☐	☐	☐	☐	☐
5. I avoid having arguments with others because I don't want them to get angry or dislike me.	☐	☐	☐	☐	☐
6. I modify my personality, opinions, or appearance in order to be accepted by others.	☐	☐	☐	☐	☐

>

Continued

SELF-CONFIDENCE	COMPLETELY TRUE	MOSTLY TRUE	SOMEWHAT TRUE/FALSE	MOSTLY FALSE	COMPLETELY FALSE
1. When I face difficulty, I feel hopeless and negative.	☐	☐	☐	☐	☐
2. If something looks difficult, I avoid doing it.	☐	☐	☐	☐	☐
3. I am not confident I've done a good job unless someone else points it out.	☐	☐	☐	☐	☐
4. Before making any decision, I ask other people if I'm doing the right thing.	☐	☐	☐	☐	☐
5. I will never be as skilled or as smart as I should be.	☐	☐	☐	☐	☐
6. I rarely achieve the goals that I set for myself.	☐	☐	☐	☐	☐
SELF-EFFICACY					
1. I am great on long endurance efforts, but I'm not very good at shorter, faster efforts.	☐	☐	☐	☐	☐
2. I'm not very good at strength work.	☐	☐	☐	☐	☐
3. I look at a scheduled workout and wonder how I'm going to get through it.	☐	☐	☐	☐	☐
4. I don't perform well in the heat.	☐	☐	☐	☐	☐
5. I avoid group workouts until I'm fast enough.	☐	☐	☐	☐	☐
6. I'm not very good at pacing.	☐	☐	☐	☐	☐

Strategy 1: Actually succeed

I know, right? Duh. The most powerful predictor of self-efficacy is "mastery experience," a posh way of saying "actually being successful." Successfully doing something, even if just once, has a tremendous effect on your self-efficacy. The reason that success boosts confidence is that it changes your brain's production and receptiveness to testosterone and dopamine—two chemicals that increase the impulse to try it again. Success also gives you a behavioral blueprint of what and how things need to be performed to get the right outcome. In Vince's case, his perception of success was changing in real time, but for most situations in sports it's a before-and-after evaluation. Increasing low self-efficacy can be tough because you tend to avoid stuff you're not good at, which keeps it low. It stays low because you never get a chance to increase it by constantly trying. This has important implications for how to boost your perception of "being successful." First, increase the number of times you attempt things. Remember as a kid when you wouldn't let yourself leave the driveway until you'd hit at least 10 consecutive shots? Yeah, start using that principle as an adult. For example, if I keep crashing on a technical part of a trail on my mountain bike, I will not continue the ride until I've cleared it. Second, set small, incremental goals so you have a better chance of actually being successful (called a "micro-success"). For example, on a fast technical descent on a mountain bike, you might try to ride it four times on the same ride but focus on a different goal each time. Four attempts makes four opportunities to affect self-efficacy through mastery experience:

1. Focus on body position and finding the best lines for each turn.
2. Focus on where you look—fix your eyes farther down the trail.
3. Focus on braking strategy and exiting with power.
4. Put it all together and focus on letting the bike roll.

Structure your training and racing to give yourself lots of opportunity to feel successful—shoot for tons of micro-successes. However, be wary of setting and accomplishing goals that are too easy. Those don't fool your Chimp. The mere whiff of a hollow victory, and your Chimp knows it's all horseshit. At the other extreme, setting goals that are too hard sets you up for efficacy-sapping failure.

What's the ideal level of challenge that will maximize the self-hug needed for self-efficacy? Something that has a 70–80 percent chance of success.[6] **Ask yourself: On a scale of 1 to 10, how likely is it that I can pull this off? If it's more than an 8, it's too easy; if it's 6 or lower, it's too hard.** You might assume that constantly training with faster athletes is a surefire way to boost self-efficacy. Sure it can be motivating, but it doesn't really help to change your beliefs about your own ability to perform at their level. Make sure you still use the 70–80 percent challenge rule, even with micro-successes, to ensure your Chimp and Professor brain "accept" the accomplishment.

A good rule of thumb is to try and start every session on your program, no matter what (the obvious caveats about injury and illness apply). If you have a hard 90-minute indoor trainer session on your program with key intensity targets to hit, and you're really thinking about putting it off because you know it's not gonna be pretty, then you need a trick to help you at least start. One strategy is the "Quarter Quit" rule—agree to do at least 25 percent of every session. Don't be tempted to avoid challenging tasks for which you have low self-efficacy—it actually makes the problem worse.

Strategy 2: Become a voyeur of success

The second most powerful strategy to increase self-efficacy is to watch it happen to someone else—a sort of mastery by proxy. Psychologists call this a "vicarious experience" and research suggests that the more similar that person is to you, the better. Watching Danny Hart crush the 2011 downhill mountain biking world championships might be motivating and jaw dropping, but it won't do much for your own self-efficacy for downhilling unless you also have mad skills and "balls so big that you can't sit down." (The commentator's phrase, not mine—you need to watch the coverage!) However, standing trailside and watching a bunch of recreational riders clear something that you struggle with will help self-efficacy. If you're a generally confident swimmer but have been hesitant to join a masters swim group, try watching a session before joining in, paying particular attention to swimmers with the same base time as you. If you're still

---

6 We made that up, but it seems reasonable given what we have learned from the psychological research on goal setting.

unsure, jump into a slower lane first to maximize the chance of a mastery experience and finish feeling good. So, for tasks in which you have low self-efficacy, the take-home message is: *Spectate, then participate.* If you can't watch the action live, find something close on YouTube.

Strategy 3: Use verbal persuasion

Receiving verbal encouragement that you can complete something increases self-efficacy. However, it pales in comparison to the power of actually succeeding and watching others. Persuasion works best when: (1) it comes from someone else whose opinion you trust, (2) it's grounded in facts and logic, and (3) it makes mention of your existing skills or experience. That's one reason why having a skilled coach can be helpful for building confidence. However, be wary of dubious attempts at encouragement. For example, here are two ways that Lesley Paterson has tried to cajole me (Simon) to go over a drop-off on a mountain bike.

Simon (screeching to a halt at the edge): Whoa. Where's the B-line? [Expletive about height, followed by expletive about bad consequences.]

Lesley (Strategy 1): Come on, Si, stop being a f*cking pussy and just ride it.

Lesley (Strategy 2): Remember—commit, pull up, sit back, and absorb. It's just like the one you cleared in Mission Trails last week. You can do this, babe.

You don't need a PhD to know which form of verbal persuasion works best. (FYI, she consistently defaults to strategy 1, and when I tell her of the science backing strategy 2, she just shouts strategy 1 even louder.)

Verbal encouragement doesn't always need to come from others. Positive self-talk and self-affirmation are forms of verbal persuasion but are less effective than feedback from a trusted outsider. This is why looking in a mirror and telling yourself that you can do it is lame. It superficially addresses self-efficacy—it's the weakest form of the third-best thing you can do.

Strategy 4: Control your body

The fourth and final evidence-based strategy for increasing self-efficacy is to change the way your body interprets or responds to confidence-threatening and nerve-racking situations. This means learning to control physical and cognitive arousal using different relaxation techniques and "reframing" negative physical sensations as positive (e.g., "I'm so nervous, I need to poop and pee again" gets reframed as "That's great! The lighter I am, the faster I am"). You can learn about the anxiety control and reframing techniques in Chapter 13.

Smile, you miserable bastard. Research in cognitive neuroscience tells us that we can change the levels of certain neurotransmitters in the brain associated with confidence by simply changing our expression and posture. Scientists call this "embodied cognition"—the curious finding that when we give certain emotions or thoughts a physical form through body language, our brain soon joins the party.[7] For example, the simple act of smiling makes you feel better because it causes dopamine to be released, the brain's pleasure juice. Even if you don't feel like smiling, faking it still gives you the neurochemical boost to actually get there. Researchers have devised creative ways to test the embodied cognition theory and the extent to which it's under your control. For example, when people are asked to smile but prevented from doing so by holding a pencil above their top lip (don't laugh; researchers do this), the mood boost doesn't appear. However, when researchers inject Botox into facial muscles to inhibit frowning, positive moods increase and negative moods decrease.[8]

Look like a boss. Changing your posture also increases confidence because it affects your brain chemistry. Recent research shows that something as simple as adopting a "power pose" for one minute increases testosterone, decreases cortisol, and increases feelings of power and tolerance for risk—important biological determinants of confidence.[9] A power pose is simply body language that is open and expansive, with chest out, shoulders back, and eyes looking straight ahead. Think Superman stance or William Wallace stepping out from the front line as if to say, "Come at me, bro."

---

7 P. M. Niedenthal, "Embodying Emotion," *Science* 316, no. 5827 (2007): 1002–1005.

8 M. Heckmann et al., "Pharmacologic Denervation of Frown Muscles Enhances Baseline Expression of Happiness and Decreases Baseline Expression of Anger, Sadness, and Fear," *Journal of the American Academy of Dermatology* 49, no. 2 (2003): 213–216.

9 D. R. Carney, A. J. Cuddy, and A. J. Yap, "Power Posing: Brief Nonverbal Displays Affect Neuroendocrine Levels and Risk Tolerance," *Psychological Science* 21, no. 10 (2010): 1363–1368.

So the next time you're standing on the beach waiting for your swim-wave to start, rather than spending the time crapping your pants or hoping you don't get punched or drown, put your hands on your hips, stick your chest out, pull your shoulders back, look straight ahead, and let your nonverbal communication scream that today is a day that you will not be f*cked with.

Dealing with low self-confidence.

Because self-confidence is a generalized version of self-efficacy but is driven by self-esteem, the strategies to improve it combine techniques used to increase self-efficacy and self-esteem. Raising self-esteem (see strategies in the next section) lays the groundwork for positive thinking, but increasing your self-efficacy across multiple tasks will backflow to your general confidence. What you target should be decided by the relative strength of your upstream self-judgments (self-esteem) as well as your downstream self-judgments (self-efficacy). If you lack general confidence as an athlete but think your overall self-esteem is strong, you should first target self-efficacy. Do this by identifying two or three specific areas in your sport where you lack self-efficacy. For example, if you're a half-marathon runner who lacks general confidence as an athlete, you might identify aggressive pacing, tolerating pain, and dealing with cramping. These are your efficacy weak points. Next, use the strategies described above to increase your efficacy beliefs in each one. If you suspect that low self-esteem is contributing to your low confidence levels, then you should prioritize challenging your inner critic and developing gratitude. Strategies to increase self-esteem and self-worth are described next.

Dealing with low self-esteem or low self-worth.

Problems with self-judgment systems that originate deep down in the tree need to be solved with strategies that target the inner critic—the voice that is constantly reprimanding you for screwing up and not being good enough.

Changing your self-worth and self-esteem is best done with the help of a professional because it's hard to clean up biased thinking using biased thinking. It's like looking at the color blue and trying to convince yourself it's red.

For athletes with low self-worth, these beliefs will be affecting all aspects of their lives, not just their Lycra-clad experiences. So here are things we strongly recommend.

Strategy 1: Talk to a professional about untangling this stuff

When we say "professional," we don't mean a sport psychologist—we mean a clinical psychologist or therapist trained in helping people correct wonky self-belief systems. A good starting point is to do an online search for a licensed therapist in your area. Here's where to start: therapists.psychologytoday.com. Alternatively, you could ask a therapy-going friend for a recommendation. Word-of-mouth is one of the best ways to find a good "shrink." In the meantime, what follows are some more helpful strategies that you can start doing today.

Strategy 2: Confront your negative thinking

The starting point for telling your Chimp brain to shut the f*ck up with the self-criticism is to first be aware that you're doing it. As any psychologist will tell you, self-awareness is the cornerstone of change, so in order to confront it, you have to know you're doing it. You could keep a log or journal, download one of the many smart phone apps that help you keep track of your thoughts, or simply put 30 paper clips in your left-hand pocket and transfer one to your right-hand pocket every time negative Nora opens her mouth. Once you're aware of your tendencies (when, how often, what), start writing down the shit you tell yourself. When you have a list of the self-criticisms, you need to start using your Professor brain to untangle fact from fiction. Psychologists call this "countering" or "reframing," but we call it "confronting the bullshit."

In the next table, contrast the two approaches in response to self-criticism. Can you tell why the right-hand column is better?

SELF-CRITICAL THOUGHT: *I am so slow, it feels pointless. I am hopeless.*

TRY TO AVOID . . .	YES, GREAT!
I'm not slow and it's not pointless. As long as I try my best, that's all that matters.	I may be slow, but I'm training in the heart rate zone that my coach wants me in and I finished the session. It wasn't pretty, but I'm no quitter.
I will be faster soon. Just suck it up and do the work.	So I'm one of the slower athletes. Who f*cking cares? If I can't keep up, the sun still rises.
It doesn't matter what other people think of me. All that matters is that I'm out here.	No matter how fast or slow I am, there will always be athletes above me and below me. Getting faster won't make me happier. I will find the joy in today.

In Exercise 2 (p. 76), we recommend tackling only five of your self-spanks rather than the entire army of crazy that swims around your head. That would feel like a battle scene from *Braveheart*. For each of the five spanks, ask yourself what evidence supports those beliefs. And just in case you're science-phobic, "evidence" refers only to stuff that can be substantiated, verified, or corroborated—not the tautological imaginary shit that your Chimp feeds you (e.g., "I'm a loser because I feel like a loser"). Because your Chimp brain can smell bullshit from a mile away, don't bother to try and use empty, fake, or totally unrealistic alternatives or affirmations. Be honest with yourself. This is essential.

Crisis planning is another variation on confronting negative thinking. Make a list of all the things that could go wrong in your event and write a plan detailing what you will do if they happen. Then develop the skills to get out of these situations. Worrying that you will get a flat on the bike will remain a concern if you have no confidence in your ability to fix it. Force yourself to learn. Similarly, losing all your nutrition because it fell out of your back pocket won't jeopardize your chances of finishing if you know exactly where all the aid stations are and what's at them. Do your homework. Starting a race knowing that you've planned for every eventuality reduces the likelihood of it being something to fret about.

EXERCISE 2

CONFRONTING THE BULLSHIT

Use the left-hand column to write five of your most common, yet specific, self-criticisms you notice. For each self-spank, create a meaningful and factually substantiated alternative way of interpreting that thought. You don't even have to agree with the alternative; just offer it and write it down. Try to develop counter-statements that focus on self-acceptance, rather than self-criticism. Follow our lead.

My Self-Critical Chimp Talk (Self-spanks)	**Alternative Interpretation** (Ask yourself, "So what?")
I'm never going to be fast enough to ride with that group.	I'm fast enough to start with them and hang in for as long as I can. No one except me cares if I get dropped.
1	
2	
3	
4	
5	

Strategy 3: Focus on gratitude

There is now good scientific evidence that expressing appreciation for what you have has a remarkable effect on your self-judgment system and your overall well-being, most likely because it confronts negativity and increases the production of dopamine—your brain's pleasure juice.[10] Scientific studies have also revealed that the simple act of looking for things to be grateful for is as important as finding them, so you need to at least f*cking try. One of the best techniques is the daily gratitude log. Finding and writing down three things that you are grateful for every day for three weeks is known to improve your mental well-being and help you calm the f*ck down.[11] I know; I know. It sounds sort of trite and trivial, but it's based on evidence and it actually works! The "daily gratefuls" can be tiny, but they need to be experienced, meaningful, and concrete. So avoid the banal, the vague, and the cheesy (e.g., "I'm grateful for the earth"), the things that haven't yet happened ("I'm grateful for the vacation I'm going on next week"), and the obviously shitty things no one wants ("I'm really grateful that I don't have bowel cancer"). Focus on things you noticed that make you smile or feel happy, even if just for a few seconds (e.g., "I'm really grateful for getting into bed the first night of clean sheets" or "I'm grateful for the smell of asparagus pee").

This works because it forces you into a habit of scouring your day for positive emotion. To do that, you need to engage in bouts of mindful behavior—concentrating on the little things hidden in your daily routines and actions that you might otherwise take for granted. These positive droplets create a micro-squirt of dopamine (pleasure) and serotonin (happiness) that are incompatible with judgment and self-criticism. Start recording your own daily gratefuls in Exercise 3.

Strategy 4: Volunteer in a meaningful way

Helping others is a great way to recalibrate your self-belief system. And we're not talking about volunteering to work the feed zone at your local Ironman; we're talking about activities that make a real difference for people living with

---

10 A. M. Wood, J. J. Froh, and A. W. Geraghty, "Gratitude and Well-Being: A Review and Theoretical Integration," *Clinical Psychology Review* 30, no. 7 (2010): 890–905.

11 R. A. Emmons and M. E. McCullough, "Counting Blessings Versus Burdens: An Experimental Investigation of Gratitude and Subjective Well-Being in Daily Life," *Journal of Personality and Social Psychology* 84, no. 2 (2003): 377–389.

EXERCISE 3

YOUR DAILY GRATITUDE LOG STARTS HERE

Write down three things you are grateful for every day for three weeks—and wtach it work.* Avoid the banal, the vague, and the cheesy, or things in the future. Focus on things you noticed that make you smile or feel happy, even if just for a few seconds. To get started, complete the first week of log entries below.

Today I am grateful for . . .

Monday
1
2
3

Tuesday
1
2
3

Wednesday
1
2
3

THursday
1
2
3

Friday
1
2
3

SAturday
1
2
3

SUnday
1
2
3

Now that you have some momentum, for Weeks 2 and 3, e-mail your daily gratitudes to yourself.

* Emmons and McCullough, "Counting Blessings Versus Burdens."

adversity. It's hard to simultaneously loathe yourself and act charitably. Focusing on the lives you're helping to improve has such incredible therapeutic power that it's on our list of "must dos" for athletes with low self-worth and low self-esteem. Volunteer for Girls on the Run, the Challenged Athletes Foundation, a homeless shelter—anything that helps stick a plug in the self-spank system and refocus your attention on people who are not you. If you're not able to volunteer (because of time, resources, or whatever), try creating a habit of doing random acts of kindness. Pay for coffee for the guy behind you in line, give three people a compliment today. You get the idea. Make it part of your day.

The problem with expecting success to come from trying hard.

If you've been told that effort (trying hard) is the only thing that matters and the only way to define success, then you've been sold a turd. In 1969, Dr. Nathaniel Branden published *The Psychology of Self-Esteem,* a book often credited with launching the self-esteem movement. To raise happy and productive kids, we were told, we needed to focus on the only thing that matters—building self-esteem.[12] It turned out to be utter bullshit, but that didn't stop it spreading like wildfire. Visit virtually any youth sports field across the country to witness the fallout: participation and "trying hard" get richly rewarded above all else. Medals for everyone. The so-called mercy rule is enacted to end games prematurely when one team gets a pummeling. This is not only a misguided interpretation of the science but a disservice to the kids we are raising. The main problem was that we got the logic ass-backwards. High self-esteem and confidence come from experiencing adversity and accomplishment. In other words, confidence is earned, not given. In case you're nodding with smug agreement, adults are on the receiving end too. Why does anyone need a participation medal and a T-shirt for finishing a Turkey Trot 5K that raises money to feed the homeless?

As we become more and more conditioned into a culture of "effort entitlement," it can play havoc with the mindset of endurance athletes. For example, if you've been told that effort is the only thing that matters, then you're more

12 N. Branden, *The Psychology of Self-Esteem* (San Francisco: Jossey-Bass, 1969).

likely to feel let down or lacking when effort clearly isn't enough. Some athletes don't just feel let down when they give it their all and still come up short; they refuse to admit that effort isn't the answer. After all, if you've been told your entire life that hard work pays off and is the only thing that matters, then effort becomes the only way to explain success and failure. When these athletes don't perform as well as they had hoped, the judgment usually turns inward—"I didn't try hard enough" or "I must have neglected something." Of course effort is critical for success, and on race day, effort and attitude are pretty much the only things you can control, aside from a handful of rudimentary tactical and nutritional decisions. However, in the wider context of training and racing, the "effort is king" mantra sets a dangerous precedent because effort only really matters if it's combined with actual learning about what works and what doesn't. When this is layered on to the relatively fixed asset of genetic talent, performance suddenly becomes much harder to make sense of. Which brings us to Andy.

ALL I WANT TO DO IS WIN

When effort is not enough

ALL HIS LIFE, Andy has been told that anything was possible with hard work. He was the golden boy of the family who could do no wrong. No goal was out of reach, he was told, if only he wanted it badly enough. Starry-eyed parents told him to dream big and commit 100 percent, and the world would be his oyster. He was praised and encouraged every step of the way. Andy was a great guy, and, at 24 years old, he wanted to conquer his new passion—triathlon. After a tough rookie season, he seemed genuinely perplexed by his mid-pack finishes. He seemed supremely confident and his goals were impossibly high: win a national championship within two years (he had yet to break the top 10 in the local sprint triathlon) and get his pro license (he was running 9-minute miles). He was trying as hard as he could but wasn't winning races. As far as Andy was concerned, some aspect of his training must be getting neglected. Why else would he not be winning? Within six months, Andy was sleeping in an altitude tent every night, battering himself with 20–25 hours per week of hard training, and constantly searching for training gadgets and gimmicks to give him the edge. Andy's life had become one-dimensional. He was putting all his energy into anything that might help him become a winning triathlete.

Andy improved dramatically, but he wasn't destined for the top ranks any time soon. What Andy lacked was the physical talent to compete at the elite level, a fact he conveniently ignored. When Andy ran out of ways to prove that effort was king, he started grasping at new but largely meaningless indicators of improvement—a new max speed on a bike descent or a new resting heart rate. Each session was scoured for ways to prove to himself that effort and hard work were paying off. Every single race was followed by a forensic analysis of things he could have done better.

The problem was that Andy's self-confidence had been learned rather than earned. Instead of succeeding through challenge and adversity (which builds confidence the correct way), his confidence was bestowed from being told how great he was. He was simply unaccustomed to staring failure in the face and trying to learn from it. Andy believed that everything should fall into place provided he tried hard enough. When effort did not bring success, his inability to interpret failure correctly got in the way of him enjoying the sport at all. Unable to enjoy the process of training, the adversity, and lacking curiosity about what lessons can be learned from setbacks, he stopped training and racing altogether. His triathlon career came to an end two years and two months after it had started. Don't be like Andy.

4

SETTING GOALS IS NOT YOUR PROBLEM

THE SECRET OF DOING

Do. Or do not. There is no try. —YODA, *THE EMPIRE STRIKES BACK*

It turns out that *just do it* is pretty shitty advice. It might make for a good marketing tag line and it's certainly one of the most commonly shrieked instructions from exasperated coaches, parents, and teachers, but the scientific reality is that this pointy-ended call to action is almost always ineffective. In fact, some evidence suggests that it can actually undermine motivation, confidence, and enjoyment. The sentiment behind *just do it* is perfectly well-intentioned—stop overthinking it, stop talking about it, stop procrastinating, and stop forcing me to keep asking you to *take action.*

Here are some of the things that athletes have told us about what they struggle to *just do:*

> I just can't seem to get out of bed super early for those workouts. I'm just not a morning person. I go to bed with good intentions, but when the alarm goes off, I convince myself that I need more sleep or that I will get it done after work. Yeah, right.
>
> —JIM, 44, MOUNTAIN BIKER

> I struggle to do long runs off the bike. I get done with the bike, and I just can't be bothered. I make up an excuse why it's not a good idea. I'm looking for every reason to not do it. —TAYLOR, 52, TRIATHLETE

> I rarely stretch and roll. I know it's on my program, and I know how important it is, but I just don't do it. I don't even know why. Well, I do. It's boring, I'm always late, and I'd rather spend the time actually training. —JANE, 39, RUNNER

> I know my coach keeps telling me to upload my data, but I often forget my heart rate strap or it doesn't work, or my watch gives me an error message when I try to upload. There's always something that gets in the way. The technology drives me nuts and I haven't had time to figure it out. —HUMBERTO, 36, ULTRARUNNER

> I miss breakfast or lunch too often, and I never remember to have healthy snacks at work. I know that preparing my weekly meals on Sunday helps, but I never have time. I end up going to the café at work and eating crap.
> —PAUL, 55, IRONMAN TRIATHLETE

> I f*cking hate doing core strength work. I know it's good for me, I know it will help me as a rider, *I know all that*!!! But urgh. I will put that shit off unless you point a gun at my head. —LISA, 28, ROAD CYCLIST

Like most things in life, knowing *what* to do isn't usually the problem—it's the *how* and the actual *doing* that's difficult. In endurance sport coaching, one of the most common go-to solutions for mobilizing our *what*, *how*, and *do* is goal setting. Need some direction? Let's set some long-term or "distal" goals. Don't know how to get there? Let's set some short goals. Having trouble starting? Let's set even smaller goals. We've not met a single athlete who doesn't have at least a rudimentary understanding of the importance of setting goals. Even if you're not well-versed in goal-setting terminology, the fact that you were born at all tells me that you already understand and implement the basic principles. This is because the human brain is wired in utero to be goal-oriented. For example, your Chimp brain gives you certain types of basic goals whether you like it or not (e.g., to stay alive, eat, sleep, and shag), and your Professor brain is biologically wired to strive for the more complex thinky stuff (e.g., finding meaning, gaining acceptance, and achieving mastery). Setting goals is part of your operating system. If you've studied coaching science or sport psychology, you also know that entire courses are devoted to the science of goal setting. Students delve deeply into the what, the why, and the how. They spend hours dissecting and workshopping each of the letters in the hallowed acronym SMARTER. Drum roll . . . effective goals need to be Specific, Measurable, Achievable, Realistic, Time-Dependent, Energizing, and whatever that last "R" stands for. Just kidding. It stands for Redundant.

Motivational Monday . . . cue the eye-roll, please.

I bet that if you were to analyze the universe of psychology-themed articles that appear in popular endurance sports magazines, the most common topic would be goal setting, followed by lame visualizations to reduce anxiety and mostly useless advice about building confidence. The online athletic community has such an insatiable appetite for goal-setting clichés that an entire day has now been reserved in Facetwitter for memes intended to shove a firecracker up your ass. If you've not been paying attention, it's called Motivational Monday. Here are a few of our favorites:

Set a goal **SO BIG** that you can't achieve it until YOU GROW INTO THE PERSON WHO CAN.

SET GOAL.
MAKE PLAN.
GET TO WORK.
STICK TO IT.
REACH GOAL.

Stop wishing.
Start doing.

If you don't like where you are, then CHANGE IT.
You are not a tree.

If you can dream it, you can do it.
—WALT DISNEY

Yup, information about goal setting has become the athletic equivalent of the inflight safety demonstration: "I know I ought to watch and read, but please, dear God, spare me!"

It's not that these memes don't serve a rah-rah function or trigger a mini-mindset change, it's just that they are behaviorally impotent. They don't help with doing. By our cynical tone, you might assume we are advocating for a goal-less and directionless athletic journey. We're certainly not. Setting high-quality goals is as important as wearing underpants. It's just that we rarely come across athletes who suffer from goal-setting problems (i.e., they don't know why or how to set a goal). Sure, many athletes need help tweaking aspects of their athletic goals—usually one of the letters in the acronym—but these are just sprinkles on the goal cake. Far more athletes suffer from not putting the *do* into it—creating, channeling, and using their energy to actually get the job done.

Goal setting in brain world.

It's easy to see why the recommendation to *just do it* is not effective. Intentional and deliberate goal setting in sport is a mental exercise that starts and ends in the prefrontal cortex. It's Professor brain porn—planning and analysis. This is also where conscious intention begins (or "I will" statements). However, we are all too fully aware from countless failed New Year's resolutions that intention is not the same thing as doing. Doing is an energy-demanding behavioral task strongly regulated by the limbic system.[1] Recent neuroscience research has opened the box on who holds the reins of motivated behavior, and the anatomical, electrophysiological, and neurochemical clues all point to the Chimp.[2]

---

1 In reality, this is simplistic because intentional, motivated behavior is theorized to be, in part, a product of a negotiation between the prefrontal cortex (in the Professor brain) and the hippocampus (in the Chimp brain). The prefrontal cortex might have an elaborate plan, but the hippocampus controls the memory banks and determines whether the expected outcome matches the actual outcome. In essence, it works like a strong-armed advisor. It does this by checking your experiences (or your memories of it) and then sending signals back to the prefrontal cortex that either strengthen or weaken the likelihood of action. See R. Numan, "A Prefrontal-Hippocampal Comparator for Goal-Directed Behavior: The Intentional Self and Episodic Memory," *Frontiers in Behavioral Neuroscience* 9 (2015): 323.

2 E. Simpson, H. Balsam, and D. Peter, eds., *The Behavioral Neuroscience of Motivation: An Overview of Concepts, Measures, and Translational Applications* (Cham, Switzerland: Springer, 2016).

Athletic goal setting can really only help cajole, channel, and direct motivation . . . it can't create the ACTUAL DOING.

Sure, your Professor brain can muster up an intellectual equivalent, or intention, but this is really only a cognitive precursor of doing, hardly a guarantee.[3] Even worse, your goal-setting Professor is no match for an unmotivated Chimp. Your Chimp is much quicker and much stronger than the logic of your Professor. When you've reached the point that you need to tell someone (even if that someone is you) to *just do it*, you're making the mistake of assuming that the Professor is in charge. Well, it isn't. The Chimp is holding the reins and riding the Professor like Ben Hur.

Think about that training session that you are always struggling to just do. Listen to the self-talk: *I mean come on, it's not complicated! How many times do we have to go over this? What is it about this that is so hard for you to get? Stop making excuses, and get it f*cking done!* All of this tough talk assumes that action (or inaction) is simply a logical exercise, but the Chimp won't budge. Which brings us back to doing.

How do we mobilize our "oomph" to start actually doing the things that will help us reach our goals? There are two complementary approaches: one grounded in behavioral neuroscience, the other in cognitive psychology. These approaches are not oppositional in theory or practice. Like ketchup and mustard, they're just different, but both are capable of dressing up a good hotdog. If you struggle with motivation, slather on some sauce. The focus of this chapter is on the first doing sauce: habit formation. Creating habits puts the doing out of reach of the meddling and procrastinating hands of conscious thought. The second doing sauce is based on understanding the building blocks of intrinsic motivation, and then trying to embed specific principles into tasks you've been struggling to just do. For now, let's see how we create habits.

---

3 For the science nerds among you, the meta-analytic correlation between intention and behavior across many different types of actions is ~ r = 0.2. (i.e., bloody abysmal). It's even worse when you only include studies that required people to prove that they did the behavior instead of trusting their word. See C. Armitage, and M. Conner, "The Efficacy of the Theory of Planned Behavior: A Meta-analytic Review," *British Journal of Social Psychology* 40 (2001): 471–499.

Makin' a recipe for doing sauce.

Your brain is biologically wired to be lazy. Actually, *efficient* is a better description because it's constantly searching for how to do the same work with less time and effort. It has been estimated that we make about 35,000 decisions a day, yet only about 5 percent of these make it through to conscious thought.[4] If you tried to think about every tiny detail in life your brain would hate you. And your brain is one organ that you don't want to piss off. **The more tasks that your brain can put on autopilot, the happier your brain is. Your brain's favorite labor-saving device is the habit—behavioral rituals or autopilots that develop through repetition.** They're mental shortcuts to get things done without having to think too much. Good habits help us stay safe (wearing a seatbelt) or healthy (cleaning your teeth), and some make us feel really good (sexy time). Other habits make us unsafe (texting while driving) or unhealthy (sugar binges at night), even though they might feel good, at least temporarily. If the habit is pleasurable and/or fulfilling, the habit wiring becomes stronger and the habit becomes harder to break. If a behavior isn't pleasurable or fulfilling, it takes a lot of willpower for it to become a habit. This is why it's so hard to make exercise a habit but really easy to eat a half pound of Red Vines while watching TV. Unpleasant or painful behaviors can still become habits if the motivation to meet an important need is strong enough (your "why"). Think about the diabetic who doesn't flinch at daily insulin injections, or the athlete who continues to run through a painful injury because the fear of weight gain has become so powerful.

Clearly, habits are extremely powerful, and it should be self-evident that if we could only force many of the things that we struggle to *just do* into a habit loop, we wouldn't have to think about them. Less thinking equals less opportunity for the daily negotiation between the Chimp and the Professor brains. That's less procrastination, less dithering, less talking about it, and more doing. The good news is that scientists have now uncovered the critical building blocks of habits. It's as if we've been handed the wiring diagram to the brain, giving us vital clues on how to take advantage of the brain chemistry that creates *want* and *do*. You can use these principles to design a strategy to *just do* things that you've been putting off or are struggling to stay on top of.

4 This oft-quoted statistic has no empirical evidence behind it. It's probably just an educated guess.

And it works. We got so tired of seeing athletes relegate core strength to the "If I have time" folder that we decided to design a program based on the principles of habit formation. The case study at the end of this chapter shows how we use it with our athletes.

The brain chemical that compels you to act.

Dopamine is dope. As you recall, dopamine is a neurotransmitter—a chemical released by nerve cells to communicate with other nerve cells. One of its primary roles is in motivation and reward. You probably know of dopamine because of its reputation as the brain's pleasure juice. When you feel pleasure, you are getting squirted on by dopamine. But that's not the whole story. Dopamine is also behind a host of other feelings that compel you to act.[5] It drives the feeling of wanting even if what you want isn't inherently pleasurable. For example, money isn't inherently pleasurable, but we want it. That's dopamine's fault. Of course, some of us associate money with pleasure, but that's a learned, or conditioned, response. In contrast, some activities are inherently pleasurable, such as sex, drugs, eating chocolate, and winning money. Dopamine works you at both ends: It creates a compulsion to act and rewards you for doing so. You will find its fingerprints on other parts of your brain too. Low levels of dopamine are associated with procrastination, lack of enthusiasm, and self-doubt. Dopamine is also partly responsible for impulse control, aggression, motivation, and competitiveness. Too much dopamine can overwhelm your brain and cause you to become addicted and/or psychotic. This is why people get addicted to cocaine and methamphetamines, which are the equivalent of shotgunning a dopamine beer. Any behavior that gives you a dopamine rush will train your brain to want to do it over and over and over again. And over time your brain will need more and more of it to get the same rush.

I know what you're thinking. *I don't want to become a crackhead, but can't I just sneak in a bit more dopamine to make getting out of bed at 5 a.m. easier?* Scientists have a few answers to this question. First, don't bother trying to inject dopamine.

5 J. D. Salamone et al., "Mesolimbic Dopamine and the Regulation of Motivated Behavior," *Current Topics in Behavioral Neuroscience* 27 (2016): 231–257.

Dopamine can't pass the blood-brain barrier to any significant degree, and so eating, snorting, injecting, or inserting it up the Hershey highway will only get you ready below the neck;[6] it won't French-kiss your Chimp brain. That said, we can influence dopamine production through our diets. You can't actually eat dopamine, but you can eat the thing that makes it—tyrosine. It is a nonessential amino acid, meaning that you must consume it in your diet because your body doesn't make its own. However, before you start rushing out to the supermarket to get a cart full of tyrosine—cheese, soybeans, beef, lamb, pork, fish, chicken, nuts, seeds, eggs, dairy, beans, and whole grains—research shows that it really only helps if you're deficient to begin with.[7] Science is a cruel mistress.

In contrast to dopamine-fueled feelings of pleasure, feelings of happiness are caused by another neurotransmitter—serotonin. Serotonin also helps create feelings of contentedness, significance, and importance. Among other functions, serotonin is a mood stabilizer. Sure, dopamine will give you the quick pleasure rush, but serotonin will keep you happy in the long term—a positive upbeat mood that chases the blues away. While we're not going to talk much more about serotonin in this chapter, you do need to recognize this one important distinction: **Dopamine is pleasure juice, but serotonin is happy juice.** It's an important distinction because it also gives us a clue as to why some habits are hard to form and others are hard to break. When dopamine's involved (the pleasure test), you've got a fight on your hands because you feel good almost immediately and that's hard to give up. The bummer is that many things that are good for us are often not pleasurable, at least not initially.

Many of the things that you struggle to *just do*, or that you desperately *want to want* to do but don't, are a struggle precisely because the benefits don't come immediately. In other words, there's hardly any dopamine involved to get you to want to do it, or to feel good once you've done it. Here's more bad news: New exercise habits are usually uncomfortable, disrupt your rituals, and often make you feel self-conscious—three strikes against making them habits. In contrast, it's easy to turn to foods high in sugar, fat, and caffeine for

---

6 Dopamine gets hydroxylated in the body to form norepinephrine, which stimulates the sympathetic nervous system.

7 A. Hase, S. E. Jung, and M. Rot, "Behavioral and Cognitive Effects of Tyrosine Intake in Healthy Human Adults," *Pharmacology of Biochemical Behavior* 133 (June 2015): 1–6.

NERD ALERT!

My striatum made me do it. The neurobiology of bad habits

YOUR PREFRONTAL CORTEX (in the Professor brain) might determine that it's good for you to stop eating a half-pint of Coconut Bliss ice cream each night, but your striatum—the brain's habit controller in the Chimp brain—isn't so rational. Stuffing your face with delicious food is pleasurable (strike 1), and you have plenty of practice doing it (strike 2). The end result is that your brain is locked in a constant cycle of trying, succeeding, failing, and trying again, failing again, and getting more and more frustrated by your apparent lack of control and willpower.

The problem is that your striatum couldn't care less about your watts per kilogram (a revered measure of "relative power" in cycling). Making things even more complicated is the fact that different areas of your striatum regulate different aspects of your habits and conspire together to get them hard-wired. For example, part of your lower striatum—the nucleus accumbens—wants you to do things that are pleasurable, whereas the upper striatum—the dorsal striatum—wants you to do things that you've done before. Your nucleus accumbens is a crafty wee bloke, responsible for giving you a squirt of dopamine at 8 p.m. when you're primed to think about sugary treats. This is called an "anticipatory reward" because you've been biologically rewarded for just thinking about something pleasurable. You're now even more motivated and excited. This leads to another dopamine squirt, which propels you further along the routine. And on it goes until you're prying open the lid and digging away at your frozen treat like a dog covering a shit. Because your routine was successful, it strengthens the dorsal striatum's grasp on the routine, and your penchant for sugary treats becomes harder and harder to resist.

This habit is destined to continue unless you interrupt the sequence of trigger, ritual, and reward. Deconstructing this holy trinity of habit and reverse engineering it is the only way to break it. Read the remainder of this chapter to learn how to actually do it.

an immediate pleasure payout. See the problem? If we can just stick with new routines long enough to start cranking out the happy juice (serotonin) or find a way to make the experience intrinsically pleasurable (dopamine), we've got a much better chance of it becoming a long-term habit. As you might expect, the actual neurobiology of habit making and breaking is rather complicated. If you're nerd-curious to dip your toes deeper into the dark side of routines—bad habits—go back and read "My striatum made me do it" (p. 91).

A DESIGN FOR DOING AND UNDOING

To master the art of doing, you need to create habits and routines in the brain that are relatively resistant to a whining Chimp and the paralysis-by-analysis ruminations of your Professor brain. For the routine to become automatic, we need to design it with such conscious and deliberate precision that it's ready-made to run on autopilot. Here are the step-by-step instructions.

Step 1: Learn the pattern, and crack the code

All habits follow very predictable and logical patterns. They are composed of a "neurological loop," which is science-speak for a predictable pattern of events in the brain and body that runs on autopilot. The loop consists of three important elements: a trigger, a ritual, and a reward.[8] If you want to break, modify, or build habits, you must first figure out which element is causing the most problem (it might be all three!).

Trigger. The event that cues the brain to start the habit, like your alarm clock going off if you need to get out of bed early. It's the habit's starting pistol. If you want to start a new behavior, you often have to choose the trigger for that behavior.

Ritual. The actual behavior that you want to start, which includes the timing and the step-by-step instructions for how it occurs. For example, if the desired behavior is to do more stretching and rolling, the ritual might start with being in

8 C. Duhigg, *The Power of Habit: Why We Do What We Do in Life and Business* (New York: Random House, 2014).

TRIGGER
REWARD
RITUAL
TRIGGER
REWARD
RITUAL

the right clothes, having any equipment you need on hand, having enough space and time, and knowing what exercises to do.

Reward. The feeling you get once you've done or are doing the behavior. For new behaviors that aren't intrinsically pleasurable, you might need to pair a separate reward (something that does provide a dopamine squirt) with the new behavior so you still feel good after completion. For bad habits, the reward is what stops the craving. It might be the intense pleasure you get from eating chocolate, or temporarily forgetting that you're lonely when you hit the booze.

A former research collaborator of mine at Stanford University, tiny habit guru Dr. B. J. Fogg, trained himself to do 10 push-ups every time he flushed the lavatory. He developed great upper body strength using this simple trick. That's a genius use of triggers. When you think of the behaviors you want to change, try to be as specific as possible. For example, instead of just saying, "Do more training," you might say, "Get up at 5 a.m. on Monday, Wednesday, and Friday to run for 45 minutes before work." Give it a shot in Exercise 1.

Step 2: Make a watertight ritual

The ritual is the sequence of behavioral steps you need in order to actually create a habit. You need to know exactly how it unfolds for you, and this takes some self-experimentation. If you're trying to start a new habit, you should design the ritual so it has a good chance of becoming automatic. If it's overly complicated or requires a lot of thought, it doesn't stand much of a chance. For example, if you want to go out for a run three mornings a week before work, you might plan the routine as follows:

1. Lay out run clothes the night before.
2. Change into run clothes immediately after getting out of bed.
3. Pee or poop.
4. Drink single espresso and eat half banana.
5. Lace up shoes while mentally visualizing run route.
6. Leave the house at exactly 6:15 a.m.!

EXERCISE 1

KNOW EXACTLY WHAT YOU ARE TRYING TO JUST DO

List two new important athlete-related behaviors and one silly behavior that you want to start (or stop) doing or want to simply become more consistent at doing. For the two important behaviors, pick actions that help you as an athlete (e.g., stretching and rolling, doing a really-early-morning training session, uploading your data, etc.).

The things I'm trying to *just do*:

1

2

For the third and silly behavior, pick something that is interesting (or amusing), simple to do, and helpful to you or someone else but doesn't require much physical effort. This third behavior helps you practice the art of ritualizing an action and doesn't have to be connected to sport in any way. It just makes you a better person. If you're stuck for ideas, here are some great ideas:

› Men: Putting the toilet seat down after you pee. › Women: Taking the trash out. › Teens: Making your bed. › Squeegeeing the shower door after each shower. › Saving your spare change for a good cause. › Unloading the dishwasher. › Doing 25 push-ups a day. › Not checking your phone after 7 p.m. › Calling your mother. › Engaging regularly with a quiet or shy work colleague. › Performing a random act of kindness every day.

A small or silly habit that I want to start or stop doing:

3

Once you have listed three behaviors, rank the two important behaviors. You will attempt to start your small or silly habit next week. Once you've made a habit of it, start number 1, and then number 2.

If you have to dig through laundry for clean shorts, or try to answer e-mails beforehand, it doesn't lend itself to becoming automatic. Lock that ritual in! If you're trying to break a bad habit, you need to deconstruct the pattern of actions that lead you there. For example, your evening snack binge ritual might involve getting off the couch, walking over to the pantry and opening it, foraging for something, and then slouching back on the couch with your treats. You may want to ask your partner or spouse to help you uncover your ritual. After all, many routines are subconscious, and you may not even be aware you're doing them. Remember, you're trying to make the ritual conscious (Exercise 2).

Step 3: Know the rewards that do and don't work for you

For some people, the reward is the driving force behind the habit. We've already established that powerful neurotransmitters cause a chemical reaction to reward the ritual and increase pleasure (dopamine) and/or feelings of happiness and positive mood (serotonin). However, other neurotransmitters may also be involved, like endorphins (which reduce stress and alleviate pain) or oxytocin (which increases a sense of trust and intimacy). If the action you're trying to just do isn't that pleasurable or enjoyable, we need to find a way to make it so. Here's an example from Lesley, the world's biggest moaner about how cold the swimming pool is.

Lesley: But babe, you don't understand! The pool is so f*cking cold! I'm literally shivering in the water. I just don't want to get up for that. Have you any idea what it's like trying to psych yourself up for a hard session in a cold pool when it's still f*cking dark out? It's miserable!!

Simon: [Resisting the urge to say: Just suck it up or fatten up a bit.] That sounds horrible, darling. Why don't you do two sessions a week in your wetsuit? It's warm, it's fast, and you won't dread it so much.

Lesley: Hmm.

Sometimes, there's really no way to make the activity itself more enjoyable. Braveheart Athlete Nadja Mueller has an on-again-off-again relationship with a masters swim group. She devised a strategy to help her look forward to swimming—after each session she goes out for breakfast with some of her friends, many of whom need a similar reward.

DEFINE YOUR STEP-BY-STEP RITUAL

Describing your ritual is a lot like writing instructions for a recipe. It's a logical, step-by-step series of instructions that spell out exactly what you plan to do. Leave no room for interpretation, and no loopholes. When you actually try it, some parts may feel awkward or a crucial step may be missing, so it may take one or two drafts to get it right. When I planned my morning run routine, my beloved act of drinking a single espresso was missing. This alone made a huge difference to helping me get my ass out the door.

1

2

3

4

5

Now, make a contingency plan to deal with all circumstances that threaten to destabilize the ritual. If you're trying to, ahem, do push-ups after flushing the toilet, you may also need to think through dealing with floor cleanliness and bystanders.

For example, if I check my phone in the morning and there is something urgent I need to respond to before my run, then I will do this: Create a new habit of putting my phone on airplane mode when I go to bed at night and not reconnecting with the Interwebs until my run is done.

If ______________________, then I will do this:

If ______________________, then I will do this:

If ______________________, then I will do this:

Here are some other occasions when you might need to pair something that is pleasurable or enjoyable with the suck.

Long, boring training sessions. Listen to audio books, a recording of a comedy show, or a new album. Train with other people, or have someone join you for the last hour.

Stretching and rolling. Only do it while binge-watching your favorite show. Treat yourself to a stretch-and-roll session from a personal trainer.

Meal planning/batch cooking. Include a foil-wrapped treat in each snack pack. Offer to swap one week of pre-prepared lunches with a fellow athlete. Treat yourself to a meal-delivery service once a month or sign up for their free trial period.

Uploading data. Buy a sports watch that does it automatically. Duh.

The bottom line is that you need to create a meaningful reward for your new routine—something that gives you pleasure or happiness. It doesn't even have to happen at the same time. Stop for a cappuccino on your way to work or play your favorite cell phone game for 10 minutes before you start your day. Set aside $1 for every mile you run to a fund that you can give to charity or use to buy a new outfit or gadget at the end of the month. Avoid rewards that sabotage your new habit—like ordering a 1,000-calorie drink after burning 250 calories during your run. Good habits need good rewards.

★ **If it's a bad habit you're trying to change.** The goal is to uncover what need or craving the reward was satisfying. Does it change a feeling, like boredom, anxiety, or loneliness? Does it change an internal physical state, like hunger or pain? If you're still not sure what reward is lurking behind a bad habit, try this experiment: Switch out the reward for a "fake" reward while keeping the exact same ritual. See what happens to the feeling or internal state. For example, you might go to the food cupboard at the same time you always do, but instead of taking the chocolate, you drink a bottle of fizzy water instead. If after 10–15 times of drinking the fizzy water the cravings have subsided or gone, you know it wasn't hunger. If you're still not sure what it is, try writing down the exact feelings you're experiencing 10–15 minutes after having the reward and then try other fake rewards (like chewing gum, drinking hot tea, or going on Facebook, etc.) and repeat the experiment.

Step 4: Know thy trigger

Once you've figured out the ritual and reward, the next step is to create a trigger for it. Remember, a trigger is the habit's starting pistol. It's the cue that triggers the routine. Triggers can be physical objects (your cell phone), circumstances (a time of day), or feelings (boredom, anxiety, hunger, etc.). Triggers are important because they remind you of what and when you need to act. All behaviors that you want to *just do* must have good triggers that get the ball rolling. For example, the act of brushing your teeth at night is usually triggered by feeling sleepy and deciding it's time for bed.

★ **If you're trying to start a new habit.** You need to design your new triggers carefully. Some people lay out their run kit the night before as a visual reminder as soon as they get out of bed. For people who are just starting a new exercise habit, it can even help to sleep (!!) in your running clothes the night before to make it harder to bail. However, it might just take a Post-it on the refrigerator or a ready-packed gym bag next to the door. Others might need the help of others. For example, a friend who texts you at 7 a.m.: "Track session@6.30 p.m. tonight. Don't U dare bail! U betta B there!" is providing a great trigger for you to quickly throw your run kit in the car before you leave for work. A well-designed trigger needs to be specific and actionable at that exact time. You also need to have the skills or ability to act on it. If it's vague or you can't act on it immediately, or you simply don't have the skill, fitness, or knowledge to do what you actually need to do, the trigger (and possibly the ritual) needs redesigning or replacing. One strategy that helps is what behavioral scientists call *habit stacking*.[9] Habit stacking is simply the process of adding a new habit on top of an existing one. Always flossing after you've cleaned your teeth is a habit stack. The existing habit (brushing teeth) becomes the trigger for a second habit (flossing). Habit

9 S. J. Scott, *Habit Stacking: 97 Small Life Changes That Take Five Minutes or Less* (Cranbury, NJ: Oldtown Publishing; 2nd ed. Amazon Digital Publishing, 2014).

stacks are great because you are leveraging triggers that are already cemented into your ritual. Here are some examples of a few novel athletic habit stacks:

- Doing 20 push-ups before you shower.
- Doing 2 minutes of core strength exercises while you wait for the coffee to brew.
- Uploading your training data only when you're on the toilet taking a dump.
- Stretching for 2 minutes during the TV commercial break.
- Doing a 1-minute body relaxation exercise after parking your car but before you open the door.

* **If you're trying to undo or replace a bad habit.** You need to become aware of the triggers for your existing habits. They can be very subtle and often appear amid a gazillion other cues that bubble up into your consciousness. For example, what triggered you to bail on your ride this morning? Was it the thought of the effort? The cold weather? How much work you have to do? Something else? If you're trying to change an existing habit, you need to eliminate or sidestep the triggering circumstances, and to do that you need to have a forensic understanding of what, how, and when those triggers occur. The good news is that psychologists have determined that you can deconstruct your trigger problems by completing Exercise 3.

Step 5: Develop your plan

Once you've uncovered your ritual, experimented with rewards, and isolated your trigger, you need to put the pieces together and write out the new habit "loop" on paper, as in Exercise 4 (p. 102). Think of this like a diagram describing each element and how you intend to create it (start a new habit) or disrupt it (break a bad habit). Then you can start with some self-experimenting to fine-tune it and practice it! Go on, *just do it.* In the case study that follows, you can see how we did this for Bill, a 52-year-old ultrarunner who couldn't manage to *just do* his weekly core strength training session.

FIND OUT WHAT TRIGGERS YOUR BAD HABITS

Answer these five questions on at least three occasions that you do your bad habit. It often takes three "recordings" to reveal noticeable patterns.

The behavior I'm trying to stop: *Trying not to have that second glass of wine.*

1. **Where were you, exactly?** *At home on the couch in my living room.*
2. **What time is it?** *8:05 pm*
3. **What is your emotional state?** *Tired from work, zoned out, feeling a bit lonely.*
4. **Who are you with?** *On my own.*
5. **What were you doing immediately prior?** *Finishing my first glass and watching TV.*

The behavior I'm trying to stop:

Occasion 1

1
2
3
4
5

Occasion 2

1
2
3
4
5

Occasion 3

1
2
3
4
5

EXERCISE 4

BUILDING OR BREAKING YOUR HABIT LOOPS

In the blank discs below, enter your triggers, rituals, and rewards for one good habit you're trying to start and one bad habit you're trying to break.

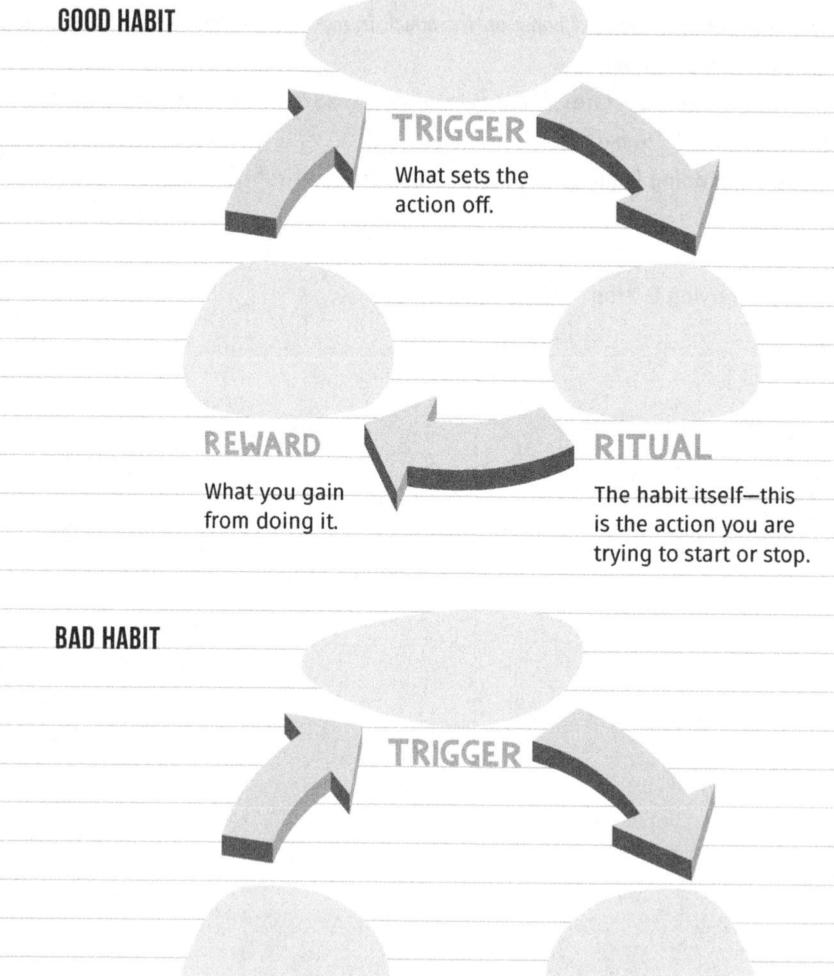

WHY CAN'T I *JUST DO IT?*

Building a habit of core strength training

BILL IS A 52-YEAR-OLD ultrarunner and marine biologist. Bill has a history of back problems and tight hips and suffers from occasional iliotibial band pain. His weekly run volume is around 50 miles, but he also trains around 5 hours per week on the bike to develop aerobic fitness and save his knees, ankles, and hips. The one session that Bill consistently fails to do is 30–60 minutes of core strength training each week that targets the glutes, hips, lower back, obliques, and hamstrings. Bill always has a reason why he misses this session, and he's frustrated with his lack of willpower. He accepts the value of this session for overall training. As his coaches, we have been nudging him to *just do it*, but encouragement alone clearly isn't working. The time has come to change tactics and focus on creating a neurological loop—a trigger, ritual, and reward—that will help Bill get it done.

The behavior Bill is trying to just do: Complete 30–60 minutes per week of core strength training to support his ultrarunning program.

We recommend that Bill use our core training "small habit" program (www.6min6pack.com) and commit to completing 6 minutes of structured core training, six days per week (36 minutes per week). The 6 exercises would be the same each day for 4 weeks to help ritualize the plan and reduce cognitive load. Every 4 weeks, we will introduce 6 new daily exercises. He will follow the structured exercises for each day, using his cell phone to log on to www.6min6pack.com. After discussing his daily routine, we mutually agree that first thing in the morning is the ideal time to get the session done.

Bill's routine:

1. Upon waking I'll turn my alarm off, get up, and visit the bathroom.
2. Put contact lenses in.
3. Go into the kitchen and put coffee machine on.

>

Continued

4. Go back to bedroom and sit down on yoga mat already laid out beside bed.
5. Make sure exercise ball, two paper plates, and two 5-pound dumbbells are within reach.
6. Set cell phone timer for 6 minutes. Log on to 6min6pack.com website.
7. Begin exercises (6 × 1-minute exercises).
8. Have coffee and read newspaper.
9. Shower and dress.

Bill's contingency plan:

If I have to be at work before 7 a.m., I will do my core routine the night before.

If I wake up late or oversleep, I will do 30 seconds of each exercise for a total of 3 minutes instead of the full 6 minutes.

If I have an urgent call or email that needs a response, I will reply as soon as I am out of the shower.

Bill's reward: Bill likes to read the news on his iPad each morning, so we urged him to splurge on a new subscription, something he could get excited about. He chose the *New York Times* online edition. The thought of sitting down for 20 minutes every morning with a coffee sounds like a real treat. However, he will only allow himself this reward upon completing his 6 minutes of core training.

Bill's triggers:

Trigger 1. Bill will put his yoga mat and equipment directly next to his bed. When he steps out of bed each morning, the first thing he sees is the mat and the equipment.

Trigger 2. Bills puts on the coffee pot each morning, which takes 7–8 minutes to brew. A Post-it note on the coffee machine says "beat the beep"—a reminder that the coffee brew time also acts as a surrogate timer for his core strength workout. His goal is to complete his routine before he hears the beeper sound on his coffee machine, indicating that the coffee is ready.

Initially, Bill found it hard to complete each minute of exercise at the beginner level. We revised the goal to have him complete just 30 seconds of each activity for the first two weeks. This also motivated him to work toward doing a full minute of each exercise. In the first 8 weeks, he completed 44 of 48 sessions. After 10 weeks, he moved up to the intermediate exercises (still just 6 minutes per day, but with modifications to make the exercises slightly more difficult). After 6 months, core work is now part of Bill's daily routine, and he rarely gives it a thought. He no longer needs to use the online exercise guides because he has them memorized.

WINGS

DEAL WITH OBSTACLES, SETBACKS, AND CONFLICT

5

OTHER ATHLETES SEEM TOUGHER, HAPPIER, AND MORE BADASS THAN ME

THE POWER AND PERIL OF COMPARISON

There are only three things that always tell the truth: drunk people, children, and Lycra.

—ANONYMOUS

Let's get a few things straight. Comparing yourself to others is essential if you want to be happy, motivated, and content. It isn't foolish, harmful, or dangerous, and it won't rob you of happiness. There are occasions when it certainly can be counterproductive. But so can drinking several gallons of orange juice and sticking a cotton swab too far into your ear. Fear not; social comparison is completely natural—in fact, your brain will hate you if you don't do it. Of course, you'd never know it from looking at the motivational meme-bots that have crapped all over the Internet with turds like this:

Comparisons are a form of violence. When you believe you are not good enough, you will compare yourself to others.
—IYANLA L'ANZANT

HAPPINESS IS FOUND WHEN YOU STOP COMPARING YOURSELF TO OTHER PEOPLE.

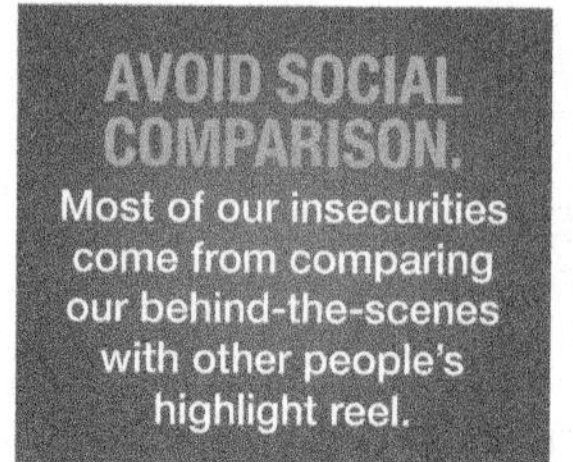

Don't get us wrong. The intention behind this advice is reasonable: Don't look to others to validate your sense of self, try to avoid perceiving yourself as inferior or unworthy, and when other people win, succeed, or look happy, it doesn't mean you have to lose, suck, or be miserable. We get it. But what these self-affirming-egocentric-avoid-negativity-at-all-costs-but-live-in-denial philosophies of life fail to point out is that you're going to do it anyway. It's as natural as peeing in the shower (Oh, c'mon . . .). But while meme-turds will scream at you not to compare yourself to others, biology will bludgeon you until you do. The trick is knowing how and when to use the inevitability of social comparison to become happier, faster, and grittier. Otherwise you'll just end up envious and resentful that everyone seems happier and more exciting than you. More on that later.

If you're a 6, then I'm an 8.

Your brain is biologically wired to compare yourself to others. This means that you can't actually stop peeking at others, even if you tried to. If you recall from Chapter 1, your Chimp brain is driven by psychological urges such as power, ego, acceptance, recognition, security, and inquisitiveness. Your Chimp is constantly scanning the world for data that helps determine where you sit in the social hierarchies of attractiveness, awesomeness, athleticism, and aptitude. And that's just the "As." By comparing yourself to others, you can see how your attributes stack up. If you're forced to make a decision about whether to fight, hide, run, or hump, you had better know if you stand a chance of pulling it off. Even when survival isn't at stake, attribute comparison helps us make better decisions about which groups to join or avoid, which sexual partner to pursue, and what situations are likely to make us happy or miserable. If there's no social comparison, you risk being left on the sidelines out of fear or, worse, in the thick of the action but ill-equipped to cope with people who have more skill, more swagger and, well, just about more of everything than you. A few million years ago, both scenarios would have left you dead, but now they just make you miserable.

Psychologists have spent decades studying social comparison, and their conclusions are invariably the same: People are virtually incapable of judging their own abilities without reference to some criteria, especially the abilities of others. Think of an occasion when you got some novel data about yourself or something you've done. Perhaps it was when you learned that you could hold 200 watts for 20 minutes on the bike, you have 23 percent body fat, or that you take 6,388 steps per day. If your first question is *What does this mean?*, your second question will almost certainly be *Is that good?* You immediately claw for a reference point. This is often called benchmarking, and we are all driven to do it because it gives meaning to our abilities. Remember that the human brain is wired to search for meaning in everything, even blathering balderdash. Fortunately, benchmarking is really easy in endurance sport. There are times, finish results, and three podium steps for every race.

People who participate in competitive sports usually find social comparison pretty rewarding, though they might not know it, admit it, or even realize the subtle ways that they do it.[1] Some people seem to enjoy the thrill of competition from an early age. Lesley entered every single race she could as a kid. Or at least as many as her increasingly exhausted parents could tolerate. If she wasn't trying to manically out-sprint other kids in the tots-trot, she would be challenging her friend's dads to eating competitions. (Her talent at inhaling food emerged at the age of two.) She would take on all comers at anything—she didn't care who; she just wanted to go head-to-head. Because endurance sports give Lesley very clear and objective criteria about how she stacks up to others, competing makes her feel like a pig in shit. It's important to point out that the power of competitive social comparison is most potent when you're stacking up against people whose abilities are within reach of yours. After all, no one gets a kick out of beating people who posed no status threat to you in the first place (cue thoughts of racing against your mum or a top pro).

---

1 K. A. Martin Ginis, M. Lindwall, and H. Prapavessis, "Who Cares What Other People Think? Self-Presentation in Exercise and Sport," in *Handbook of Sport Psychology*, ed. Gershon Tenenbaum and Robert C. Eklund, 3rd ed. (Hoboken, NJ: John Wiley and Sons, 2007), 136–157.

Even in sports known to be inherently explorative and self-referential like big-wall climbing, mountaineering, and recreational skiing, we can find breadcrumbs of social comparison in the stats: completions of climbs with different technical ratings, number of summits without oxygen, the type of ski runs you're competent at, and so on. Even the most noncompetitive version of a sport or activity will often be adapted to create an illusion of comparison—as is the case when one person assumes the role of two different players during a solo game of pool, billiards, or darts. Human versus human. It's what we do.

It is possible to go overboard in the hunt for social comparison information. Do too much of it, and your brain will throw a tantrum because it feels bullied. No one appreciates constantly hearing about how fast or fit other people are. I learned this the hard way when, approaching the 2016 XTERRA World Championships, I thought that giving Lesley regular updates about Flora Duffy, her nemesis in off-road triathlon, would be a good idea. Turns out it wasn't. Lesley told me to shut the f*ck up about her. Oops.

Self-presentation as a performance.

Scouting the opposition is only part of the equation for determining your social standing. After all, your social standing is also determined by how others see you—or more correctly, how you think they see you. This means that your brain also needs to sell itself and the attributes and abilities of the body it lives in. Psychologists call this self-presentation, and how we actually go about doing it is called impression management. Technically speaking, *impression management* refers to conscious and subconscious attempts to influence the perceptions of other people about an object or thing (in this case, you) by regulating and controlling information during social interaction.[2] Impression management is often compared to running your own broadcast channel that tries to tell the world how attractive, awesome, athletic, and smart you are, among other

2 M. Leary, *Self-Presentation: Impression Management and Interpersonal Behavior* (Boulder, CO: Westview Press, 1996).

ONLINE

IRL

things.[3] However, impression management isn't necessarily pretense; it's just "selective nondisclosure"—because you will leave out certain, ahem, details so that you are portrayed in a way that is consistent with how you see (or want to see) yourself. For most athletes, this is fast, fit, competent, smart, exciting, fun, and shaggable,[4] which may be a frequent departure from how you feel in real life (IRL).

When you're on the receiving end of someone else's in-your-face impression management, it's annoying precisely because you're on the opposing team. Shrinks call this a self-evaluation threat. It sends the message that their social standing is higher than yours because they're fitter, leaner, faster, grittier, happier (need we go on?) than you. And it's f*cking irritating. Sometimes it's really overt, such as someone telling you literally how great they are. Sometimes it's less overt but still noticeable—when a person's anecdotes are only about how they saved the day or were proved right. At other times, impression

3 In reality, it's far more complicated. For example, it's theorized that impression management comprises two constructs: the motivation to be concerned about self-presentation (impression motivation) and the actual way we go about it (impression construction). For simplicity, we do not distinguish between the two constructs here.

4 From an evolutionary perspective, the importance of sexual attractiveness matters most to mating preferences when it's reproductively most relevant—a polite way of saying that young people care more about looking sexy.

management can also be really subtle, as in when and where people "check in" on Facebook. It can be plain nauseating, but only if you know about esoteric rules, such as when to call yourself "Dr." or add "PhD" after your name (answer: only when that professional capacity is relevant, which it certainly isn't for a hotel reservation, a credit card, a gym membership, or a personal social media account). Some people prefer to reverse engineer the process entirely by faking inadequacy, in order to fish for compliments or to create a personal handicap, portraying themselves as deficient in order to catch opponents off-guard and gain an advantage.

The one thing we know for certain about impression management is that we all do it—at least to some degree. And make no bones about it: It's a performance in every sense of the word. Interestingly, research suggests that you're less likely to do it with your relatives, perhaps because you'd catch shit for doing it and there are genetic reasons not to.[5] Reacting negatively to other people's blatant impression management is probably also encoded in your DNA at some level. This may be why scientific studies show that humans take great pleasure in seeing other people get knocked down a peg or two, especially if they are considered to have deserved it. Read the nerd alert "The guilty pleasure of seeing other people get what they deserve."

Athletic "truthiness" and why your pants are probably also on fire.

Impression management isn't always about complete and utter honesty. Like advertising, the goal is to shape or change people's perceptions. In this case, about you. You don't have to be a sociopath to rationalize away a few misrepresentations of yourself in public. We just can't help wanting to portray ourselves in a flattering light. Why else would the phrase "you look nothing like your picture"

5 Richard Dawkins, the award-winning evolutionary biologist and author of *The Selfish Gene*, noted that selfishness and self-promotion are genetically encoded and will lead to behavior that is in one's self-interest, except possibly when people are related. Selflessness among genetically related individuals (which is common) is theorized to help increase the possibility that the common gene survives, not necessarily the individual. This appears more consistent with contemporary evolutionary theory. And in a comical turn (at least for this book), Dawkins also coined the term "meme" to refer to the fact that some cultural "entities" (e.g., ideas, norms) self-replicate and transmit through groups, which helps ensure their survival. Thus, it is likely that selflessness and other traits are perpetuated with both biological and cultural "help."

The guilty pleasure of seeing other people get what they deserve

NERD ALERT!

WHEN WE RECEIVE incoming information that threatens our self-perceptions (e.g., the badass chick on Facebook who always seem fitter, faster, tougher, and happier than you), the part of the brain that processes social pain and mental conflict—the dorsal anterior cingulate cortex—goes apeshit. And why wouldn't it? After all, your brain is motivated to maintain a positive self-perception at all times. When social comparison information from [Facebook/your mother/your unimpressible sister/work colleague/whomever] kicks your self-evaluation in the nuts, it creates envy. Here's what it might sound like in your head: *I thought I did okay until I saw Billy Badass with the perfect f*cking family win again. Man, he's irritating.* Underneath the envy is a feeling of inadequacy or disappointment. Congratulations, you're now primed to enjoy other people's suffering.

People do seem to enjoy seeing bad things happen to certain people. The Germans call it "schadenfreude"—taking pleasure from someone else's misfortune. It's why the human brain enjoys seeing bullies get their comeuppance, fraudsters get exposed, the rich and privileged be embroiled in scandal, and yes, the arrogant Olympian get busted for performance-enhancing drugs. And don't just take our word for it. Neuroimaging studies show that parts of the ventral striatum—a key reward node in the brain—light up like the Fourth of July when people we envy catch shit. It's also the reason you might get a smug but guilt-ridden pleasure from learning that the badass triathlete next door flatted on the bike or got a drafting penalty, even if he still beat you by 12 minutes. Empathy goes out the window, compassion is tossed aside, and who gives a f*ck about pity when someone who has consistently won the self-presentation battle against you gets knocked down a peg or two. It's important to point out that when we believe the person does not deserve the misfortune, most of us respond with compassion or pity. After all, we're not total assholes. Or psychopaths.

Research reveals that we show the most schadenfreude when we are envious of someone's position, hold some level of resentment toward them, >

Continued

benefit in some way from their misfortune, or have lower self-worth or self-esteem ourselves.* Even when there is zero tangible benefit to us as a result of someone's misfortune, it still feels good because it makes us feel better about ourselves. Don't worry, that doesn't make you a loser or a bitter and malicious old bastard; it's just biology's way of rewarding a perceived upward shift in your social status. Even the German philosopher Friedrich Nietzsche thought it not only natural but important: "To see others suffer does one good, to make others suffer, even more. This is a hard saying but an ancient, mighty, human, all-too-human, principle."† Admittedly, Freddy Nietzsche wasn't exactly a cuddly fellow, and this position can quickly spiral into moral quicksand, but in the fluffy and trivial world of endurance sport, schadenfreude provides an explanation for why we enjoy seeing the local star athlete get dropped. When we play an active role in their misfortune, it causes a related emotion. If you've ever put people "in the hurt locker" on the local club ride or a group run and enjoyed it, gloating would be your official psychological diagnosis. And while you can't argue with science, you don't have to be a dick. Be nice and gloat in private.

* M. Cikara and S. T. Fiske, "Their Pain, Our Pleasure: Stereotype Content and Schadenfreude," *Annals of the New York Academy of Sciences* 1299 (2013): 52–59.

† F. Nietzsche, *On the Genealogy of Morals*, trans. W. Kaufmann and R. J. Hollingdale (1887; New York: Random House, 1967), p. 67.

be the most commonly uttered words by members of www.[redacted to stop us being sued].com? After all, if you want to zoom up a league table of social status, cherry-picking examples of your own awesomeness and broadcasting them to the world seems entirely sensible. For endurance athletes, it's not even considered lying. After all, you did run 18 miles on Saturday in your new kit and wear a run visor that hides the zit on your forehead but makes your cheekbones pop. And, as luck would have it, you managed to selfie an exhausted but not unattractive pose prior to collapsing. Who cares that your six other runs lasted less than 28 minutes because you were mildly hungover and had the face of a swollen otter and, if the truth be known, you just couldn't be arsed to run any farther. Welcome to athletic "truthiness." Nope, if it's your broadcast channel, you might as well give 'em the Heisman Trophy reel. If people conclude that being you is wall-to-wall awesome, then who are you to protest? (Your Chimp certainly won't.)

If the psychological purpose of impression management is to broadcast a version of yourself that influences people's perceptions in a way that enhances your status (self-presentation), then it's entirely unrealistic to expect people to hose down the public with things that decrease status—weaknesses, failures, stupidity, and, yes, unflattering photos. That is, of course, unless it suddenly becomes socially advantageous to do exactly that. For example, showing embarrassment or vulnerability can enhance your status when there is normative adulation to do so (meaning that enough people agree that it's a good thing). For example, if you completed the 2014 ice-bucket challenge,[6] posted on your Facebook wall about dealing with mental illness, or put up pictures of yourself doing something stupid in order to make a point about, well, the importance of being stupid, then it's still a status-enhancing impression management strategy (despite your good intentions, of course).

We now snort, inject, and inhale impression management.

Technology has taken a lot of the effort out of impression management by helping us broadcast truthiness about our abilities and all-around awesomeness. Social media is a particularly grand stage for your performance because an audience is guaranteed if you have an account. With the click of a button, you can instantly pebble-dash your social network with photos, updates, check-ins, plans, trips, experiences, and mood states—the golden currency of impression management. Strava has built an entire business around athletes' psychological need to compare themselves to others, and there is ample evidence that no segment of road is too ridiculous for some cyclist, somewhere, to want to claim victory as the fastest person across it. If you want to induce a mild panic attack in Stravaholics, just send them an e-mail with the subject heading: "Uh oh, someone just took your KOM."

---

6 In 2014, the *ice-bucket challenge* took the Internet by storm. It involved dumping a bucket of ice and water over your own head, or someone else's, to promote awareness of amyotrophic lateral sclerosis (ALS).

Of course, Facebook is the mother ship of impression management. It is sophisticated software that is used almost exclusively to enhance social status. Even allowing for the fact that people are unlikely to admit that they participate mostly for show and are just as unlikely to know why they're doing it, the research still indicates that self-presentation and the need to belong are the primary motivations for using Facebook and that many are blissfully unaware that they come across as total tools.[7] It doesn't help that it can also be addictive because it almost certainly triggers the brain's dopaminergic reward system. Regardless of the motives for impression management, you may find it motivating and enjoyable to keep checking on the status of others as well as updating your own—mostly to feed your self-presentation drive. **Unfortunately, when impression management is done on a computer you are denied access to the vital nonverbal cues that can be used to detect bullshit.** There are now so many scientific studies showing that people craft their self-presentation on Facebook with such precision that it would take an entire book to cover the manipulative art of message crafting, photo editing, tagging, and sharing.[8] Of note is that neuroticism, narcissism, and low levels of self-esteem and self-worth are all associated with higher Facebook use.[9] Jesus, no wonder triathletes love it. Kidding. Sorta.

HOW TO FILTER TRUTHINESS AND BULLSHIT

Because of the psychological drive for self-presentation, it's impossible to expect impression management software—Facebook, LinkedIn, Instagram, Tumblr, Snapchat, Strava, Endomondo, RunKeeper, Runtastic, MapMyRIDE, Garmin Connect, or the 2,479 other data-logging social networks—to be suddenly used for sharing stories of your own perceived failures, inadequacies or awkwardness, or evidence of your otherwise humdrum life. Because

---

7 A. Nadkarni, and S. G. Hofmann, "Why Do People Use Facebook?" *Personality and Individual Differences* 52, no. 3 (2012): 243–249; V. Barash et al., "Faceplant: Impression (Mis)management in Facebook Status Updates," *Proceedings of the Fourth International AAAI Conference on Weblogs and Social Media* 2010, 207–210.

8 But if you're interested and have the nerd-chops to cope with it, try this for starters: J. B. Walther, "Selective Self-Presentation in Computer-Mediated Communication: Hyperpersonal Dimensions Of Technology, Language, and Cognition," *Computers in Human Behavior* 23 (2007): 2538–2557.

9 Nadkarni and Hofmann, "Why Do People Use Facebook?"

impression management software is everywhere and always on, your brain gets exhausted. Your dorsal anterior cingulate cortex, the brain's processor of social pain and emotional discomfort, is getting worked like a distance runner at CrossFit. The trick is to know how to manage this barrage so you don't feel like you're losing a social status game. After all, if obesity, happiness, smoking, substance abuse, and voting habits can spread through online social networks, you better believe that impression management tactics of athletes can too.[10]

Facebook isn't the problem; you are

See social networks for what they are: carefully designed opportunities for people to "self-present" in the most favorable way possible. If you find yourself looking at other people's profiles, run-group selfies, screen grabs from their sports watch, or their badass training sessions—and you think *WOW, this person is the real deal,* closely followed by *I wish I had their life,* know that you've been duped.[11] You are seeing selective nondisclosure. They show you only the parts that are literally awesome or give off an aroma of awesome. They're not as fit, strong, happy, and as perfect as they seem. No one is. This isn't a criticism of them, either. They're simply very good at impression management. For every single instance of masterful impression management that is uploaded, posted, or selfied, there are 10 hiding behind it of a straggly, exhausted, disorganized mess. This is the human condition. The more perfection they sell you, the worse the problem usually is. Trust me.

★ **What to do about it.** Constantly remind yourself that you are seeing a sanitized and heavily edited version of someone's reality, even if it looks totally authentic. What you see and read is usually the best of the best—their highlight reel. It's rarely overt and almost guaranteed to be subtle, but never forget that you are still watching a performance. If you still find it hard to see through other people's impression management, you may have a behavioral habit that's kicking. As you learned in Chapter 4, habits are comprised of triggers, rituals, and

10 N. A. Christakis, and J. H. Fowler, *Connected: The Surprising Power of Our Social Networks and How They Shape Our Lives: How Your Friends' Friends' Friends Affect Everything You Feel, Think, and Do* (New York: Back Bay Books, 2011).

11 H. T. Chou, and N. Edge, "They Are Happier and Having Better Lives Than I Am: The Impact of Using Facebook on Perceptions of Others' Lives," *Cyberpsychology, Behavior, and Social Networking* 15, no. 2 (2012): 117–121.

rewards. Delete the Facebook app from your mobile phone and you've eliminated one of the biggest triggers for the problem.

Stalking versus grazing—know the dangers

If you've been surviving on a diet of social media grazing and stalking (observing, not posting), then you might want to reconsider why you do it. First, you need to know whether you're predominantly a grazer or a stalker. A Facebook "grazer" is someone who cares little for social media but still enjoys the sort of pseudo-connection that it creates—perhaps seeing what family members are up to or being able to vicariously enjoy the micro-successes of your loved ones without actually being there in person. No harm in that. Enjoy. Conversely, a Facebook "stalker" is someone who enters the Facebook world a little deeper but with targeted, lingering, and slightly more sinister motivations. We're not talking about "stalking" in the sense of illegal harassment, but in urban dictionary terms—peering anonymously (but legally) into someone's public presence online for the purpose of curiosity, judgment, or plain ol' voyeuristic pleasure. We all do it. It's what makes Facebook fun. That said, we prefer not to use the word "stalking" because, well, it isn't really that. It's more akin to intrigue fishing, helped by a modicum of reciprocity and passive consent, at least in the Facebook world. (My Professor brain has clearly rationalized it well.) It's mostly guilt and shame that helps the healthy brain know where to draw the line. Our goal here isn't to help you draw moral lines in the sand over whom you choose to peek at, how frequently, or why, but we do offer you this general word of caution: If you find yourself doing this a lot, research suggests that you're probably headed down an emotional dark alley.[12] Excessive intrigue fishing seems partly fueled by feelings of inadequacy—the breeding ground for envy. And envy rarely ends well. It's a gateway drug to depression, resentment, and schadenfreude.[13]

If you're an athlete who only grazes or stalks on Facebook, you could also be a kind of bully. All take and no give. A healthy self-presentation requires a broadcast channel. So use it. If you're feeling self-conscious about making a dis-

---

12 P. Verduyn et al., "Passive Facebook Usage Undermines Affective Well-Being: Experimental and Longitudinal Evidence," *Journal of Experimental Psychology General* 144, no. 2 (2015): 480–488.

13 M. N. Steers, R. E. Wickham, and L. K. Acitelli, "Seeing Everyone Else's Highlight Reels: How Facebook Usage Is Linked to Depressive Symptoms," *Journal of Social and Clinical Psychology* 33 (2014): 701–731.

closure, losing anonymity, or being poked fun at, your impression management system needs a bit of foreplay from your self-judgment system. Read Chapter 3, "I Don't Think I Can: Building confidence and self-belief."

★ **What to do about it.** If you only stalk, start to talk (and by "talk," we mean post). If you're just never sure of what to say or phobic about pretense, start by being honest. Tell your network about something you've enjoyed doing today, something you found hard to cope with, or something you're grateful for. It's not about getting "likes," it's about telling your dorsal anterior cingulate cortex that you care enough about it to at least field an offensive team. If you find yourself feeling increasingly envious or resentful of other people on Facebook, logging out or letting it go is your best strategy. After all, it's your mental health that suffers, not theirs. As the saying goes, "Resentment is like swallowing a poison and waiting for the other person to die."

Low self-worth or low self-esteem might be your problem

Envy is an emotional response born out of a sense of discontent or inadequacy about someone else's possessions or attributes, like success, attractiveness, popularity, talent, or fitness. It represents a self-evaluation threat that pisses off your Chimp. When your Chimp brain doesn't feel threatened by another person's self-presentation shenanigans, you don't feel envious. Simple as that. You might feel slightly annoyed, indifferent, or even a twinge of scorn and condescension—but envy isn't in the mix, for three reasons:

1. Your self-judgment system (self-worth, -esteem, and -confidence) is sufficiently strong to not internalize threats to self,
2. The incoming impression management tactic is so blatant and exaggerated that it's actually funny, or worse, tragic (e.g., the questionable behavior of some men experiencing a "midlife crisis"), or
3. The person you are being compared to is already lower on the totem pole on the attribute or possession in question. Hence social status was never under threat in the first place.

When an athlete has low self-worth or low self-esteem, the "threat threshold" is artificially low. He or she lives in an ever-present state of inadequacy and discontent, and the slightest whiff of another person's impression management broadcast is invariably perceived as a threat. This leads to a cascade of negative emotion that feeds into the existing narrative—*Oh that's just great. Yet more proof that I'm talentless and slow*. Some athletes respond by amplifying their own self-presentation even more—greater pretense, more exaggeration, and more selective disclosure—flattering selfies, podium shots, accomplishments, and race results dominate their posts. The grazers and stalkers, those with low self-worth or self-esteem who don't put an offensive team on the field, simmer with disappointment, resentment, and envy—a breeding ground for depression. Let's try to break those cycles.

★ **What to do about it.** First, read or reread Chapter 3. It doesn't provide a magical cure for self-judgment problems, but it does lay out a game plan to get you started. If you're only a grazer or stalker, stop it. Try to give your impression management team a fighting chance by posting and sharing about things you can do. You probably don't have to worry about being a show-off. And even if you are, it will probably help. Screw it. If you feel motivated to cut down on your Facebook activity, then this will certainly help, especially if it's dominated by stalking. Ahem, we mean intrigue fishing.

Remember your brain is biased

As we've discussed elsewhere in this book, your brain takes shortcuts (175 at the last count) to reduce cognitive effort and become quicker and more efficient at making decisions.[14] The strategies it uses are often named according to the mistakes it makes along the way—referred to as cognitive biases. When you look at other people with envy or admiration, you tend to fall into the trap of the *halo effect*. The halo effect refers to our tendency to let an impression about someone in one area influence our impression about them in another. It need not be as obvious as thinking they're probably good at everything, but instead can be extremely subtle, such as giving them the benefit of the doubt, being more forgiving of their bad decisions, or assuming their intentions must be good. Just because the badass athlete next door posts pictures of her smiling husband on Facebook, it doesn't mean that her relationship is perfect or

14 For a list and description, see https://betterhumans.coach.me/cognitive-bias-cheat-sheet-55a472476b18#.ax0cpydmr.

that she's even happy. Of course, she might well be, but that's not the point (or your business). It's the fact you may be using information from one aspect of someone's life to make assumptions about another. This can fan the flames of envy even more.

Another mental shortcut we use is called an "availability bias," which refers to our tendency to use information that is close to hand when forming opinions about people and things. In this context, "close to hand" simply means things that you can most readily recall about them. Facebook serves up so many examples that are curated for quick-access memory (e.g., short pieces of text, photos, shares) that it's no wonder we think certain people are better than they are—we're often just subconsciously regurgitating their own highlight reel. Conversely, if you hold negative opinions about a certain race team, you might automatically assume that you probably won't get on with Dave, an athlete who races for that team.

★ **What to do about it.** When thinking about a person you are growing increasingly envious of, stop to think about what information you actually have to support your conclusions that they are any faster, fitter, happier, or more content than you. Even if the evidence might be overwhelming that they are faster than you (or whatever), stop to think whether you've given them a halo and have now become envious of areas of their life that you actually know nothing about. To avoid the availability bias, stop and force yourself to consider more information than first springs to mind. What do you know about them from in-person interactions? The same goes for confronting stereotypes you might have about certain people based on incomplete or biased information. After all, not all triathletes are neurotic, are terrible bike handlers, and wear mid-calf compression socks out to dinner.

WHY CAN'T I BE HER?

An impression management intervention

CATHERINE IS A 42-YEAR-OLD teacher, triathlete, mother, and wife. She's a pretty kick-ass chick. She has a successful career, is smart and capable, and gets stuck in to triathlon training and racing even though she's pretty scared of failing, crashing, and not being prepared enough. Catherine's eldest son and husband started to race cyclocross, and after growing bored on the sidelines clapping in the freezing cold, she decided to give it a go. "Cross" quickly became a passion for her. She bought a new bike, took a few skills classes, and faced up to even more fears. Eager to learn more, she found herself doing some "intrigue fishing" of the local big hitters.

Two women in particular seemed to win everything. One woman, Annie, was only two years younger than Catherine, had three kids, and raced for a sponsored team. Catherine started to become a bit obsessed with Annie. Not only was she a beast on the bike, but she owned her own business, appeared to do a lot of volunteer work, and always seemed so put together—her kit was impeccably matched, her bikes (she had two!) were high-end, and she always looked so happy and successful. Catherine began to envy Annie, not just because she seemed to have it all but because nothing seemed to bother her. Then, Catherine became increasingly annoyed at the little things she noticed Annie doing on Facebook. The book she was reading in her book club, the awards her kids won at school, and the fact that she still found time to coordinate the f*cking Christmas toy drive. Catherine found herself saying, "Why can't I be like that?" and "What's wrong with me that I can't enjoy life as much as Annie?" The more she raced, the more she compared herself to Annie. If she did well, she put it down to Annie not racing. If she felt strong and confident on the pre-ride, getting passed by Annie would lead to a spiral of self-doubt and self-criticism about her own skills and abilities. Catherine rarely tooted her own horn about her accomplishments but appeared to have a PhD in everyone else's, especially Annie's.

When Catherine approached us about coaching for cyclocross racing we discovered her obsession with Annie in about 15 minutes. It soon became clear that Catherine had low self-esteem. Nothing she did was ever going to be good enough. She found it hard to accept praise from us and was suspicious of our motives when we gave it. We discussed how she saw herself as an athlete but decided to focus initially on her self-presentation as an athlete. I (Simon) introduced Catherine to her Chimp and the concept of impression management. We talked through how her current "stalking" habits and limited posting were making the problem worse, not better. Catherine had hinted at wanting to cut down on using Facebook anyway, so we developed a plan of action to do so. First, she deleted the app on her mobile phone.

Second, we instituted a rule of "post to read." This meant that when Catherine felt the urge to graze or stalk she only could do so if she also contributed to her network by writing a post (a "like" was not sufficient). We developed a list of post types that were positive and self-affirming. These two strategies alone cut Catherine's Facebook time in half.

Finally, we encouraged Catherine to reach out to Annie in person and tell her that she found her inspiring and to ask for tips to help manage the things she found challenging. She was initially too embarrassed and intimidated to do so, so we developed a plan to help it feel natural and less stressful. Two months later, Catherine told us that she and Annie had become training partners and friends. She was surprised to learn that Annie struggled with just as many things as she did and couldn't help but laugh when Annie told her, "Oh, don't believe everything you read on Facebook!" Even though Annie still kicks Catherine's ass and Catherine still feels the occasional pang of envy toward her, having a real friendship helps her cope better with negative emotion and feel supported—two things she was missing before meeting Annie.

6

I FEEL FAT

DEALING WITH BODY IMAGE IN A WORLD OF ATHLETES

And I said to my body. Softly, "I want to be your friend." It took a long breath. And replied "I have been waiting my whole life for this."

—NAYYIRAH WAHEED

Feeling unhappy about the way you look is something almost all of us have experienced at some point in our lives. Whether it's your sticky-out ears, the size of your forehead, your skin, or your thighs, there's not a single body part that hasn't caused untold anxiety to someone, somewhere. However, when it comes to sport, the common culprits behind body dissatisfaction are fat and muscle. Too little or too much of either can wreak havoc with your Chimp and Professor brains. For endurance athletes, problems with body image are impossible to ignore because you routinely squeeze yourself into Lycra and prance about in public. While parts of your body might feel like taut guitar strings, other parts can feel more like a lava lamp where blobs drift around trying to find a home. Because as athletes we put our bodies on display more often than nonathletes, we also open ourselves up to a larger-than-normal dollop of judgment and evaluation from other people.

What many people fail to realize is that athletes struggle with body image issues just as nonathletes do. The problem is easier to understand in the so-called aesthetic sports, like diving, figure skating, and gymnastics, where judges evaluate an athlete's appearance. But body dissatisfaction will always be prevalent in sports where certain shapes and sizes provide a clear functional advantage. We know that cyclists and runners are more metabolically and biomechanically efficient when they drag around less fat and have limited excess muscle. For many athletes, striving for an elusive size or shape can be miserable, unsustainable, or medically unwise. Add in all the other ways that athletes want their bodies to look or feel different (after all, athletes are still human), and you have the requisite conditions to seed unhealthy behaviors. The truth is, unhealthy behaviors can change the way our bodies look and perform, at least in the short term. When a cyclist loses 10 pounds of fat and gains 2 pounds of muscle (almost regardless of means), they will look leaner and be measurably faster. Because these attributes are part and parcel of an athlete's self-schema, our cyclist is likely to feel happier too.

Athletes find themselves in a shit storm when behaviors (healthy or otherwise) become motivated by a need to suppress negative thoughts and feelings that are increasingly disconnected from performance. Some motives start off well-intentioned but morph into something a bit darker, while others intensify to the point that they become self-destructive. Most athletes prioritize healthy eating, but some become so obsessive about it that they develop a rigid and righteous fixation on food purity and quality that restricts their diets to the point of compromising their health instead of enhancing it. This obsession can also interfere with other areas of life, cramping their cash flow or stunting their social life. Left unchecked, the athlete's commitment to eating healthy can evolve into a need to control consumption, avoid fear and anxiety, create an identity through food, or even a search for meaning and spirituality through it.

When negative thoughts and feelings about food, eating, or appearance reach critically high levels and have a life-altering impact, psychologists diagnose it as a clinical disorder. For example, eating disorders are characterized by *consistently* irregular eating habits and severe distress or concern about body weight or shape. Similarly, when an obsession with healthy eating becomes severe and debilitating, it may be diagnosed as orthorexia nervosa.[1] People who feel overwhelmed by negative thoughts and feelings about perceived flaws in their physical appearance that aren't weight- or fat-related could have body dysmorphic disorder (BDD, which is explained in the sidebar on p. 146). If you think you might be suffering from a clinical disorder about food, eating, or parts of your body, read the section at the end of this chapter titled "Help! I think it might be a bit more serious than that." Because eating and body-perception disorders can coexist with compulsive and excessive exercise, you might also benefit from reading Chapter 8, "People Are Worried About Me. Exercise dependence and the incessant need to do more."

Navigating the no-man's land between normal and clinically significant.

Fortunately, the vast majority of athletes do not experience clinically significant levels of emotional distress, which is psychology-speak for "diagnosable." If you're interested generally in how psychologists and other mental health professionals diagnose mental disorders, then read the nerd alert about their bible, the *DSM-5*. After all, it is perfectly normal to eat more on some days and less on others, crave certain foods at certain times, and periodically fall in and out of love with parts of your own body. Although normal is a relative term, there are a few signposts that can help you determine if you are wandering off the path a bit too far. Take your relationship with food, for example. How you think and feel about food as well as how, when, and why you eat or stop eating gives us a little window into how you think and feel about your body generally. It also reveals the role that food plays in managing the inner backchat coming from your Chimp and Professor. Here are some of the questions you can ask yourself to determine whether you have a healthy relationship with food:

- Do you make food choices that are a combination of healthy and enjoyable?
- Are you comfortable not always choosing foods based on calorie content?

1 For more information about orthorexia nervosa, see www.nationaleatingdisorders.org/orthorexia-nervosa.

- Do you balance the time spent thinking about food, weight, and dieting with other aspects of life?
- Are you able to deviate from a routine pattern of eating without distress?
- Do you find pleasure in eating, or do you eat simply for sustenance or fuel?
- Are your portions based on energy needs rather than what other people are eating or social pressure to eat?
- Can you routinely eat or stop eating in response to hunger rather than out of adherence to a strict diet or feelings of guilt?

As athletes, we all deviate from healthy behaviors depending on our emotional state, different situations we find ourselves in, the demands of training and racing, and myriad other factors. In fact, it's perfectly normal to periodically find yourself off the rails, providing that you have a handle on what periodically means. For obvious reasons, this calibration needs to be done by your Professor

The psychologist's bible for diagnosing your brand of crazy

NERD ALERT!

BEFORE YOU OBJECT to our use of the word "crazy" or think that we're poking fun at people with serious mental health issues, calm the f*ck down. A little light-hearted humor can go a long way in helping the inaccessible become accessible. Besides, we're all a little crazy. As Carl Jung once said, "Show me a sane man, and I will cure him for you."

The *Diagnostic and Statistical Manual of Mental Disorders,* 5th Edition *(DSM-5),* is what most mental health care professionals around the world use to diagnose and classify mental illness. This 991-page, $25 million behemoth represents the entire universe of recognized psychiatric illnesses and mental disorders and is the culmination of decades of research and clinical judgment from hundreds of experts. It offers no treatment guidance, but it does provide critical validation of different illnesses to help you get treatment, and it helps clinicians and researchers share a common language for a consistent and reliable identification of the different mental health issues.

As you can imagine, classifying and diagnosing mental illnesses is not without controversy, fueled in part by the ballooning number of official disorders. The *DSM-I* from 1952 had 106 listed disorders, the *DSM-III* from 1980 had 265, and the *DSM-IV* and *DSM-5* have 297. Are we really getting that much nuttier, or are we getting better at identifying and labeling mental illness? Are we too quick to pathologize quirkiness, or are advances in brain science helping us to better understand distinct neurological causes of distress? Probably all of the above. Even though all changes in the *DSM* must be backed up by evidence-based science, cynics are quick to point out that there is a financial incentive to creating more diagnostic categories, and companies with aggressive drug-marketing cultures are keen to convince you that the problems of everyday life are actually undiagnosed mental illnesses for which there is pharmaceutical solution. In the fifth edition, some disorders have become more clearly differentiated (e.g., hoarding disorder is now considered distinct from obsessive-compulsive disorder), whereas others have become less so (e.g., Asperger's disorder is now part of autism spectrum disorder). Some diagnoses have been added (e.g., gender identity disorder), some have been deleted (e.g., hypochondria), and some are intensely controversial because they appear to over-pathologize natural responses (e.g., caffeine withdrawal disorder). Regardless, the *DSM-5* represents the latest science on understanding and diagnosing mental health conditions. It's not exactly bedtime reading, but it is a fascinating glimpse into the world of clinical psychology.

brain, not your Chimp.

For most of us, feeling fat comes and goes, but for others the level of distress can be more overwhelming or more frequent. It's a particular brand of Chimp crazy that beats down far too many athletes. We want to give you a toolbox of strategies to combat the unwanted thoughts and feelings that distort your relationship with your body and how you nourish it. Our focus is deliberately narrow and self-centered. It's very much a "save yourself" approach that targets winning a very personal fight rather than a larger battle. This means that we won't tackle the sociocultural influences that scream at women and girls to be thin. That's not because this battle is unimportant . . . it's just that you can't hope to make much of a dent in it at 8 p.m. on a Thursday night, and it certainly won't help you calm the f*ck down if you mistakenly grab a roll of belly fat.

The skinny on feeling fat.

Having occasional and disheartening thoughts of "feeling fat" is a bit like coping with a racist aunt or uncle at Thanksgiving—you wish they hadn't invited themselves to begin with, arguing with them seems to make things worse, and you just try to bite your lip until they leave. Sometimes they never really leave—they just camp out in the basement waiting for the right moment to surprise you again.

When athletes have an "I feel fat" moment, it manifests as cognition, or thought. As we discussed in Chapter 1, "Hello, Brain!" cognitions or thoughts are simply things you say to yourself in your head. All cognition is self-talk because thoughts appear in our head as words or sentences. Here are some examples of the thoughts that athletes tell us they have during a fat moment:

> I feel like a McChunk-Chunk today.
> I just feel so bloated.
> Urgh, I'm bulging out of my clothes. F*ck, why did I eat that last night?
> I feel like a sausage in my kit today.
> When I bend over, I can feel rolls.
> I can't look at my legs in the mirror. I just see cellulite.
> Flab. I just feel and see flab.

All of these examples come from female athletes. That's not because feeling fat is only experienced by women, but it is far more prevalent among women, and women are far more likely to admit it. Even still, it's hard to know exactly how common it is for women to have these kinds of thoughts. There aren't good scientific data on the prevalence of feeling fat among women who don't have a clinical disorder of eating or appearance or who aren't experiencing feelings of being bloated or gassy in response to normal hormonal shifts prior to menstruation. However, we do know that body dissatisfaction is related to ethnicity, and white women are more likely to experience these feelings than nonwhite women.[2] That said, based on our own anecdotal experience, we can conclude wholly unscientifically that feeling fat is as common as socks.

As you might suspect, feeling fat and being fat are not the same thing. Sure, some of us don't just *feel* fat. Some of us *are* fat. Let's not argue here about what being fat actually means. That's a hornet's nest at the best of times, even for the scholars who study it. It reflects intellectual tensions between the medical definition of excess fat and its health consequences versus the importance of self-acceptance and body positivity (a.k.a. "all the right junk in all the right places").[3]

However, it is important to make the distinction between feeling fat and being fat: Although the distress caused by feeling fat is related to actual fatness, it's certainly not the same thing.[4] So, the next time your size 2 friend complains about having to wear her "fat jeans" because she feels bloated, take a moment to think before you blurt out, "But you're not fat. Look at you!" More on that in a moment.

Fat is not a feeling: The psychopathology of hating your inner thighs.

We've already established that we experience "feeling fat" through self-talk. If we want to get even more scientific about it, there's no such thing as feeling fat. This is not just about semantics but actual neurological differences between a thought and a feeling and an emotion. For the purposes of this chapter, we use the terms "emotion" and "feeling" interchangeably even though it's not technically accurate to do this. Emotions precede feelings, neurologically speaking. Emotions originate in the limbic system (Chimp brain) and cause physical changes in your body, whereas feelings add a layer of interpretation from your frontal cor-

2 S. Grabe, and J. S. Hyde, "Ethnicity and Body Dissatisfaction Among Women in the United States: A Meta-analysis," *Psychological Bulletin* 132 (2006): 622–640.

3 E. D. Rosen and B. M. Spiegelman, "What We Talk About When We Talk About Fat," *Cell* 156, nos. 1–2 (2014): 20–44; N. M. McKinley, "Resisting Body Dissatisfaction: Fat Women Who Endorse Fat Acceptance," *Body Image* 1, no. 2 (2004): 213–219.

4 R. Pingitore, B. Spring, and D. Garfield, "Gender Differences in Body Satisfaction," *Obesity Research* 5 (September 1997): 402–409.

tex (your Professor brain)—a sort of mental representation of what's going on. These mental representations appear as thoughts or self-talk. For example, being scared is an emotion that may give rise to feelings of being fearful or nervous, which, in turn, may give rise to the following self-talk: "You need to back away from the dog very slowly"—a thought. Ok, back to feeling fat.

When you feel fat, you're actually feeling something else. Feeling fat is a smokescreen for other feelings. For example, you might feel frustrated that you don't feel in control of your exercise or eating habits, or depressed that with all the exercise you do, your body still doesn't look the way you want it to. Perhaps you feel jealous or envious of the badass athlete with the great legs, or you're worried about gaining weight. Before we start digging into what your "something else" feelings are, we need to uncover what triggers the "I feel fat" in the first place. Then we need to deconstruct why we have the underlying feelings. The following exercises are designed to help you do just that.

EXERCISE 1

MY TRIGGERS FOR FEELING FAT

As we learned in Chapter 4, a trigger is simply the circumstance or event that prompted you to think or feel something. For example, if you happen to catch yourself in the mirror a certain way and notice the back of your thighs, which leads to feelings of fatness, then the glance in the mirror would be the trigger. If you sit down in a certain way and notice a roll of fat around your middle, which triggers "I feel fat," then sitting down a certain way would be the trigger, and so on. The next three times you feel fat, make a note of the triggers, the context, and who you were with. Alternatively, you can think back to the last time you felt fat and record the same information.

1 **I felt fat when . . .**

The trigger:

Where I was:

Who I was with:

2 **I felt fat when . . .**

The trigger:

Where I was:

Who I was with:

3 **I felt fat when . . .**

The trigger:

Where I was:

Who I was with:

EXERCISE 2

NAME IT, DON'T SHAME IT! THE FAT FEELING FINDER

For each example in Exercise 1, use the Fat Feeling Finder to try and uncover what it is you are really feeling. First, identify the big emotion(s) on the top line that best correspond to the feeling. Next, circle up to five applicable words in the column below that explore this emotion in more detail. If you find it hard to think about what's behind your fat feelings, you can also use this grid to uncover the emotions behind your relationship with food. In this context, you would complete the exercise while thinking about food or your current eating habits.

MY SHITTY FEELINGS

Angry	Depressed	Confused	Helpless	Indifferent	Afraid	Hurt	Sad
irritated	lousy	upset	incapable	insensitive	fearful	crushed	tearful
enraged	disappointed	doubtful	alone	dull	terrified	tormented	sorrowful
hostile	discouraged	uncertain	paralyzed	nonchalant	suspicious	deprived	pained
insulting	ashamed	indecisive	fatigued	neutral	anxious	pained	grieving
sore	powerless	perplexed	useless	reserved	alarmed	tortured	anguished
annoyed	diminished	embarrassed	inferior	weary	panicky	dejected	desolate
upset	guilty	hesitant	vulnerable	bored	nervous	rejected	desperate
hateful	dissatisfied	shy	empty	preoccupied	scared	injured	pessimistic
unpleasant	miserable	stupefied	forced	cold	worried	offended	unhappy
offensive	detestable	disillusioned	hesitant	disinterested	frightened	afflicted	lonely
bitter	repugnant	disbelieving	despairing	lifeless	timid	aching	mournful
aggressive	despicable	skeptical	frustrated		shaky	victimized	dismayed
resentful	disgusting	distrustful	distressed		restless	heartbroken	
inflamed	abominable	misgiving	woeful		doubtful	agonized	
provoked	terrible	lost	pathetic		threatened	appalled	
incensed	in despair	unsure	tragic		cowardly	humiliated	
infuriated	sulky	uneasy	in a stew		quaking	wronged	
cross	bad	pessimistic	dominated		menaced	alienated	
worked up	sense of loss	tense			wary		
boiling							
fuming							
indignant							

Adapted from http://www.psychpage.com/learning/library/assess/feelings.html.

FINDING PATTERNS AND EXPLANATIONS

Write down any patterns that you notice from the triggers you identified in Exercise 1 and the underlying emotions you have circled in the Fat Feeling Finder. Take some time to think about the reasons behind these feelings. For example, if you notice a pattern of feeling frustrated and resentful that you can't seem to lose belly fat despite all your training, you might reflect that you feel helpless because you're doing everything you can, or because you expect there to be a concrete relationship between training and fat loss. Perhaps it's something else entirely.

From my triggers and my Fat Feeling Finder, I notice the following patterns:

I think I feel this way because:

HOW TO SEPARATE FACT FROM FICTION

When it comes to coping with feeling fat, a few simple self-help strategies can go a long way to minimize the mental disruption. When feeling fat becomes so overwhelming that it begins to impact your quality of life or your overall mental health, it's usually a sign that we need to bring in reinforcements. We'll get to that in a moment. In the meantime, let's keep building your self-help toolbox.

Fat-talk. Yeah, don't do that.

When we talk about our feelings of being fat, it's referred to as "fat-talk." Research shows that fat-talk is extremely common among women. For example, one study found that 90 percent of college-aged women did it, even though only 9 percent were overweight. Before you start rolling your eyes, you might be surprised to learn that 25 percent of guys do it too. Fat-talk matters. A lot. Even though women believe that talking about their fat makes them feel better about their bodies, scientific studies show that it actually increases feelings of body dissatisfaction.[5] Increasing evidence also suggests that talking about your fatness can contribute to your actually becoming fat, at least among young women, probably because it causes psychosocial stress and may fuel unsustainable dietary habits that contribute to weight gain.[6] It also seems to matter who does the fat talking and who's listening. Even though talking to other women about feeling fat is clearly a strategy to cope with one's own distress (by seeking reassurance or a cathartic release of guilt), it doesn't actually do that and can add to the stress of the person listening. For example, when women described as "slim" start fat-talking it makes other women feel even worse.[7] Because self-inflicted fat-shaming is contagious and destructive, you need to confront the

---

5 R. Salk and R. Engeln-Maddox, "'If You're Fat, Then I'm Humongous!' Frequency, Content, and Impact of Fat Talk Among College Women," *Psychology of Women Quarterly* 35, no. 1 (March 2011): 18–28; H. Sharpe et al., "Is Fat Talking a Causal Risk Factor for Body Dissatisfaction? A Systematic Review and Meta-analysis," *International Journal of Eating Disorders* 46, no. 7 (November 2013): 643–652.

6 Koenraad Cuypers et al., "Being Normal Weight but Feeling Overweight in Adolescence May Affect Weight Development into Young Adulthood: An 11-Year Follow-Up: The HUNT Study, Norway," *Journal of Obesity* (2012): 601872.

7 A. F. Corning, M. M. Bucchianeri, and C. M. Pick, "Thin or Overweight Women's Fat Talk: Which Is Worse for Other Women's Body Satisfaction?" *Eating Disorders* 22, no. 2 (2014): 121–135.

EXERCISE 3

WATCHING FAT FEELINGS FROM AFAR

First practice this exercise while sitting comfortably and in a quiet environment. Recall a recent experience in which you felt fat.

Recreate that experience in your head—the sights and sounds around you, everything that makes it come back to life. Pay attention to what triggered or prompted the feelings.

Once you've got the movie playing, leave your body and hover above it, as if you were a human drone. Just hang there for a moment and watch. You can see yourself, but you are not you in the moment.

While staying in your drone, try to pick out the thoughts and feelings the "you" down on the ground is experiencing. Try to be aware enough to label the experience but not actually have it. If it helps, see thought bubbles appear with the stuff that was going through your head. See each one evaporate or float into the distance so you can no longer read it. Notice, acknowledge, let it float by.

Now start describing and labeling what you see and the thoughts and feelings you remember yourself having: *Yup, that's when I sat down in that bean bag chair. See how it made my stomach roll up? Yes, that's the moment I noticed it. Watch, I put my hand over my stomach to inspect the rolls of fat. Urgh. Watch my expression. And there come the thoughts . . . F*ck, why am I so fat? Urgh, I hate these jeans too because they really pinch the fat and make it worse. I wonder if people can notice it. They must! I mean look at it. I knew I shouldn't have had dessert last night. . . .* And so on. If you find yourself wandering down into the body of the you below, get back up to your drone! You are observing, not experiencing. As you watch yourself, now see each thought or feeling float past as if it's a thought bubble.

› What kinds of thoughts did you notice? › What was it like to just see your thoughts without having to follow or experience them? › What does it feel like to see thoughts and feelings but not *be* them? › How easy was it to let go of the thought or feeling after it evaporated or floated out of sight?

Once you have a good grasp on recreating your fat moments, try to repeat this exercise soon after you experience your next fat moment. With practice, you will be able to do it "live"—as soon as you notice a trigger.

misguided thinking that it will lead to some sort of awakening or added motivation to get your shit together. It doesn't. So (1) be kind to yourself, and (2) care about who's listening.

Acknowledge the feelings but don't indulge them

The long-term goal is to be able to recognize—in the moment—that you have encountered a trigger to feel fat, but instead of letting the feelings run wild, you let them float by. Think of this shift in perception as watching people pass you by in the street, walking in the opposite direction. You notice them, but you can't stare because they're gone in a flash. That's what we want to do with your feelings of fatness. This takes practice. Exercise 3 (p. 140) is designed to help you do this. It's a detachment exercise common to many forms of meditation and passive attention to help you detach yourself from the actual experience and simply observe it. We used the same exercise in Chapter 2, "I Wish I Felt More Like an Athlete." The overall goals of the exercise are to (1) recognize that you are not your thoughts and feelings but rather a container for them, and (2) you don't have to "react" to the feelings that your brain feeds you.

Don't feed the fat-talk, especially around others

Fat-talk might seem like a good idea, but evidence suggests that it is likely to make things worse for you and the people around you. So we need to stop or divert these conversations when they occur. You've heard these conversations before:

You: Ugh, I feel so fat.

Friend: Are you serious? You are definitely not fat.

You: Yes I am. Look at my muffin top.

Friend: Look at my stomach.

You: Oh, come on. You're a stick.

Friend: So are you!

If you feel the urge to start commenting about how fat or chunky you feel, stop yourself. Acknowledge the feelings, but don't let the words come out of your mouth. Be a good role model by avoiding fat-talk. If your friend starts talking about her body in a self-shaming or derogatory way, divert the conversation to things she has done or accomplished rather than indulging the fat feelings. You don't have to be preachy or cold and unrealistic to pull this off. In virtually all instances, we recommend using humor to your advantage:

Friend: Ugh, I feel so fat.

You: You want my opinion? I say, f*ck the fat!

Friend: Ha ha.

You: Listen, hon, these feelings are here to test us. To get us moping around. We're bigger than that.

Friend: In my case, literally!

You: Don't sweat it. We all get visits from fatso. We've got to rise above it. It's not the real us. The real you is a badass tough chick. Here's your new motto: F*ck the fat!

Friend: F*ck the fat!

Accentuate the positive

So far, we've focused on the strategies of awareness, detachment, and avoidance of fat-talk to help stem the tide of feeling fat. If we left it at that, we would be in danger of leaving behind a vacuum for the festering fat feelings to keep growing back. It would be like going to the dentist with a toothache, getting lidocaine for the pain, having the decayed bits drilled away, and then leaving the office with a clean but gaping hole. Hardly ideal. We need some mental amalgam.

Research on healing destructive cognition about our body's lumps and bumps finds that self-acceptance is key. Self-acceptance isn't pop-psychology drivel for standing in front of the mirror and telling yourself that you're beautiful (although that might work for a short while). Self-acceptance is about embracing and accepting our strengths, weaknesses, limitations, quirks, kick-ass attributes, and annoying habits—in other words, ALL of us—without judgment or qualification (no more "Oh, I'm just a . . ."). The goal isn't to ignore annoying traits or gloss over gross character deficiencies (as in "People say I'm rude and manipulative, but I think I'm f*cking awesome"), but to be aware of which parts of us are great, which aspects are okay, and which bits need a bit of work—*and*—this awareness

NAME IT AND FAME IT!

On the word grid, circle one or more of the big emotions, attributes, characteristics, or tendencies on the top line that best correspond to how you see yourself generally or how you think other people would describe you. Yes, we know this isn't very scientific, but it also doesn't need to be. And no, of course you don't feel like this all the time. However, you probably do feel some of these things more than others, and other people might use some of these words to describe you. Next, circle up to three words in those categories that best describe you. These are your superpowers.

MY HAPPY FEELINGS

Open	Happy	Feisty	Good	Loving	Interested	Positive	Strong
understanding	joyous	playful	calm	considerate	concerned	eager	free
confident	lucky	courageous	peaceful	affectionate	fascinated	keen	sure
reliable	fortunate	energetic	at ease	sensitive	intrigued	earnest	certain
easy	delighted	liberated	comfortable	tender	absorbed	inspired	rebellious
amazed	overjoyed	optimistic	pleased	devoted	inquisitive	determined	unique
free	gleeful	provocative	encouraged	attracted	engrossed	excited	dynamic
sympathetic	thankful	impulsive	content	passionate	curious	enthusiastic	tenacious
interested	ecstatic	frisky	quiet	admiring		bold	hardy
satisfied	satisfied	animated	relaxed	warm		brave	secure
receptive	cheerful	spirited	serene	close		daring	
accepting	sunny	thrilled	free & easy			optimistic	
kind	merry		bright			reinforced	
	elated		reassured			confident	
	jubilant					hopeful	

Adapted from http://www.psychpage.com/learning/library/assess/feelings.html.

Continued

FINDING YOUR AWESOME

After you have identified your emotional superpowers, we want you to think about how you can turn these positive emotions into an action. The important point is that you focus on doing something that is grounded in a personal strength—in this case, your emotional superpower. Here are some examples:

Emotional superpower: FEISTY and Courageous.

How I plan to act on this feeling today: I will be feisty and courageous today by apologizing to someone I recently offended.

Emotional superpower: GOOD and Calm.

How I plan to act on this feeling today: I will be good and calm today by smiling as I sit in traffic on the way to work. The worse the traffic, the more I will smile and laugh.

Emotional superpower: STRONG and Rebellious.

How I plan to act on this feeling today: I will be strong and rebellious today by wearing my bright yellow pants to work.

Okay, now it's your turn.

Emotional superpower:

How I plan to act on this feeling today:

Emotional superpower:

How I plan to act on this feeling today:

Emotional superpower:

How I plan to act on this feeling today:

doesn't get in the way of our acceptance of ourselves. You know your wavy hair that gave you nothing but misery in high school? Or your turned-in feet? Or your belly button inspired by Stephen King? (We could go on.) Well, you don't really think about those things much now, do you? Yeah, so that kind of acceptance.

We can't tackle the entire psychopathology of self-loathing here, nor cover the 10,000-piece jigsaw puzzle that is meaningful self-acceptance, but we can lay down a corner piece. We dealt with self-acceptance in more detail in Chapter 3, "I Don't Think I Can: Building confidence and self-belief." For now, let's make a start by focusing on things you do like about yourself. This might seem like self-help, but anchoring ourselves around positive attributes and then acting on these attributes when we feel a wholelottashittola is a great strategy to change our tune. If attitude and gratitude are the yellow brick road to happiness, then "things I like about myself" are the bricks.

The following exercise focuses on your emotional self, not your physical capabilities, your intellectual smarts, or the fact that you can make a mean risotto or crush the beer mile. This exercise is designed to single out the positive emotions, feelings, and attributes that define your personality. It's like the B-side of Exercise 2, "Name it; don't shame it." We call it "Name it and fame it" because you first identify your emotional superpowers and then you escort them to the front of the line when you feel fat.

Help! I think it might be a bit more serious than that.

If your thoughts and feelings about food, eating habits, and/or your body cause you great distress on a regular basis, it might be worth exploring whether something more serious is going on. If you do think it's a bit more serious then we urge you to make an appointment with a professional, preferably a clinical psychologist with postdoctoral training and expertise in the specific issue you face. Many of the recognized clinical disorders about eating, anxiety, and body perceptions are so interrelated that trying to separate the diagnoses can be difficult, even for trained professionals. For example, very similar obsessive worries, intrusive thoughts, and repetitive behaviors are hallmarks of both eating disorders and certain anxiety disorders such as body dysmorphic disorder (excessive anxiety about perceived flaws in appearance, usually not related to fat or weight, see sidebar "Mirror, Mirror on the Wall: A Look Inside Body Dismorphic Disorder," p. 146). Because diagnostic criteria have so much overlap as well as lots of "fuzzy" edges, in-person interviews by specialized clinical psychologists are often the only way to know who has what, and even that's not great. That said, here's what we do know.

Feeding and eating disorders

Feeding and eating disorders refer to serious and sometimes fatal illnesses that severely disturb a person's eating behavior. Obsessive thoughts about food, body weight, and shape are also telltale signs. There are currently three recognized types of eating disorders: anorexia nervosa, bulimia nervosa, and binge-eating

MIRROR, MIRROR ON THE WALL: A LOOK INSIDE BODY DYSMORPHIC DISORDER

IF YOU FEEL OVERWHELMED by negative thoughts and feelings about perceived flaws in your physical appearance that don't seem to be weight- or fat-related, you might be experiencing symptoms of BDD, a type of anxiety disorder. Before you get too paranoid or convinced you have BDD because you've always hated your nose or because you really want bigger pecs, hold your horses. BDD isn't a vanity-inspired gripe about parts of your body or a wish to feel awesome naked; it's a serious mental illness that's often accompanied by a psychiatric shit storm of other conditions such as depression, substance abuse, an eating disorder, exercise dependence, obsessive-compulsive disorder, or a social phobia. Yeah, it's no picnic. Fortunately, the prevalence of BDD as a diagnosable condition is pretty low—about 2.4 percent of US adults are estimated to be sufferers. So, statistically speaking, it's pretty unlikely you have it. That said, here are the criteria for BDD, as listed in the *DSM-5* (and adapted from https://bdd.iocdf.org/professionals/diagnosis). These can't be used for self-diagnosis, but they can help you to decide if you want to see a specialist to talk more about it.

8 S. Bratland-Sanda and J. Sundgot-Borgen, "Eating Disorders in Athletes: Overview of Prevalence, Risk Factors and Recommendations for Prevention and Treatment," *European Journal of Sport Science* 13, no. 5 (2013): 499–508.

Appearance preoccupations. The individual must be preoccupied with one or more nonexistent or slight defects or flaws in their physical appearance. "Preoccupation" means thinking about the perceived defects for at least an hour a day. A distressing preoccupation with obvious appearance flaws (for example, those that are easily noticeable or clearly visible at conversational distance) is not diagnosed as BDD.

Repetitive behaviors. At some point, the individual must perform repetitive, compulsive behaviors in response to the appearance concerns. These compulsions can be behavioral and thus observed by others—for example, checking the mirror, grooming to excess, picking at the skin, seeking reassurance, or changing clothes. Other BDD compulsions are mental acts—such as comparing one's appearance with that of other people.

Clinical significance. The preoccupation must cause clinically significant distress or impairment in social, occupational, or other important areas of functioning.

Differentiation from an eating disorder. If the preoccupation with appearance focuses on being too fat or weighing too much, the clinician must determine that these concerns are not better explained by an eating disorder. If the patient's only appearance concern focuses on excessive fat or weight and the patient's symptoms meet diagnostic criteria for an eating disorder, then he or she should be diagnosed with an eating disorder, not BDD. However, if the criteria for an eating disorder are not met, then BDD can be diagnosed, as concerns with fat or weight in a person of normal weight can be a symptom of BDD. It is not uncommon for patients to have both an eating disorder and BDD (the latter focusing on concerns other than weight or body fat).

For more information, resources, and tips to get help, go to https://bdd.iocdf.org.

disorder (as defined in the *DSM-5*).

Anorexia nervosa. Characterized by distorted body image and excessive dieting that leads to severe weight loss with a pathological fear of becoming fat. It primarily affects adolescent girls and young women. Estimated population prevalence: men, 0.3 percent; women, 0.9 percent.

Bulimia nervosa. Characterized by recurring episodes (at least one per week) of binge eating, followed by inappropriate behaviors such as self-induced vomiting to avoid weight gain. Estimated population prevalence: men, 0.5 percent; women, 1.5 percent.

Binge-eating disorder. Defined by recurring episodes (at least one a week for three months) of eating significantly more food in a short period of time than most people would eat under similar circumstances, with episodes marked by feelings of lack of control. The person may eat too quickly, even when he or she is not hungry. The person may have feelings of guilt, embarrassment, or disgust and may binge eat alone to hide the behavior. Estimated population prevalence: men, 2 percent; women, 3.5 percent.

There are other types of eating disorders, but they are all clumped under "Not one of the above" in the *DSM-5*. If you're interested in learning more about these other disorders, just search online for "Other Specified Feeding and Eating Disorders (OSFED)," a phrase that's guaranteed to be a conversation stopper.

People who show some of the symptoms of an eating disorder, but with less frequency or severity, are often diagnosed with a subclinical eating disorder called "disordered eating." The main difference between an eating disorder and disordered eating is the frequency and severity of the symptoms. Endurance athletes have a higher risk of both disordered eating and eating disorders because of the overvalued belief that leanness and lower body weight gives a competitive advantage. A recent study estimated the prevalence of either disordered eating or eating disorder to be 6–45 percent among female athletes and 0–19 percent among male athletes.[8]

Other risk factors among athletes include training for a sport since childhood,

HOW TO TALK ABOUT EATING DISORDERS

THINGS TO SAY OR DO	THINGS *NOT* TO SAY OR DO
Use "I" statements when sharing your concerns, such as "I care about you" or "I'm worried about you."	Don't focus on the food. Don't say "You don't eat enough" or "You need to eat more." At first you might want to talk about the behaviors you notice, but then try to focus on how the person is feeling.
Let them know that it's safe to talk to you and that you won't judge or criticize them. "As your friend, I really care about you. I won't judge or criticize you; I just want to know how I can help."	Do not use language that implies blame or that the person is doing something wrong. Of course, we know that they probably *are* doing something wrong, but pointing out the obvious forces them to be defensive.
Encourage them to express how they feel, and remember, it is important to understand how they feel rather than just state how you feel. "I know this stuff is really hard to talk about, but can you help me understand what it feels like for you?"	Don't assume the role of a therapist or try to fix things. You don't need to have all the answers; it's more important that you listen and help the person feel comfortable opening up to you.
If the person isn't very talkative, try to let silences linger longer than normal to give them more opportunity to speak. People don't like awkward silences. They will usually fill them if you can fight your urge to talk.	Don't use manipulative statements or phrases that focus on the impact the problem is having on other people. This can make things worse or increase the person's level of denial. "Do you have any idea how this is affecting your mom?" or "If you loved me, you would start eating properly."
Encourage them to seek help and explain that you will be there with them each step of the way. "Why don't we go and see someone together? Just to chat through some of the feelings you have. I'll be right there with you."	Don't use threats, especially if you have some control or authority over the person as a parent or coach. This only heightens an already stressful experience for the individual and can make the behavior worse. "If you don't eat properly, you can't [play, practice, join in, go out]."

low self-esteem family dysfunction (which includes parents who live through the success of their child in sport), families with eating disorders, chronic dieting, a history of physical or sexual abuse, or other traumatic life experiences. Female athletes also tend to experience more performance anxiety and self-criticism than male athletes, both of which further increase the risk. Of course, one of the most pervasive and pernicious causes of body bashing that targets women and girls almost exclusively is cultural: the promotion of the thin, and often sexualized, ideal from our media that bombards women and girls on a daily basis.

What to do if you suspect a friend has an eating disorder

Many people are reluctant to voice their concerns about people's eating habits for fear of being offensive or causing embarrassment. Get over it. However, before you share your concerns, take some time to educate yourself about the illness and to learn how to have difficult and awkward conversations. Remember, an eating disorder is a coping mechanism, and denial is the psychological defense. For this reason, you need to be prepared for resistance. Although you cannot force someone to change or get help, you can share your honest concerns, provide support, and tell them where they can get proper help. As with all sensitive topics, the language you use is really important. Our cheat sheet will keep you from sounding like a judgmental old nag (see p. 149).

It's never easy to talk about intensely private, awkward, or embarrassing stuff. Here's one example of how you might have that conversation with Amy, your roommate you suspect is suffering from a binge-eating disorder. It goes without saying that it's important to have these conversations in a private and quiet environment.

You: Hey, Amy, you got time for a quick chat?

Amy: Sure. What's up?

You: I feel a bit awkward saying this, but I'm concerned about you. It's about your eating. I've noticed that you follow a really strict diet, but you don't seem to eat that much when we're out. You also visit the bathroom a lot just after we've eaten. At home, I can hear you going into the kitchen after we've all gone to bed, and I think you must be eating because things in the fridge are gone by the morning. I get a sense that you might need some help. What's your take on this?

Amy: Oh no, I'm fine. I appreciate your concern but you're reading into things. I mean, I've just got a weak bladder. I might get up a few times in the night, but it's usually because I can't sleep. Seriously, I'm totally fine.

You: Okay, I understand that. Yeah, I may have got things wrong, but can you help me understand how you've concluded that you're fine? I still see things differently. You hardly drink at dinner, and I know you're eating things in the fridge most nights. I don't care about the food stuff; I'm just worried about you and think that some of these behaviors aren't good for you. You're a great athlete, and your health is really important. What about talking to someone about it?

Amy: I'm not going to see anyone. I don't want to, and I don't need to.

You: I get it. I mean, it's pretty normal to not want to discuss something that's scary or embarrassing. But as your friend, I really want to make sure you're okay. I don't know that much about eating disorders, but I do know that between friends, it's okay to admit when we're struggling. And you seem to be showing some of the telltale signs. I'm not saying you're some sort of wacko, but I do think that talking to someone could help, even just as a precaution. Would you be open to that?

Amy: No. There's nothing wrong with me. I'm just conscious about my weight because I know how much better I do [as an athlete] when I'm lean. My training is pretty heavy, so I get hungry at weird times.

You: I hear you on that. Me too. But here's what I see differently: You seem to be doing a lot of these other things too. The bathroom visits, eating in the middle of the night. The thing about eating disorders is that they're not really about food and weight, but about coping with problems, with anxiety, feeling in control, and so on. It might be that you're not only frightened about gaining weight or losing control over your eating, but perhaps of other things, too. You know, how you think and feel about yourself in general. Have you considered that?

Amy: Yeah, I suppose. I get stressed just like everyone else. But I've got it all under control.

You: You may well have, but it seems like this gives you a lot of anxiety. Can you imagine how it would feel to not have to worry about this sort of stuff?

Amy: Urgh. I know.

You: So how about this. Why don't we go and see someone together? Just to chat through some of the feelings you have. I'll be right there with you.

7

I DON'T COPE WELL WITH INJURY

HOW TO RESPOND TO SETBACKS, BIG AND SMALL

Note to self: Let shit go. —CONFUCIUS

Athletes do not enjoy being injured. Sure, there are some athletes who might feel relieved when they get injured because the pressure to perform has become overwhelming, and some athletes might even feign or exaggerate injury for the same reason, but it's fair to say that most athletes f*cking hate it. Knowing the medical facts about your injury and why it occurred is a small, albeit important, part of coping with it, but this information will be insufficient if you start to experience despair, anxiety, frustration, rage, depression, or the gazillion other emotions that can panic-rush your brain. As an athlete, it's hard to find science-based information about how to mentally cope with injury. Endurance sports magazines often feature advice from physical therapists or doctors who have little, if any, training on dealing with your 3-pound lump of crazy. You become a headless body of pain, swelling, mobility, and strength, and advice is often laced with bemusement at why athletes can't follow simple instructions. Any mention of psychology usually comes in 100-word nuggets of advice based on anecdotal nonsense, or in trite prescriptions like this: "Rest . . . and don't worry about losing fitness. You won't get anywhere fast injured." Oh for God's sake. Shut up.

Checkup from the neck up.

How an athlete copes with an injury depends on so many interconnected factors that attempts to study this subject yield theoretical models that look like spaghetti and meatballs.[1] The challenge is in knowing why some athletes respond so differently than others. How can one athlete feel mild indifference to developing plantar fasciitis while another feels suicidal? Of course, most athletes are somewhere in between, but it can still be a roller coaster—some days you are calm and accepting, but on other days you're a psychotic Medusa with a nasty passive-aggressive streak. What fascinates sport psychologists is how these reactions influence rehabilitation.[2] As coaches, we are interested in helping injured athletes become better at dealing with the thoughts and feelings they don't want so the recovery process can be as smooth and productive as possible.

If you've experienced a significant injury,[3] you can probably relate to mood swings, grouchiness, and some level of social withdrawal, not to mention hearing yourself say the same shit over and over again. If you're the partner of an injured athlete, you're forced to deal with the fallout. Speaking from personal experience, I need to tell you to avoid this verbal cluster bomb: "Can you just shut up about it?" It feels so cathartic to say it, but who would have guessed that it has zero therapeutic impact on the athlete? This much we know—injury can bring fire and brimstone to even the most optimistic and bubbly of sporty households. If you don't cope well with injury or you have to live with athletes who don't cope well with injury, help is on the way.

What kind of patient are you?

Research on the psychology of sports injury helps us understand the types of emotions that athletes have when injured and the factors that cause these emotions. That said, no research can prepare you for the psychological messiness

---

1 Current research suggests about 55 interrelated factors influence your injury coping skills. When you see these in a diagram with causative paths, it looks like something the cat threw up. See D. M. Wiese-Bjornstal et al., "An Integrated Model of Response to Sport Injury: Psychological and Sociological Dynamics," *Journal of Applied Sport Psychology* 10 (1998): 46–69.

2 N. Walker, J. Thatcher, and D. Lavallee, "Psychological Responses to Injury in Competitive Sport: A Critical Review," *Journal of the Royal Society for the Promotion of Health* 127, no. 4 (2007): 174–180.

3 Which is a can of worms to define, let me assure you.

that is the actual experience. For example, we know plenty of athletes who are very motivated and goal-oriented about their training, but they suddenly become unfocused and apathetic in dealing with their injuries. We call it *passive patient syndrome*. The training mindset leaves them, their hustle-muscle skedaddles, and they do virtually nothing to help themselves get better. They simply wait. Even worse, some athletes don't bother to connect the dots of bad decisions that led to injury. Some get lost in a fog of emotional *meh* or disappear down a hole of envy or resentment. Like Ian, 41, who said this upon getting plantar fasciitis just weeks after successfully rehabbing a long-standing Achilles tendon injury:

> I'm so sick of being injured. I see all these happy athletes out there but instead of thinking, "Hey, good for you," I think, "Damn you. It's so unfair."

Compare this mindset to that of Jessica, a 34-year-old professional cyclist who's had her fair share of injuries. Jessica rolled a tubular (i.e., she crashed) at pro road nationals in 2014. She broke her collarbone, separated her shoulder, and got a concussion. She was hating life. In 2015, she had surgery to repair a left iliac artery and a second surgery to fix nerve compression. Just as she recovered, she crashed again and needed two surgeries on her wrist. Two other surgeries were needed to fix complications from the previous surgeries. All this happened during her first pro contract. This would be enough to send many athletes over the edge. But not Jess. Here's how she puts it:

> I am so lucky to be waking up knowing this injury will pass, it's not chronic, it's not life threatening, and I promise I will return as a more gracious, patient, and positive person/athlete. I'm not kidding you; I had that thought daily! It helped me deal with it. It helped me keep positive and I've really stuck with it. No more ninnies over bad days, flats, colds, etc. That said, I still have plenty of what ifs . . . what if I put all the work into rehabbing, days and nights of managing pain, weeks of feeling behind, digging and clawing to get myself back, and I get taken out in a crash my first race back?

After the crash in 2015, Jessica felt an overwhelming sense of gratitude and fear, all smushed into the same injury experience. That speaks volumes about her recovery mindset, which undoubtedly played a big role in her ability to be back on the bike sooner than expected. Who knows how Ian would respond if he was injured a third time?

So what is a normal response to injury?

Every athlete deals with injury in a unique way, but frustration, depression, anger, and tension are the emotions most commonly reported by injured athletes.[4]

Sport psychologists noticed right away that many of the response profiles of injured athletes appeared similar to that of people who were told they were going to die. The "grief model" by Elisabeth Kübler-Ross revealed that patients with a terminal illness tended to experience five distinct and sequential emotional stages after getting the news: denial, anger, bargaining, depression, and, finally, acceptance.[5] Although there are obvious differences between coping with imminent death and coping with a sports injury, psychologists and athletes have still drawn parallels. For example, some injured athletes experience denial by refusing to acknowledge the severity of their injury or trying to train through it. Some athletes are angry with themselves for making silly decisions that led to injury, or they get angry at others for not understanding "how hard it is" to deal with their injury. Many report symptoms of depression. Some athletes, like Jessica, can eventually reach acceptance and approach their injury with a positive attitude.

The grief model applied to injury has not stood up to more recent scientific scrutiny because emotional responses to injury appear more general, are more varied, and don't always follow a staged progression. That said, some injured athletes do respond as if they're grieving. Based on the injured endurance athletes that we've coached, we guesstimate the prevalence of this response to be about 10 percent, and it's usually among those with more traumatic injuries. If you think this might be you (or you know an athlete who might be exhibiting this response), it's important that you have some strategies to deal with it.

---

4 Walker, Thatcher, and Lavallee, "Psychological Responses to Injury in Competitive Sport."

5 Elisabeth Kübler-Ross, *On Death and Dying* (London: Macmillan, 1969).

When a grief response is suspected

When we suspect that injured athletes are on a grief trajectory, we offer specific strategies to help them accept these emotions and, critically, help them work through the stages to reach a more calm acceptance of it.

Denial. You try to pretend that the news isn't that bad or that you can still race in the upcoming event. "It's not that bad. I can continue and train through it."

★ **What to do about it:** Use third-person thinking. What advice would you give to another athlete in the same situation? Focus on how a small hiatus in your training could prevent losing your entire season. If this fails to work, fast-track the anger by confronting yourself with the facts. Write down what you know about your diagnosis and prognosis and read it back to yourself.

Anger. An outburst of bottled-up feelings directed at whoever is in the way. Blame is often emphasized, or thoughts of "Why me?" over and over again. "Why me? I can't believe this is happening now! I'm so pissed. It was such a stupid little fall!"

★ **What to do about it:** Let yourself get mad. Verbalize your feelings with intensity and gusto. For some, meditation works better. Either way, give yourself permission to embrace the feelings and focus on them.

Bargaining. You cling to the vain hope that the bad news about your injury is reversible or you can find a shortcut to get back to full health. Perhaps you search for alternative therapies or try experimental procedures or drugs. Either way, you're desperately trying to cut a deal to make things better than they actually are. "If I do 20 percent more than my PT suggested, I'll be back even quicker." Or this: "I need to find another specialist because my doctor clearly doesn't know what she's talking about."

★ **What to do about it:** Avoid false hope at all costs. When a therapist tells you that they have all the answers and can fix you despite the prognosis of others, use critical thinking to evaluate the advice. Remember, your brain is wired to cling to false hope. Recognize when you've started to shop around for medical advice that agrees with you. There's a fine line between hustling and refusing to accept facts.

Depression. You find yourself in an emotional funk. You're lethargic and negative, most things feel like an effort, and nothing seems enjoyable anymore. The difference between this and clinical depression is that these feelings should go away when the injury has healed. For long-lasting or chronic injuries, athletes are susceptible to lingering in this stage the longest. "I just feel so incredibly sad and pessimistic. I'm sort of anxious a lot of the time and don't want to go out."

★ **What to do about it:** Become a scheduling ninja. Get jobs done that you've been putting off, focusing specifically on the time when you know you're going to be vulnerable. Reward yourself *daily* with treats other than food. If you or the athlete you love "lingers" in this stage for longer than expected, you might consider seeking professional help.

Acceptance. You're at peace with your injury, and you've come to terms with what's wrong and what you need to do about it. You are realistic about your rehabilitation and are committed to doing what's been recommended. "I am so lucky to be waking up knowing this injury will pass, it's not chronic, it's not life threatening, and I promise I will return as a more gracious, patient and positive person/athlete."

★ **What to do about it:** Nothing. You're emotionally home free.

Maybe it's not a grief response

Although some athletes do experience a grief-like response, most don't. Science now supports a cognitive appraisal model for understanding why some athletes can take everything in stride while others release the kraken. Cognitive appraisal is just a fancy way of saying that an athlete's reaction to injury depends on what the injury means to the athlete. I know, right? It's hardly rocket science. But this is where things get interesting. In this approach, injury is simply a stressor, a threat that causes a physical and psychological reaction. The nature of the injury itself is largely inconsequential—it's how we think and feel about it that gets us into trouble. This is why the advice "Don't worry, it's just a . . ." rarely works because your cognitive appraisal of the injury isn't necessarily the same as the person limping.

It's important that you train yourself to manage the APPRAISAL PROCESS because this not only determines how well you cope with the injury itself but also the likelihood of you getting injured again.

Yes, you read that correctly. The risk of reinjury is partly determined by your history of coping with injuries you've had in the past.[6] In other words, learn how to better cope with injuries and you're likely to have fewer of them, even after factoring in the physical predisposing factors. We don't exactly know why the psychological piece is so important here, but we think it's due to the fear of reinjury. It has been shown to decrease confidence, change movement biomechanics, and negatively affect decision-making, all of which are risk factors for reinjury.

Injury assessment as your brain sees it.

When your brain "appraises" your injury, it does so via a two-step process called primary and secondary appraisal. The primary appraisal involves your Professor and Chimp brains arguing about what's at stake, how threatening or harmful the injury is to your physical and psychological future, what you've lost or will miss out on, the level of disruption it's likely to cause, and so on. In essence, the primary appraisal comprises the thoughts and feelings you have about the injury itself and its significance. Predictably, it can cause psychological stress such as anxiety, fear, or doubt—as well as thoughts based on your injury history: "Oh shit, not this again. Please, not again!" Your Computer brain then very quickly produces a memory in order to help you make sense of a current experience. You're having thoughts and feelings you don't want before you've even had a chance to realize it.

The goal is to reprogram your primary appraisal mechanism to stop your Computer brain from clouding your interpretation of current events and instead let your Professor brain take charge by using its superpowers: facts and logic. More on that later.

---

6 A. Ivarsson et al., "Psychosocial Factors and Sport Injuries: Meta-analyses for Prediction and Prevention," *Sports Medicine*, July 12, 2016.

The secondary appraisal follows the first and involves an evaluation of your ability to cope with the implications of injury—your physical and psychological capacity to deal with what lies ahead. Of course, this is strongly influenced by the conclusions from your primary appraisal as well as your experience coping with injury, your self-confidence, the perceptions you have of your body and abilities, the level of social support you have to get through it, and practical and logistical factors such as the cost of treatment and the likely disruptions to work, transportation, your social engagements, and so on. When results of the secondary appraisal aren't good (meaning that you're shitting bricks about how you're going to deal with everything), emotional responses head south. Let's look at what these appraisal mechanisms look like in the heads of real athletes.

Fear of injury causes denial and inevitable injury

Olivia is a 42-year-old runner. She experiences chronic hip pain on her long runs but hasn't seen a doctor and does not change her training. Olivia's primary appraisal is that her injury is manageable and not threatening because, in her words, "I only feel it on my long runs," and she appears to manage her symptoms using over-the-counter pain medication, insisting that "it doesn't really affect my training." Except it does. Upon talking to Olivia, it becomes clear that she is often forced to miss her long Sunday run because of pain. This gives her anxiety, which she redirects into training harder on other days. Olivia has a history of overuse injuries, has low self-confidence as an athlete, does not cope well with injury, and worries about weight gain during periods of not training. Eight weeks later she develops a hip stress fracture and a stress reaction in her opposite foot.

★ **Interpretation:** Olivia's Chimp brain has bullied her Professor brain into believing that things are under control. Her history of injury and her fear of what the rehab will likely entail (which her Computer brain shoves in her face on a regular basis) means that her primary appraisal is extremely biased. Because it's stressful for the human brain to live with a permanent internal argument (or "cognitive dissonance" in psych terms) and her Chimp is five times stronger than her Professor brain, she is forced to rationalize her bad decisions (e.g., *It doesn't hurt if I take pain meds*). Adding to her problems is the fact that her low confidence clouds her judgment: She sees injury as evidence of weakness and an inability to tolerate hard training. This creates a mindset in which she is so

YOU'RE IN PAIN!
WHOA!
SERIOUS DAMAGE AHEAD!
HURT ALERT!
STOP TAKING PAIN MEDS!

scared of injury that her primary and secondary appraisal mechanisms are virtually devoid of facts and logic. Ultimately, this mindset leads to the full-blown stress fracture and contralateral foot pain.

Not all warped appraisals lead to problems. For example, some athletes need to feel as though they are doing absolutely everything in their power during rehab, not just to heal quickly, but to help cope with the emotions of being injured. Let's look at one of these athletes next: my wife, Lesley Paterson.

Acceptance paves the way for investigative health hustle

Some athletes become worryingly obsessive about understanding and treating their injury. If their pre-injury training volume was 25 hours per week, then 25 hours per week will be devoted to rehab behaviors. They devour research articles about treatment modalities, speed-date specialists and therapists, and schedule treatment sessions like most people schedule lunch. It's exhausting. Trust me, I'm married to one of these athletes. I've watched her become a quasi-expert on upper hamstring tendinopathy, Lyme disease, piriformis syndrome, the pectineus pinch (don't ask), medial tibial stress syndrome, bone-healing biology, the gut microbiome, the placebo effect, you name it. She wouldn't think twice about flying across the country to meet with a specialist for 30 minutes or to book a treatment with a local physical therapist while we were on a romantic weekend away. At first, I thought this was nuts and she seemed stuck in the bargaining stage of a grief response. As a supportive spouse, it was hard to understand this. I was desperately trying to empathize with the emotional upheaval and identity threat that comes with injury, but I spent more time biting my lip and trying not to be preachy about the limitations of an "everything but the kitchen sink" treatment philosophy, or the dangers of shopping around for a therapist that agrees with you. Lesley calls her approach "investigative health hustle," but for a while I called it bargaining, laced with substitutive addiction. That never went down well. Here's her take:

> This is my body. I love training and racing and it's how I make a living. Why wouldn't I try to find every possible solution to help me get back? Some of the best and worst advice I've had has come from leading medical experts. If I waited for the first doctor I meet to fix me, I'd have given up long ago. You have to hustle to find

out what's wrong and get to the bottom of why you're there in the first place. My opinion is that one person never has all the answers, despite their qualifications or insistence that they do. In fact, in my experience, the more they insist that they have all the answers, the more likely it is that they don't.

★ **Interpretation:** Lurking beneath this philosophy are logistical and financial implications that can wreak havoc. While I was stewing over Lesley's need to consult everyone, it became clear that she wasn't bargaining because she seemed able to critically evaluate the evidence she was getting, something that "bargainers" don't do. Lesley's increased effort and intensity toward her rehabilitation was creating a secondary appraisal of her injury. In other words, when injured, Lesley conjures up a mindset of being proactive and "doing something about it," which she perceives to favorably impact her recovery time. This creates an emotional response of its own—she feels more optimistic and less negative about being injured. Thus, Lesley's "investigative health hustle" is her way of managing the emotions that come with being injured—it's psychologically self-medicating and motivates her to be compliant with what her therapists prescribe. It's her coping response, not just a treatment philosophy. My attempts to intervene on her philosophy about treatment only removed her ability to cope. (Note to self: Don't do that.) So I left the hustle alone, focusing instead on helping with logistics, filtering out quackery, and making the financial cost of it manageable. Bingo. We had developed a therapeutic alliance.

A note about types of injury.

Some endurance athletes get injured because of an acute impact trauma—a crash, fall, smack, or thwack that occurs quickly and with force. Sometimes it's obvious that an impact trauma is serious because it hurts like f*ck (e.g., a broken collarbone) or you can tell that your body is not supposed to look like that (e.g., you lacerate your calf on a bike part). While acute impact trauma injuries can be emotionally devastating, they are generally easier for athletes (the primary appraisal) because the cause has a distinctive beginning, middle, and end. Even if the seriousness of an impact trauma takes a while to creep up on you, it's usually not difficult to trace it back to a specific event. For example, you might notice a painful rib that gets worse and worse across the week until you realize that the fall you took last week on the mountain bike must have been worse than you first thought. Contrast this with chronic or degenerative injuries. The most common cause of chronic and degenerative injury among endurance athletes is overuse (e.g., tendinopathy, tendonitis, stress fractures). What makes the primary appraisal of overuse injuries so challenging is that the injury stressor—the cause—rarely appears waving a big flag telling you that you've just f*cked something up. It creeps up on you, and when you finally recognize what's happened, it's often too late. Your brain either missed the signs or refused to act on them.

BRAIN TREATMENT TO HELP YOU COPE

If you've realized that you're an athlete who doesn't cope well with injury, your primary and/or secondary appraisal mechanisms are plagued by gremlins gnawing away at your ability to think and act rationally and logically. The key is to figure out where these injury gremlins are hiding and put things in place to get you back on track.

Hunting for gremlins in your primary appraisal system.

Primary appraisal gremlins are crafty wee bastards. They're very good at hiding. But if you know where to look and you let others help you in the search, it's possible to do some brain cleaning. Let's go gremlin hunting.

Gremlin 1: Not knowing what's wrong with you

If you cannot answer some basic questions about your injury, we've found the first gremlin in your primary appraisal system: an inability (can't, won't, or just haven't bothered) to get a medical diagnosis of what's causing the pain. Of course, some medical experts can't give you an accurate diagnosis either, not because of incompetence but because some injuries are really hard to diagnose. That isn't a gremlin. The gremlin we're talking about here is the absence of fact-finding behavior. Start to face the facts in Exercise 1.

★ **What you can do about it:** Seek out medical advice to diagnose your injury correctly. There's nothing wrong with getting a second opinion or consulting

PINPOINT THE PROBLEM

If you are already injured, a good primary appraisal depends on knowing exactly what's wrong. Try to answer the following.

Describe what's wrong with you as explained by your doctor, physical therapist, or someone qualified. Use only information from your medical diagnosis, not things that you "think" are going on.

EX. *Stress fracture in my 4th metatarsal, diagnosed by MRI.*

My injury:

Describe anything else you know that might have contributed to your injury or any complications or consequences that might have arisen from the injury itself (compensation patterns, secondary injuries, etc.).

EX. *Caused by increased mileage and probably exacerbated by using a negative drop shoe.*

Other things I know about my injury:

from different specialties. If the thought of this scares you, just ...ageable chunk of behavior change that you can do today—make an ...ointment with someone. It's a start.

Gremlin 2: Delusion funnels and tipping points

This gremlin hides in your pre-injury experience. Overuse injuries are almost always accompanied by physical and psychological warning signs that tell you trouble is brewing. This might be felt as unusual tightness in a certain part of your body, a "niggle," or just a general sense of localized discomfort. In our experience, these warning signs bubble up into conscious attention, and athletes often choose to ignore, downplay, or simply rationalize them away. We call this period the "delusion funnel" because this gremlin forces your brain to ignore, misinterpret, or cope ineffectively with the warning signs, but it's still leading you in one direction—injury. For example, you might have noticed a few little niggles in your Achilles tendon or a tightness in your hamstring, so you decided to do a bit more mobility work, double down on the foam roller, take some ibuprofen, and hope it resolves itself. These compensatory behaviors are akin to the bargaining stage of the grief response. The delusion funnel tends to last less than two weeks because once the pain reaches conscious awareness and you can no longer ignore it, the fuse has often been lit for a bigger injury.

Dealing with pain takes a large emotional toll on the athlete, and an athlete's brain will play all sorts of tricks (rationalization, reframing, distraction) to cope with it. When the pain finally forces a disruption to your training program, you reach a cognitive and emotional tipping point. This is simply the moment you realize that something is really wrong. It's the "Oh, f*ck, I really think I'm injured" moment. This might be when you first notice a strong emotional response like frustration, despair, anger, or depression. In Exercise 2, let's see how you recognize these moments in your own injury experience.

★ **What you can do about it:** Simply being aware of delusion funnels and tipping points can help inoculate you against their future reoccurrence. However, a more robust strategy is to keep a diary or journal of niggles, tightness, and unusual thoughts and feelings that accompany your training. Make sure you review these journal entries on a regular basis. If you have a coach, share these observations with her too. Reading and evaluating these responses on paper

GO BACK TO THE SCENE TO FIND THE WARNING SIGNS

Describe the moment when you reached your cognitive and emotional tipping point—when you realized your niggle was more serious than you first thought. Try to describe what event led to this realization as well as the thoughts and feelings that came with it.

EX. *I got out of bed with heel pain three mornings in a row. I remember thinking, "Oh shit, this isn't good. It no longer feels like just stiffness or a heel bruise, it feels like plantar fasciitis." This realization hit me like a truck. I felt really down.*

The moment:

Retrace your steps and piece together the warning signs that you missed prior to your tipping point. Some of these might be physical (e.g., tightness in calf), but some could be cognitive or emotional.

EX. *On Tuesday, I remember debating whether I should run or not but decided to just try 30 minutes. I only had two more hard days before my rest week and felt pressure to make sure I got all the training in.*

The warning signs:

EXERCISE 3

CONFRONT THE BULLSHIT YOU TELL YOURSELF ABOUT YOUR INJURY

Things I Currently Say to Myself	Evidence to the Contrary (alternative ways of thinking)
That's it. My season is over.	It's way too early to know this. I'll focus on having a strong end to the season, and the added rest will help all my other niggles clear up. I'll be fresh and motivated when most other athletes are fatigued and getting burned out.
1	
2	
3	
4	
5	

forces your Professor brain to take charge because reading and comprehension are skills only the frontal cortex can do. This helps prevent your emotional Chimp hijacking your brain with feelings and impressions fueled by powerful neurotransmitters.

Gremlin 3: Catastrophizing, awfulizing, and thinking that everything's ruined

This gremlin in your primary appraisal system is planted and watered by your devious Chimp. Catastrophizing is a form of cognitive bias in which you believe things are far worse than they actually are. The less confident you are, the worse your catastrophizing becomes. The most destructive form of catastrophizing during an athletic injury has arrived when you're convinced that things in the future are no longer possible or that there's really no point in trying anymore. This is when we need your Professor brain to step up to the plate and deconstruct the bullshit.

★ **What you can do about it:** The key to changing your shitty self-talk is to confront it with meaningful and factually substantiated evidence. As you may recall from the exercises in Chapter 3 on confidence building, the first step to changing your tune is to offer alternative yet plausible interpretations of the same events. You don't even have to agree with the alternative; just offer it and write it down. We're trying to develop counterstatements that focus on positive outcomes instead of your current doom-and-gloom scenarios. Remember that your Chimp brain can smell bullshit from a mile away, so don't bother trying to offer up ludicrous and naive alternatives. Focus on things that are factually plausible, even if they don't feel realistic to you right now, and things that are preferably in your control. Complete Exercise 3 to get started.

Hunting for gremlins in your secondary appraisal system.

After identifying the gremlins in how you make sense of the injury itself, we now need to turn our attention to finding gremlins in your secondary appraisal system—managing the thoughts and feelings about rehab and recovery.

Gremlin 4: Becoming a passive patient

We've worked with hundreds of injured athletes, and we've noticed that they tend to fall into one of three groups, based on how they approach their rehabilitation and recovery. "Passive patients" are unfocused, often apathetic, and seemingly unmotivated to get better. "Active patients" are much more proactive about learning about what injury they have, why they got it, how to recover from it, and how to avoid developing it again. In our experience, most athletes fall into this category. A third group of athletes are characterized by an investigative health hustle (like Lesley) where the patients are overachievers—constantly reading, learning, and searching for new information about their injury or their rehabilitation. These athletes always seem to ask us the same question: "What else can I do to get better?"

Over the years, we've found that passive patients tend to report the most adverse emotional responses to injury—more pessimism, more negativity bias, more mood disturbance. On the face of it, it seems like a paradox: Passive patients are the most likely to moan about being injured but the least likely to do anything about it. It soon became clear to us why passivity is a gremlin. Some athletes hated that they were passive but felt powerless to change it. They felt stuck, but their passivity sank them deeper into an emotional hole. In an ensuing downward spiral, negative emotion would give rise to behavioral passivity, creating more negative emotion, which would increase passivity, and so on. We noticed that kick-starting proactive behaviors (e.g., seeking information, learning about what different specialists do, finding athletes who have the same injury) not only helps the physical rehabilitation process but becomes a form of adaptation to the injury itself. Even if your efforts don't impact your treatment outcomes, they help you manage the emotional journey to get there. It's secondary appraisal working for you instead of against you, just as it does for Lesley.

★ **What you can do about it:** Give yourself rehab homework. We're not talking about home-based exercises but educational goals to become a more informed

A NOTE ABOUT LETTING SHIT GO, GENERALLY

YOU'VE SPENT MONTHS preparing for a race. You're fit, injury-free, and tapered. Expectations are high. And then it happens: You have a shitty race. Perhaps race morning is wet and cold and you don't like wet and cold. Perhaps your goggles got knocked off and you wear contacts. Perhaps you cramp on the run, and three people tell you to drink f*cking pickle juice. Perhaps nothing specific happens at all; you're just bewilderingly slow on the day. Letting go of the past needs to be learned because we're biologically wired to focus on things that went wrong and gloss over stuff that goes right. Psychologists call this "negativity bias," and it is the reason educators are trained to give praise sandwiches.* Negativity bias serves an important evolutionary function because it helps the human brain adjust future thinking and behavior by learning from mistakes. However, when we spend too much time on the "mistake" part instead of the "learning," it has the opposite effect—we carry around a backpack full of frustration, annoyance, or anger. When it's directed at other people, we call it a grudge. When a grudge puts down roots, we call it bitterness. The longer it stays, the harder it is to extract. Ironically, the secret to letting things go isn't to "let it go" at all but instead to park it somewhere else in Brainsville. It's the intrusiveness of the emotion that causes the problem, not the fact that it's in the memory bank. If you have trouble letting go of bad races, try these strategies:

1. **Verbalize your anger or frustration.** We now know that releasing anger through physical aggression is ineffective. However, what does work is verbalizing it because it connects the emotional outlet (verbal) with the thing that caused it (describing the events). So go on, scream and shout about what just happened.

>

* A praise sandwich is criticism delivered between two pieces of positive feedback "bread": If you're on the receiving end, it's often known as a "shit" sandwich. Turns out it's also pretty ineffective. See I. A. James, "The Rightful Demise of the Sh*t Sandwich: Providing Effective Feedback," *Behavioral and Cognitive Psychotherapy* 43, no. 6 (2015): 759–766.

Continued

2. **Determine if the cause was under your control.** Think through all the elements that contributed to the bad race and categorize each as either "Under My Control" or "Not Under My Control." For example, cramping on the run might have been caused by poor nutrition on the bike but exacerbated by the hot conditions. That's one cause under each column. Now go through each Under-My-Control item and devise a strategy to reduce the likelihood of it happening again. For example, for goggles getting knocked off, you could wear two caps, one under and one over your goggles.

3. **Identify a positive from the race.** Force yourself to identify at least one thing that went well. For example, you had a great swim because you found good feet, controlled your intensity, and sighted really well. You might have refused to quit and still finished (even if slow). That takes mental toughness.

4. **Sweep that shit under the rug.** But before you do, write down your frustration or regret on a piece of paper. Read it back to yourself three times. Fold the paper in half four times and put it in a closeable box that sits under your bed, in a closet, or wherever you hide shit that you don't want people to find. When the box containing your gremlin is hidden, smile for five seconds.

Now get on with your day knowing that the problem has been dealt with. You might laugh at this technique, but it works. Trust me. And yes, it's important that you follow these instructions exactly as they are written.

patient. Set aside 30 minutes each evening to get your Google on. Don't misinterpret this as seeing Dr. Google—yeah, try not to do that[7]—what we're advocating for is taking time to learn what questions to ask your doctor, how to find a good specialist, and what other athletes have tried—perhaps by asking your network on social media. Either way, f*cking hustle!

7 "Self-Diagnosing Online Yields Mostly Irrelevant Results, Researchers Say," *Science Alert*, accessed November 28, 2016, http://www.sciencealert.com/self-diagnosing-online-yields-mostly-irrelevant-results-researchers-say.

Gremlin 5: Holding onto negative emotions

As we learned from the grief response, experiencing negative emotions during injury is a normal and adaptive response. Thankfully, the human body and brain are so robust that occasional bouts of negative emotion probably have minimal, if any, long-term consequences for health. However, it is long-term or chronic negativity that affects the brain and body the most. Unfortunately, it's virtually impossible to set a time frame in which smart people all agree that you should be over this by now. Defining reliable clinical thresholds when an acute mood disturbance becomes chronic is challenging even for psychologists, and varies by diagnosis. For example, for clinical depression, the symptoms have to occur "nearly every day for at least 2 weeks," but for a generalized anxiety disorder they have to appear "frequently for at least 6 months."[8]

When it comes to dealing with an athletic injury, we take a different approach. We consider a gremlin to be present when the standard of "informed reasonableness" can no longer be met—when your negative thoughts, feelings, and actions are lingering longer than is considered reasonable by most informed people. In this case, "informed people" refers to your treatment team, your spouse, your training partners, and/or those who know you well enough and the injury you have. We know that all sounds rather vague and unscientific—it is—but it's remarkable how well it works because informed people tend to notice things, such as how your attitude is affecting your treatment and recovery, or how your mood is affecting your relationship, or just your overall ability to get on with life and enjoy yourself. The only way to know this is to talk to them about it. After all, you're only part of the equation for determining informed reasonableness. Psychologists often refer to the process of consulting others to see if you're totally nuts as "triangulation," and it's a great practical way to reach a consensus about subjective opinions.

★ **What you can do about it:** The first strategy we use for all injured athletes who are experiencing a negative emotional response to injury is to encourage a mourning period. We avoid doling out the sympathetic platitudes, such as "You'll come back even stronger" or "Don't worry, you'll be back in no time!"

8 American Psychiatric Association, *Diagnostic and Statistical Manual of Mental Disorders*, 5th ed. (Arlington, VA: American Psychiatric Publishing, 2013).

These are well-intentioned but they rarely work, are often inaccurate, and are almost never comforting. The best policy is to designate a mourning window or "pissy period" in which the gloves can come off and you have permission to act as bratty as you like. However, this comes with a provision that when the mourning period has officially ended (we typically limit it to 2–7 days, depending on the severity of the injury), the athlete must switch to a positive mindset, even if it's an act.

When athletes hold on to negative emotions longer than is warranted (i.e., they mourn for way too long by the "informed reasonableness" standard), we teach them how to be positive and grateful. We train athletes to be positive and grateful because there's compelling scientific evidence that the best way to dig yourself out of a lingering negative mood is to *force* yourself to be positive.[9] That's right, even when the last thing you feel like is being positive, simply faking it can trick your brain's neurochemistry into believing things are better than they are. This creates a snowball effect that makes positive emotion easier to sustain. One evidence-based technique to accomplish this is gratefulness training. Finding and writing down three things that you are grateful for every day for three weeks is known to help initiate and sustain a positive mood.[10] How to actually do this is described in more detail in Chapter 3, "I Don't Think I Can: Building confidence and self-belief."

A second evidence-based technique for creating an upward spiral of positive emotion is mindfulness training. As we've discussed in other chapters, mindfulness is known to regulate emotion.[11] The central feature of mindfulness is paying conscious attention to the distress itself, but instead of holding a pity party with only one guest, you resist the temptation to judge it. This means no more talk of "No one understands how hard this is" or "My season is totally ruined." Just like gratefulness training, mindfulness can stage the neurochemical foundations

---

9 E. I. Garland et al., "Upward Spirals of Positive Emotions Counter Downward Spirals of Negativity: Insights from the Broaden-and-Build Theory and Affective Neuroscience on the Treatment of Emotion Dysfunctions and Deficits in Psychopathology," *Clinical Psychologist Reviews* 30, no. 7 (2010): 849–864.

10 R. A. Emmons and M. E. McCullough, "Counting Blessings Versus Burdens: An Experimental Investigation of Gratitude and Subjective Well-Being in Daily Life," *Journal of Personality and Social Psychology* 84, no. 2 (2003): 377–389.

11 A. Grecucci et al., "Mindful Emotion Regulation: Exploring the Neurocognitive Mechanisms Behind Mindfulness," *Biomedical Research International*, 670724, Epub June 7, 2015.

of positive emotion and help build momentum to keep the positivity going.[12] We describe mindfulness training in more detail in Chapter 11, "I Need to Harden the F*ck Up."

Gremlin 6: Failing to set aggressive fitness goals during rehabilitation

There's a pervasive mindset among athletes that injury rehabilitation is a period of measured convalescence, a time to put your athletic identify on a shelf, accept the physical losses that come with limited (if any) training, and, well, just suck it up until this whole nightmare is over. One of the biggest causes of emotional concern to injured athletes is a loss of athletic identity. As we learned in Chapter 2, "I Wish I Felt More Like an Athlete," athletic identity is built on a belief system (your self-schema) that feeds into your overall sense of self (your self-concept). When your self-concept receives a jarring blow from an upstream identity getting kicked in the teeth—which happens during injury—it triggers an emotional response from your Chimp that makes you feel like crap. One reason injured athletes are encouraged to channel their mental energy into a different identity during the hiatus (e.g., "You've always wanted to learn to cook; now's a great time to learn!") is that it helps to stop your overall sense of who you are from wobbling too much. It's a bit like diversifying an investment portfolio in case one stock tanks. While this helps shore up your overall self-concept, it does little to help the identity that took a kicking. A much stronger approach is to keep focusing on your athletic identity. Unless you're in a full body cast, there's a good chance you can still work on physical, technical, or tactical aspects of your sport that usually get neglected. For this reason, we strongly encourage athletes to view injury as an opportunity to focus on their physical, mental, technical, or tactical preparation for sport, not just try to attenuate declines.

Take Melanie McQuaid, a top professional triathlete with three world titles under her belt in XTERRA and multiple 70.3 wins. Her sights were set on nailing long-distance racing. In March 2016, Mel broke her left ankle, which put the brakes on running and biking. With the help of her coach, Kelly Guest, Mel saw

12 N. Geschwind et al., "Mindfulness Training Increases Momentary Positive Emotions and Reward Experience in Adults Vulnerable to Depression: A Randomized Controlled Trial," *Journal of Consulting and Clinical Psychology* 79, no. 5 (2011): 618–628.

this as an opportunity to increase her potential as a long-course athlete by completely overhauling her run mechanics. But with a busted ankle, doing so would take confidence and ingenuity. And water. Here's how she described it:

> I started out as a mountain biker racing triathlons, muscling and over-striding my way through some pretty fast running. I suffered a dislocated/fractured left ankle that required two surgeries over three months. The prognosis from the surgeon was 3.5 months to run and likely one year to return to my previous level in triathlon. In the weeks following my first surgery, I was non-weight bearing for 6 weeks and, because I had screws through my tibia/fibula that would be broken if I applied too much force, I wasn't allowed to run or jump for 3.5 months. At first, this didn't look like much of an "opportunity." However, my coach and I decided that a long layoff from running would allow me to completely overhaul my run mechanics and thus improve my potential over the marathon. During this time, I was allowed to water run and, eventually, I could run in the shallow pool (about 1.1 m deep). Using low-impact environments for run training allowed me to focus more on core engagement, arm mechanics, and turnover. These aspects of running are easily overlooked when you focus on foot strike and mileage, but they are really important if you want to achieve proper form. Post-accident I am an efficient triathlon runner with high turnover. When I am 100 percent healed from this injury, I will be able to complete a much faster run over the marathon distance due to this opportunity to unravel some muscle patterning that has limited my potential in Ironman racing.

★ **What you can do about it:** Hone in on a current weakness, limitation, or just something you've always wanted to get better at that does not jeopardize your injury healing. Set aggressive goals for fitness, injury risk reduction, or technical proficiency and create an intensive block of training around those goals. If you struggle to think of a weakness or limitation (ahem), then try completing a performance profile analysis as in Exercise 4 to prioritize your efforts.

CREATE A PERFORMANCE PROFILE

A performance profile is simply a graphical display of the qualities or characteristics that are important to be successful in your sport. You can create separate or combined profiles for different aspects of your sport, such as technical skills, physical skills, psychological skills, and so on. For example, a triathlete might identify skills such as core strength, hip flexibility, swim technique, swim-specific muscular power, functional power threshold on the run, pain tolerance, mindfulness, and so on.

Come up with several attributes on which you can rank yourself from 1 to 10 (where 1 = *I'm terrible at it*, and 10 = *I'm awesome at it*).

Write each attribute in the outer ring on the segments below, and shade in your self-rating score.

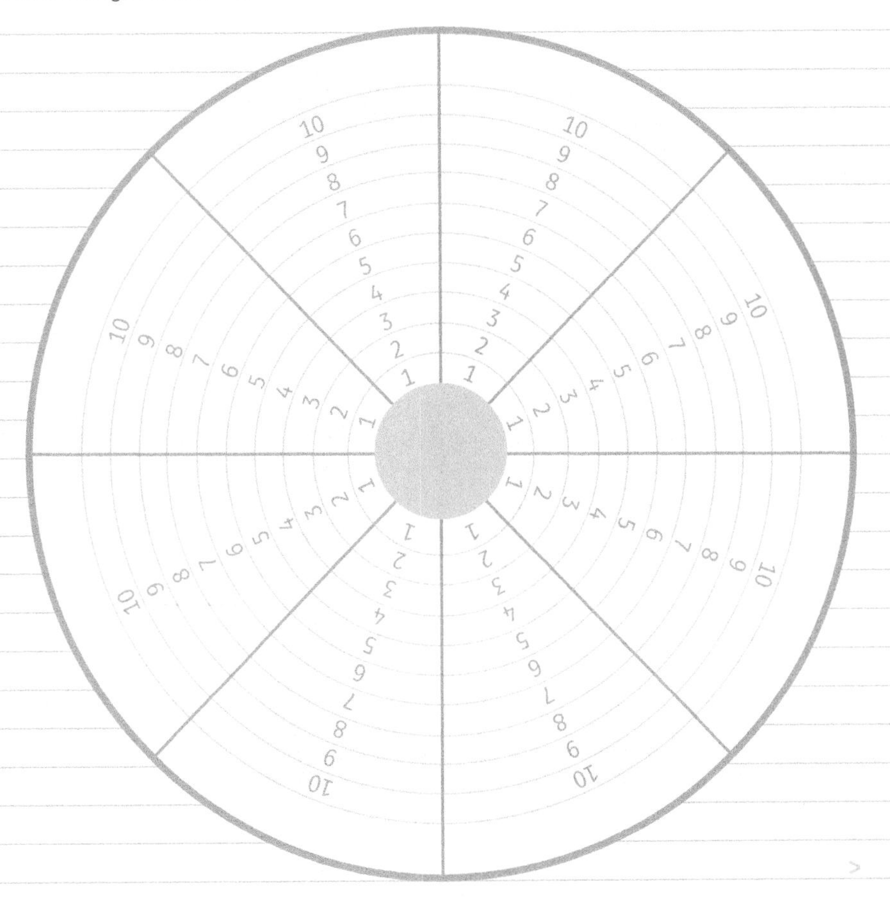

Continued

LOOK FOR OPPORTUNITIES

When you have finalized the key attributes, narrow down the list to those skills that you can still work on with your injury. Prioritize those skills that you have rated yourself the lowest on. Run this list by your coach or a fellow athlete to validate the list and your self-ratings (it's triangulation, baby!), make the necessary adjustments, and then prioritize one or two of your lowest-rated skills.

Now it's time to develop aggressive or ambitious goals to improve these skills during the course of your rehabilitation and recovery.

Goal	Time Frame
1	
2	
3	
4	
5	

Gremlin 7: Dealing with symptom anxiety and a fear of reinjury

A common concern of the injured athlete is anxiety and fear of an injury getting worse or of an old injury returning. It's understandable that athletes feel like this. When you have spent weeks, months, or even years living with an injury symptom,[13] you become extremely sensitive to it. It's like an old friend, except this friend is one you f*cking hate. During the spiral into chronic injury, we've noticed that the attention athletes give to their symptoms ranges from utter denial to paranoid hypochondriasis, but mostly somewhere in between. However, in rehab and recovery, we notice that athletes tend to change how they think about their symptoms. They seem better able to differentiate and understand soreness, tightness, and pain—usually because treatment experts have been educating them. However, during the recovery phase when training has resumed, one psychological gremlin stands out: anxiety over the return of pain and subsequent reinjury.

In our work with athletes returning from injury, we usually look for a manifestation of this anxiety, what we call "symptom hypervigilance." This refers to an athlete's obsessive focus on micro-sensations in and around the injured site that often get exaggerated and/or overanalyzed. Attention narrows in on the affected body part and amplifies the slightest whiff of pain still present or that may return soon. It dominates the psychological experience of training. It's almost as if every other sensation becomes irrelevant or ignored. While symptom vigilance is normal (i.e., periodically scanning for signs of pain, tightness, and soreness), hypervigilance is maladaptive—a posh way of saying "faulty and not very good for you." If you're not sure of the difference or whether you're prone to hypervigilance, take this 5-second survey.

13 If you're reading this as a sports medicine professional or a coach and feel the need to saddle up onto a moral high horse with "Athletes should never let things get that bad!" or "If you're training with pain, you're an idiot," then you might also be part of the problem. The reality is that athletes routinely do things you tell them not to, and medical finger-wagging or eye-rolling doesn't change their behavior (an evidence-based statement), it simply encourages them to hide symptom onset or severity from you even more (another evidence-based statement). This doesn't mean that we need to endorse bad decision-making and behavior, but we do need to understand the mindset that creates it and develop skills to circumvent greater self-sabotage. After all, you can't really help an athlete in, say, denial if you don't try and unpack the psychological reasons behind the denial.

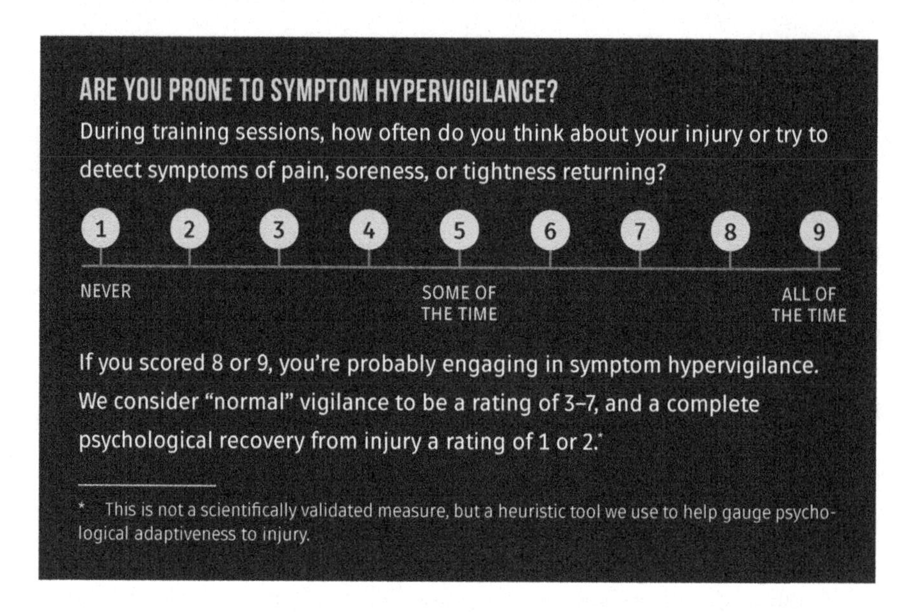

You might be tempted to say, "So what? Surely it's better to be in tune with your body?" Well, the biggest problem of symptom hypervigilance is what's behind it. It often reflects unrealistic expectations about recovery, excessive outside pressures, threats to athletic identity, and a mindset of anxiety and fear. Plus we know that anxiety and fears about reinjury are negatively associated with good rehabilitation outcomes.[14] While fear stems from a specific fear-provoking situation (e.g., running hills during recovery from a calf injury), reinjury anxiety is a conditioned generalized response that something might happen (e.g., "I'm really nervous that the pain will come back"). Both get exacerbated during symptom hypervigilance, and that's a problem. Feeling pain, or the expectation of pain, is no longer simply an indicator of tissue damage, but conjures up the entire injury experience that forces you to repeat the primary and secondary appraisals that created the anxiety and fear in the first place. In addition to being exhausting and making you miserable, symptom hypervigilance can also reinforce bad biomechanical and neurological patterns that lead to new injuries. For example, running with knee pain can cause a movement compensation that

14 D. Forsdyke et al., "Psychosocial Factors Associated with Outcomes of Sports Injury Rehabilitation in Competitive Athletes: A Mixed Studies Systematic Review," *British Journal of Sports Medicine* 50, no. 9 (2016): 537–544.

contributes to another injury, or, running in the absence of knee pain during recovery can contribute to "protecting" the knee, which reinforces the maladaptive compensation. If that doesn't convince you, symptom hypervigilance also uses up critical attentional bandwidth that is better allocated to making good in-the-moment decisions that keep you fast, efficient, and grateful. It's not good for you, so stop it.

★ **What you can do about it:** First, recognize that you're doing it. Just having an awareness that you're being symptom hypervigilant helps develop the readiness to change it. When you notice your amplifiers are on, picture a big red stop sign in your head accompanied by the sound you associate with a screeching halt. This becomes your cue to change the attentional channel and self-talk from a narrow/internal channel to an external channel of attention, such as other people or the world around you (see Chapter 12 for a detailed explanation of attentional channels). You can even force a channel change by listening to music or an audiobook while training (the usual caveats about safety apply).

Another strategy is to train with chatty Kathy. There are times when it's tough to be around a chatterbox, but injury rehab is not one of them. Training with talkative athletes can be great therapy when your head is a laser-guided missile of symptom hypervigilance. Chatterboxes are great company for helping you get out of your own head and into random conversations about life, love, and everything in between. Of course, a really good idea is to deal with the anxiety itself. We've described key techniques to reduce anxiety in Chapter 13, but other techniques like "detachment" are also really helpful.

Gremlin 8: Failing to do things that make you feel good

There are plenty of reasons why treating yourself to something pleasurable is a good idea when you're feeling down in the dumps. In psychological terms, this is called a "lifestyle buffer" because it's not necessarily related to the stressor itself (the injury), but it helps mediate the stress response caused by it. Lifestyle buffers can take many forms, but we prefer ones that help to micro-dose dopamine and serotonin, the brain's feel-good neurotransmitters. You know it as treating yourself.

★ **What you can do about it:** One of the best rewards for an injured body and a depressed brain is massage. The nice kind. Most endurance athletes do not need to be sold on the benefits of regular massage. The physiological, circulatory, and musculoskeletal benefits are so well accepted that most athletes would submit their bodies to the kneading and digging every week if money permitted. That said, and as most athletes will attest, a sports massage is rarely a spa-like experience that rains down pleasure. Deep-tissue massage can be an eye-welling, sweat-inducing pummeling. When athletes are injured, routine massages often fall by the wayside because the thought of getting finger punched for 60 minutes isn't that appealing. However, a grossly undervalued benefit of massage is its efficacy as psychological therapy. Classical or gentle massage (i.e., not the teeth-clenching, punchy kind) causes a surge in oxytocin that reduces anxiety and pain perception. Massage causes brain neurochemistry to change so you feel better emotionally. After massage, dopamine is up 31 percent and serotonin 28 percent, and the stress hormone cortisol drops.[15] Simply put, massage is brain therapy for the injured athlete. So when you're feeling especially crappy, schedule a massage. The gentler kind. Screw the body; this one's for your head.

When nothing seems to help.

Some injuries never really leave you, physically or emotionally. They can end careers, change your life outlook, or just make you miserable for years on end. What's more, an injury or illness experience might be so impervious to the strategies discussed in this chapter that no matter what you do, nothing seems to help. If you find yourself dealing with an injury that has left such strong emotional or physical scars, then a useful place to start is learning how to repair and rebuild self-schema and identity. Languishing with a victim mentality ("Why me?" or "Life is so unfair") might feel entirely justified to your Chimp brain but does little to restore psychological well-being in the long term. Finding a new normal (the *survivor* mindset) takes courage and honest reflection, but, most of all, homework. After all, it's hard to have to work out who you are again and to develop the mindset and confidence that a new identity needs to survive and thrive. Start by reading Chapter 2 to learn about the building blocks of self-

15 T. Field et al., "Cortisol Decreases and Serotonin and Dopamine Increase Following Massage Therapy," *International Journal of Neuroscience* 115, no. 10 (2005): 1397–1413.

schema (the thoughts you have about yourself) that create the scaffolding for a strong, vibrant new identity. It's far from a solution, but it's the right place to begin.

Advice to partners of injured athletes.

Dealing with an injured athlete can be like opening a box of chocolates. You never know what you're gonna get (although nuts are probably in there). When your loved one has a wailing Chimp, your Professor brain can easily tire of playing super-nanny, and so your Chimp comes out too. Arguments can escalate, moodiness and withdrawal can dominate, and you run short of compassion after hearing the same words over and over again. So even if your own Chimp wants to scream, "Can you just shut the f*ck up about your Achilles?" try to bite your lip, clench those buttocks, and follow these steps for dealing with your favorite basket case.

Focus on empathy, not sympathy

Sympathy is the skill of caring for someone in distress by being understanding and compassionate toward them. I know that all sounds rather noble, but the scientific evidence tells us that it doesn't really help. In fact, being overly sympathetic can actually delay someone's ability to get though distress because sympathy requires emotionally siding with them, regardless of whether that emotion is productive or helpful to their recovery. Think of the ugly breakup: "Yes, she is a horrible person, and she doesn't deserve you." That's sympathy. In contrast, empathy is a nonjudgmental attempt to climb into their world and imagine what it feels like to be them, even for just a moment. When you get there, you try to communicate this understanding to them (e.g., "It's horrible to feel rejected and betrayed"). Empathy has lots of therapeutic value, whereas sympathy is like getting drunk to cope with bad news. Empathy requires lots of listening and reflection, lots of questions about someone's emotions, and lots of avoiding the tendency to solve problems even if the solutions seem obvious. Here are some go-to leads on empathy responses to help you support your injured bundle of joy:

HOW TO TALK TO YOUR INJURED ATHLETE

Help me understand what it feels like to . . .	[have to deal with this] [be in your shoes] [put all that hard work in] [not feel motivated]
You must be feeling . . .	[pretty overwhelmed] [frustrated] [sad] [at a loss] [exhausted at having to deal with all this] [anxious]
How can I help you . . .	[get through this] [focus on the positive] [cope with today]
It sounds like you're . . .	[nervous about . . .] [really pissed at. . .] [worried that . . .] [frustrated by . . .] [confused about . . .]
You seem to get really [emotion] when . . .	[your treatment session doesn't go as well as you'd hoped] [we talk about . . .] [I mention that . . .]

Help them solve their injury appraisal problem

Remember that athletes who don't cope well with injury almost always have a gremlin in their cognitive appraisal of the injury itself or their ability to cope with it. Invite them to outsource part of their Professor brain mindset to you. You can act as a third party to audit their flawed thinking that leads to negative emotion. For example, you could ask them to send you their training diary of pain, tightness, or weird sensations described earlier. You can help prevent them entering another delusion tunnel. Look for patterns or warning signs and use your empathic responses to help talk things through.

Help build or prompt their use of social support

Numerous scientific studies now show that social support plays a big role in buffering the emotional effect of athletic injury. As a loved one, you can play a role in making sure that your injured athlete doesn't become socially isolated.[16] Social support can take many forms. It doesn't just involve "being there to talk" or giving them a ride to a treatment session, although those things are certainly helpful. You might consider reaching out to their training partners to let them

16 I. Mitchell et al., "Stressors, Social Support, and Tests of the Buffering Hypothesis: Effects on Psychological Responses of Injured Athletes," *British Journal of Health Psychology* 19, no. 3 (2014): 486–508.

know that your athlete would probably welcome a pep-talk from someone other than you.

Take the time to learn about their injury

You can also support your basket case by studying up on their injury so you can talk about it in an informed way. I've (Simon) read so many articles about Lyme disease, tendinopathy, and piriformis syndrome that I've now suffered them by proxy. Aside from making you smarter and better at understanding the medical terms that come out of your athlete's mouth, doing homework communicates that you care about them. That's love. I do mine with a strong IPA.

I'M SIDELINED AND MAD AS HELL!

A positive plan for rehab

MASON IS A 34-YEAR-OLD TRIATHLETE who has just been diagnosed with a stress fracture in the fourth metatarsal of his left foot. He's three weeks out from his "A" race—the age group sprint-distance national championships. And he's pissed. He's had shin splints before but never a stress fracture in his foot. He'd been having foot pain for about seven days, and an MRI confirmed the diagnosis. He doesn't experience pain when walking but has been told to avoid weight-bearing exercise that causes pain for at least four weeks. When he realizes that he will not be able to race, he's devastated. He's angry at himself for running through the pain for as long as he did and feels depressed when he thinks about the entire season being "ruined." He knows what he needs to do for successful rehabilitation and is committed to doing it, but it doesn't change the fact that he feels like shit. He becomes really argumentative with his girlfriend, who doesn't know what to say or do to help him feel better.

★ **Interpretation:** Mason's primary appraisal of his injury is a healthy one. He is understandably dejected at the thought of all his hard work "going to waste" and missing the biggest race of his career. His big regret was not resting the first day he felt pain. His doctor had told him that the initial >

Continued

pain was likely a symptom of a stress reaction, which, with rest, would not have developed into a full-blown stress fracture. This knowledge is burning him up. However, the fact that he is committed to not taking pain medication and adhering to rehabilitation without trying to still race means that his secondary appraisal is also healthy.

We identify a mourning period of 48 hours during which he is allowed to get pissed, irate, or angry. Rather than fighting these feelings, he is encouraged to let himself wallow in them. We explain the purpose of the mourning period to his girlfriend and devise some empathic responses for her to use to help diffuse conflict and be a cathartic release for his emotions. At the end of the 48-hour period, he is instructed to "flick the switch" on a new rehabilitation mindset using gratefulness training and learning mindfulness.

During the 4-week rehabilitation phase (weeks 1–4) we also agreed on two aggressive fitness goals to channel his competitive energy without jeopardizing the healing of his foot. The goals are to increase hip flexibility by 20 percent and decrease his 1,000-yard swim time by 15 seconds using a pull-buoy but without flip-turns. In his recovery phase (weeks 5–8), we decide to focus on biomechanical analyses and run technique coaching to reduce the risk of reinjury. Mason missed the national championships, but he returned to full training sooner than expected. More importantly, he now has mad injury-coping skills.

8

PEOPLE ARE WORRIED ABOUT ME

EXERCISE DEPENDENCE AND THE INCESSANT NEED TO DO MORE

The price of anything is the amount of life you exchange for it. —HENRY THOREAU

Being an endurance athlete has its problems. You already spend a bewildering amount of money on your sport and its accoutrements, you almost certainly wear things that embarrass children and scare small animals, and it's quite likely that you have a reputation for being a little obsessive about your training. While some athletes relish the family holiday or weekend away, some see only anxiety about how to fit in training without (1) a pool, track, or nearby trail; (2) too many people noticing; and (3) getting into an argument about your selfishness if (2) cannot be avoided. So when does a healthy habit become a destructive obsession? Consider these athletes:

> Neal is a triathlete who trains 30–35 hours per week. Three days per week he will train four times in 1 day. He has 3 days off per year, but 1 day per week is in active recovery. He avoids non-race travel so he doesn't have to think too much about how to find places to train.

> Jenny is a marathoner who trains 15–20 hours per week. Her training partners have learned to accept that a 90-minute run usually ends up being closer to 2 hours. Jenny gets irritated with stops and regrouping and has a reputation for going too hard on easy days.
>
> Matt is an ultrarunner who trains 18–20 hours per week. He started as a cross-country and middle-distance runner but now prefers the challenge of the longer distance events, although he's been plagued by chronic injury. He frequently creates his own charitable endurance runs to raise money for causes that he believes in, and on his birthday each year he "runs his age."
>
> Natalie is a road cyclist. Natalie trains 12–15 hours per week because, in her words, "I like food too much." She frequently skips breakfast before riding, and if she eats out at night, she will usually train longer or harder the following day.

Without knowing too much more about each of these athletes, it's hard to say whether their training habits are unhealthy, but we can probably agree that their relationship with exercise seems complicated. How does your perception of these athletes change if I told you that Neal is a professional triathlete, Jenny has an anxiety disorder, Matt is a former drug addict, and Natalie had an eating disorder as a teen? Can training be "excessive" if you make your living doing it, like Neal? After all, sommeliers can still be drunks. Does it matter if someone *uses* exercise to help keep a mental illness under control, perhaps like Matt, Jenny, or Natalie? Questions like this are important to think through if you're going to understand the role that exercise plays in people's lives and whether it has become "too much of a good thing."

Excessive exercise habits are pretty controversial, at least from a scientific point of view.[1] This topic is so fraught with contentious debate that psychologists, sport scientists, and researchers can't even agree on what the problem actually is and, more importantly, whether we should and can diagnose it as something akin to, say, biological addiction. As we shall see, the devil is in the details. This chapter is about those details—knowing where the line in the sand is for you, and what to do about it if you or your loved ones think you've crossed it.

1 "Excessive exercise" doesn't adequately capture this phenomenon, but it's easier to say and understand at this point.

Nuts about exercise, or an exerciser who's nuts?

Here's the consensus: Excessive exercise is probably a dependency or a form of behavioral addiction. Both descriptions have roots in the criteria for substance addiction—the failure to resist an impulse, drive, or temptation to use a drug that is harmful to the person or to others.[2] (Read the next nerd alert for a more detailed description of how shrinks understand and diagnose variants of an illness characterized by "You really ought to stop doing that.") When excessive exercise is understood within an addiction framework, it raises more questions than answers. Using exercise is not like using heroin or cocaine, in which the benefit-to-harm ratio looks like a soccer score between the Faroe Islands and Brazil. It's indisputable that exercise conveys lots of benefits even to the most hardened user. So when does exercise become harmful to the athlete or others? When you are training through an injury? Not seeing enough of your kids? Being habitually late for work because of your training? Arguing about how to spend your precious vacation time? Sinking into a depressive state when you're prevented from exercising? Shrinks often define "harmful" as the repetitive engagement that ultimately interferes with functioning in other domains.[3] Hmm. Hardly helpful. And what defines "failure to resist exercise"? Getting up at 3:00 a.m. to train? Choosing exercise over an important family event? Many of us would be automatically indicted. Oh dear, we're now in quite a pickle. And that's just the diagnosis. When it comes to treatment, we know even less.

In this chapter we will not focus on the complex psychobiological causes of excessive exercise but instead what to do about it.[4] A few academically brave souls have tried and succeeded to nail down some usable criteria to help figure out if you've got a problem with exercise. Among the best are Heather Hausenblas and Danielle Symons-Downs, who reviewed the scientific evidence and modified the *DSM-IV* diagnostic criteria for substance addiction

2 American Psychiatric Association, *Diagnostic and Statistical Manual of Mental Disorders*, 5th ed. (Arlington, VA: American Psychiatric Publishing, 2013).

3 J. E. Grant, "Introduction to Behavioral Addictions," *American Journal of Drug and Alcohol Abuse* 36, no. 5 (2010): 233–241.

4 But if you're interested, here's a great start: A. Weinstein and Y. Weinstein, "Exercise Addiction: Diagnosis, Bio-Psychological Mechanisms and Treatment Issues," *Current Pharmaceutical Design* 20, no. 25 (2014): 4062–4069.

to fit with exercise habits.[5] They concluded that "exercise dependence" was a better characterization of this complex, confusing, and surprisingly common phenomenon. You can take the test they developed later in this chapter. More recent research has helped to distinguish exercise dependence from frequently co-occurring disorders, such as anorexia athletica, to better understand the progression from first-time exerciser to full-blown dependent or addict.[6] However, when it comes to the diagnostic criteria, there is a virtually unanimous scientific consensus that the Hausenblas and Symons-Downs modified *DSM-IV* criteria hold the most promise for determining if you have a problem with exercise. Let's take a look.

Diagnostic criteria for exercise dependence.

There are seven criteria that must be considered before we can figure out if you, or your loved one, has a problem with exercise. We will address the issue of how these criteria fit for professional athletes later in the chapter.

1. **Tolerance.** Increased amounts (in frequency, duration, and/or intensity) of exercise are needed to achieve the desired exercise "buzz," or there is diminished effect with continued use of the same amount of exercise. Note that this is not to be confused with an increase in training stimulus required to increase physical fitness. In this context, tolerance refers to the need for a bigger acute exercise "hit" for the "feel-good" sensation.
2. **Withdrawal.** This is manifested by either the characteristic withdrawal symptoms for exercise (e.g., anxiety, fatigue, irritability, restlessness, sleep problems) or a similar amount of exercise is taken to relieve or avoid withdrawal symptoms. Some athletes develop withdrawal symptoms when they cut down their training deliberately. For an example of this, read the sidebar on taper tantrums.
3. **Intention effect.** Exercise is often taken in larger amounts or over a longer period than was intended. For example, you may frequently train longer or harder than prescribed or initially planned. From the athletes described at the

5 H. Hausenblas and D. Symons-Downs, "Exercise Dependence: A Systematic Review," *Psychology of Sport and Exercise* 3 (2002): 89–123.

6 Anorexia athletica is not yet recognized by the DSM-5. M. Freimuth, S. Moniz, and S. R. Kim, "Clarifying Exercise Addiction: Differential Diagnosis, Co-occurring Disorders, and Phases of Addiction," *International Journal of Environmental Research and Public Health* 8 (2011): 4069–4081.

"WTF is wrong with you?" Addictions, compulsions, dependencies, and obsessions

NERD ALERT!

IF YOU'VE EVER BEEN accused of excessive exercise, you've probably also had to fend off accusations of compulsive training, obsessiveness, or being an exercise "addict." The psychological bases and diagnoses of addictions, compulsions, and obsessions are distinct, and while knowing the difference isn't critical to helping you deal with your own nutty exercise habits, it might help to know what you've got (or might have). Get your shrink on; we're going in . . .

An **addiction** is the compulsive use of a substance (e.g., a drug) or a non-substance (e.g., a behavior) that the user is unable to stop, despite harmful consequences, because it's both rewarding (it feels good) and reinforcing (doing it increases the likelihood that you will do it again).* The key words to focus on here are *compulsive, pleasurable, harmful,* and *unable to stop*. It's a disorder of the brain's reward system. In some cases, more and more of the substance or behavior is needed to get the same level of pleasure, and when it's abruptly stopped, the user experiences a psychophysiological withdrawal that feels f*cking awful. When it's a drug, it's called substance addiction. When it's a behavior, it's called a behavioral addiction. At present, the only behavioral addiction officially recognized is gambling, but that's likely to change now that behavioral addictions have finally been added to the shrink's bible, the *DSM-5*.†

A **dependency** is when you experience physical and/or psychological withdrawal symptoms after stopping use of a substance or behavior. In the brain, neurons have adapted to the repeated exposure to the drug or the neurochemical consequences of a behavior. This adaptation means that the neurons only function normally when they are exposed to the drug or the neurochemical outcomes of the behavior. When the drug or behavior stops, you feel crappy. If the dependency becomes compulsive and out of control, it elevates to an addiction. Most of us have caffeine dependency, but some have caffeine addiction. Excessive exercise is most correctly labeled >

* Meaning that it activates reward circuitry of the mesolimbic dopamine system.

† American Psychiatric Association, *DSM-5*.

Continued

a dependency because it rarely meets all the criteria for being compulsive, harmful, and unable to stop.

A **compulsion** is a repetitive action or behavior that serves one purpose: to reduce feelings of anxiety. In psychology terms, this is called "negative reinforcement" because when you do it, it lessens or takes away something unpleasant (in this case, anxiety). Compulsions aren't necessarily rational and do not involve feelings of pleasure. Compulsions include things like repeatedly checking things, ordering and arranging things, counting, or cleaning or washing your hands excessively. Compulsions are diagnosed when you feel that you are no longer in control of them, you spend at least one hour per day doing them, and they significantly interfere with your normal day-to-day life.[‡] When the anxiety driving the compulsion is caused by repeated and unwanted thoughts or urges, it is diagnosed as obsessive-compulsive disorder (OCD). OCD can also be accompanied by motor tics—sudden, brief repetitive movements such as blinking or facial twitches. Motor tics also help reduce anxiety. Exercise isn't really a compulsive behavior because it can be rational, is not necessarily repetitive, and is often rewarding in and of itself, even if it's a bit out of control.

An **impulse control disorder (ICD)** refers to your inability to resist an urge or temptation to do something that could harm you or others. Think of an ICD as something bad your Chimp brain begs you to do and then slips roofies to your Professor brain so it is powerless to resist. And we're not talking about your inability to resist tiramisu, or your terrible self-control when you're already one glass in—no, this stuff can be ruinous, like pathological gambling, stealing, and setting stuff on fire for no f*cking reason.

---

‡ Ibid.

beginning of the chapter, Jenny would be considered to be suffering from an intention effect.

4. **Lack of control.** There is a persistent desire or unsuccessful effort to cut down or control exercise. For example, you might know that you ought to cut down and have even had periods when you tried to, but you end up going back to old habits.
5. **Time.** A great deal of time is spent in activities necessary to obtain exercise. This refers not only to a lot of time spent actually training, but also considerable time spent planning how, when, and where you can train when you know you're going into unfamiliar environments (e.g., on family vacations or business trips).
6. **Reductions in other activities.** As a direct result of exercise, your social, occupational, or recreational activities are given up or reduced. For example, you might consistently pass on social activities because they require staying up too late, or you avoid early morning commitments because of your training plans. You might also prefer to simply cancel social engagements if they don't involve exercise, or consistently subordinate them to fitting your training sessions in.
7. **Continuance.** Exercise is continued despite knowledge of having a persistent or recurrent physical or psychological problem that is likely to have been caused or exacerbated by the exercise. This might include training through an injury, exercising despite knowing that it will cause interpersonal conflict, blaming yourself for not being able to meet expanding expectations or goals of exercise, exercising to increase feelings of control over your body, and so on.

When exercise dependence is attributed solely to feelings associated with exercise (the "feel-good" factor), it's known as *primary* exercise dependence. When exercise dependence is motivated primarily by an attempt to manipulate or control body composition (or thoughts and feelings about body composition), it's referred to as secondary exercise dependence. This differentiation isn't reflected in the diagnostic criteria but does have implications for how it's treated.

How common is exercise dependence?

Given the challenge of diagnosing exercise dependence, it's no wonder that estimates of its prevalence vary. That said, it's thought that approximately 3 percent of the exercising public meet the criteria for dependence.[7] However, it does

7 K. Berczik et al., "Exercise Addiction: Symptoms, Diagnosis, Epidemiology, and Etiology," *Substance Use & Misuse* 47, no. 4 (2012): 403–417.

seem to be much more common in endurance sports, especially triathlon, with one study finding that 52 percent of triathletes met the diagnostic criteria for dependence.[8] If you're a runner and find yourself nodding in smug agreement, easy, tiger, you're next at 25 percent.[9] Given that exercise dependence is also highly prevalent among elite athletes—estimates are 30–35 percent—exercise dependence among elite triathletes is likely to be especially high.[10] It's difficult to know if the sport of triathlon creates the dependence, or if dependent-prone individuals simply gravitate to triathlon. However, research does hint at, and anecdotal evidence supports, that triathlon seems to attract . . . how can we put this gently . . . chocolate with more nuts? And to all those triathletes out there: Don't worry, we use the word "nuts" as a term of endearment to indicate that you're passionate and driven, if not a little neurotic. Ahem. *Psst.* If you're not a triathlete, then we use the word "nuts" to mean nuts. If you know triathletes, you know exactly what we mean. Wink.

Are you "addicted" to exercise?

By now you should know that we're not actually measuring exercise "addiction," but exercise dependence. That was a test to see if you're still awake. Diagnosing an addiction, a compulsion, an obsession, or a dependency—or any other mental disorder—requires a clinical interview with a trained professional. When only paper and pencil "tests" are used, the professionals tend to use hesitant phrases like "may indicate," and "possibly at risk for" when we see the results. This might seem a cop-out, but even psychologists know that most psychometric measures have the diagnostic validity of tasseography (look it up). The last thing we want is to have you convinced that you're a raving lunatic when all you do is overtrain and moan. With those disclaimers in place, let's see what brand of nuts you might be dealing with.

---

8 M. J. Blaydon and K. J. Lindner, "Eating Disorders and Exercise Dependence in Triathletes," *Eating Disorders* 10, no. 1 (2002): 49–60.

9 H. A. Slay et al., "Motivations for Running and Eating Attitudes in Obligatory Versus Nonobligatory Runners," *International Journal of Eating Disorders* 23, no. 3 (1998): 267–275.

10 J. McNamara and M. P. McCabe, "Striving for Success or Addiction? Exercise Dependence Among Elite Australian Athletes," *Journal of Sports Science* 30, no. 8 (2012): 755–766.

THE EXERCISE DEPENDENCE SCALE

Using the scale provided below, please rate the following statements as honestly as possible. The statements refer to current exercise beliefs and behaviors that have occurred in the past 3 months.

	NEVER					ALWAYS
1. I exercise to avoid feeling irritable	1	2	3	4	5	6
2. I exercise despite recurring physical problems	1	2	3	4	5	6
3. I continually increase my exercise intensity to achieve the desired effects/benefits	1	2	3	4	5	6
4. I am unable to reduce how long I exercise	1	2	3	4	5	6
5. I would rather exercise than spend time with family/friends	1	2	3	4	5	6
6. I spend a lot of time exercising	1	2	3	4	5	6
7. I exercise longer than I intend to	1	2	3	4	5	6
8. I exercise to avoid feeling anxious	1	2	3	4	5	6
9. I exercise when injured	1	2	3	4	5	6
10. I continually increase my exercise frequency to achieve the desired effects/benefits	1	2	3	4	5	6
11. I am unable to reduce how often I exercise	1	2	3	4	5	6
12. I think about exercise when I should be concentrating on work or school	1	2	3	4	5	6
13. I spend most of my free time exercising	1	2	3	4	5	6
14. I exercise longer than I expect I will	1	2	3	4	5	6
15. I exercise to avoid feeling tense	1	2	3	4	5	6
16. I exercise despite persistent physical problems	1	2	3	4	5	6
17. I continually increase my exercise duration to achieve the desired effects/benefits	1	2	3	4	5	6
18. I am unable to reduce how intensely I exercise	1	2	3	4	5	6
19. I choose to exercise so that I can get out of spending time with family/friends	1	2	3	4	5	6
20. I spend considerable time finding opportunities for and planning exercise for when I'm going to be away*	1	2	3	4	5	6
21. I exercise longer than I plan to	1	2	3	4	5	6

Continued

Phew. Now that's over with, let's do some basic math. In the table below, add up your scores for the questions in each criterion and enter them in the column "Score." Next, for each criterion, circle the level of dependency corresponding to your score on that criterion. Finally, tally up the number of circled criteria for each level of dependency.

			Level of Dependency, by Criterion (circle the level based on your score)		
Diagnostic Criteria of Dependency	**Add Score for Statements . . .**	**Score**	**Nondependent, Asymptomatic** (i.e., NA, you're good)	**Nondependent, Symptomatic** (i.e., a few warning signs are there)	**At Risk for Dependence** (i.e., you might need some help)
Withdrawal effects	1, 8, 15		<7	7–14	15+
Continuance	2, 9, 16		<7	7–14	15+
Tolerance	3, 10, 17		<7	7–14	15+
Lack of control	4, 11, 18		<7	7–14	15+
Reduction in other activities	5, 12, 19		<7	7–14	15+
Time	6, 13, 20		<7	7–14	15+
Intention effects	7, 14, 21		<7	7–14	15+
Total Score (Range 21–126):			Count up the number of circled responses in each column		
Number of criteria in each category:					

The higher your total score, the more exercise-dependent you are. However, psychologists look beyond your total score and instead focus on the total number of *DSM-5* criteria that you meet. If you have three of more in the "At Risk for Dependence" column, you would be considered to have exercise dependence. Congratulations. It's official. Well, pending validation by a clinical interview with a trained professional. Ahem.

Reproduced by permission from H. A. Hausenblas and D. Symons-Downs, "How Much Is Too Much? The Development and Validation of the Exercise Dependence Scale," *Psychology and Health* 17 (2000): 387–404.

---

* This statement differs slightly from the original to better reflect exercising when away.

But I'm a professional athlete—of course I meet these criteria. It's my job!

If you earn your living as an athlete or are *trying* to earn a living as an athlete, you might have skipped down this list with bemusement at how easy it is to rack up the "Yup, that's me" responses, and this may explain why the prevalence of exercise dependence in elite athletes appears to be so high. In reality, a few of these criteria (e.g., "Time," "Reduction in Other Activities") are de facto *requirements* to even be a pro. If your rent or mortgage payment depends on your physical and mental fitness, then you *need* to be extremely focused (read: moderately obsessive) about training and recovery. After all, the life of a professional endurance athlete is often anything but balanced by conventional standards (physically, mentally, socially, financially—you name it).

To date, no one has tried to adapt the criteria of exercise dependence to professional athletes or investigate the extent to which the status of "professional athlete" can actually mask exercise dependence.[11] Pro athletes usually get a free pass on the Time and Reduction in Other Activities criteria, even if these criteria are exceeded far beyond what is actually helpful to perform at a top level. Even in the presence of considerable self-harm, training longer and harder is often seen as a badge of honor (e.g., "He's a beast!" or "She's an animal") that is rarely accompanied by the judgment or raised eyebrows shown to athletes doing it for "fun." The only people to have explored this phenomenon in any detail appear to be sport sociologists, although their work rarely reaches ordinary humans because of their tendency to write with such impenetrable complexity. It makes one wonder how their research will ever make a difference where it's needed most. That said, if you feel up to learning more about "deviant over conformity" and "normative moral ambivalence toward supranormal actions in high-performance cultures," give it a go.[12] Grandiloquent bullshit aside, the insights in this literature are exceptionally relevant to professional athletes because they help us understand why burnout is so prevalent, why autocratic and dictatorial coaches who run sequestered athlete "squads" become successful, and why it's

11 The previous statistic on the prevalence of exercise dependence among elite athletes was based on standard diagnostic criteria.

12 Jay Coakley, "Positive Deviance in Sports—An Explanation," 2014, https://www.academia.edu/7982733/Positive_Deviance_in_Sports_-_An_Explanation.

so hard to get out from under the cosh of arduous training and racing and just quit to find more balance or happiness in life.

★ **So where does that leave the pro?** Academic insights aside, we prefer to take a pragmatic approach to determine the likelihood of exercise dependence among professional endurance athletes. Here are the criteria and additional warning signs that we look for:

1. The athlete meets at least *five* of the diagnostic criteria. Any five. This is in contrast to the three diagnostic criteria required of recreational exercisers. This allows for pros to meet the criteria of "Time" and "Reduction in Other Activities" without biasing the diagnosis.
2. The athlete appears unable or unwilling to periodize his or her training. This is often demonstrated by consistently high volume and/or intensity year-round, limited variability in training volume within a micro- or meso-cycle, or the lack of an off-season.
3. There is evidence of the athlete being indiscriminate when it comes to the type of training. "Exercise indiscriminancy" happens when the type of exercise appears to be less important than keeping the dependency going. For example, if an athlete can't participate in his or her preferred activity, another activity lasting for a similar or greater period of time is substituted: He or she might go to the gym for three hours to make up for not being able to run or bike for two hours.

HOW TO DEAL WITH EXERCISE DEPENDENCE

Unlike substance addiction, exercise has many benefits. It's neither reasonable or healthy to expect someone to stop exercising altogether. The goal of all exercise dependency treatment is to help people get their exercise habits under control, not eliminate them entirely. If you think you might be suffering from *secondary* exercise dependence (i.e., excessive exercise with a possible eating disorder), then read and complete the exercises in Chapter 6, "I Feel Fat." The following recommendations are intended to help both primary and secondary exercise dependence, but when a concurrent eating disorder is present, treatment needs to focus specifically on distorted perceptions about your body. As novel treatments for exercise dependence emerge, recommendations are likely to change. For example, some evidence suggests that transcranial magnetic stimulation and drug therapy might help, but data are sparse and limited to studies of people with other stuff going on.[13]

Identifying the memory feed coming from your Computer brain.

When we introduced you to your brain(s) in Chapter 1, we learned that our Computer brain is continually feeding us memories that are drenched in association, meaning, and automatic responses. Your Computer brain trawls, retrieves, and serves up memories with such lightning speed that your Chimp and Professor don't get much of a chance to write a new script (a new way of responding) when you encounter a familiar situation. Before you're even barely aware of what's happening, you're probably thinking, feeling, and acting the way your Computer brain has reminded you that you've responded in the past. For example, thinking about a new environment, away from the comfort of your exercise routine, might make you feel instantly on edge because you know what this means for your training habits—planning and confrontation. This is what has happened before. After these memories leave the subconscious world of your Computer brain, the next fastest brain—your Chimp—gets its grubby hands on them. Your Chimp brain filters it further using emotionally charged insight. Thoughts of family vacations suddenly become riddled with anxiety about scheduling exercise and not pissing people off. By the time these experiences reach your Professor brain, they've gathered so much emotional momentum that your Professor brain often just rolls over and plays dead—you're now exhausted just thinking about the family vacation.

The same phenomenon occurs with compulsive completion. We all know what it's like to finish a ride with 49.9 miles on the clock, or a run that lasted 59 minutes and 30 seconds. Because our brains are goal oriented, there's nothing

---

13 For example, one study found that the drug Quetiapine may help reduce the compulsion to exercise. Quetiapine is an antipsychotic with affinity for the D1 and D2 dopamine receptors and the α1 and α2 adrenergic receptors, and is antagonistic to the 5-HT1A and 5-HT2 serotonin receptors. See M. Di Nicola et al., "Quetiapine As Add-On Treatment for Bipolar I Disorder with Comorbid Compulsive Buying and Physical Exercise Addiction," *Progress in Neuro-Psychopharmacology and Biological Psychiatry* 34 (2010): 713–714.

wrong (or right, for that matter) with wanting to add on a few extra minutes to make the session finish on a nice round number. It's the same feeling that comes from "topping off" at the gas station. While most of us have a sensible threshold where we are willing to "top off'" (translation: Professor brain says to Chimp brain, "Okay, I'll give you that reward, but any more and it could have negative consequences"), some athletes are unable to summon their Professor brain to pump the brakes at all. The Chimp's grubby hands create an anticipation of anxiety and disappointment (with themselves) from not completing the session *exactly* as written despite all the facts and logic telling them that they've done enough. "I won't be happy with myself unless I do this exactly," or "the entire session is ruined if it's not 100 percent complete." They know how miserable this makes them because they remember from past experience.

Although the Chimp and Professor brains are responsible for all the content that fills your Computer brain, it's not Nordstrom's—you can't take memories back and ask for a refund. You're stuck with them. And when the memories are put there by the Chimp under protest by your Professor, we have a huge problem. It's really hard to change the thoughts and feelings that accompany these memories. But it *is* possible, and this is our way in. Our strategy is to confront the automatic and biased memories that Computer-then-Chimp throws at us, and try to use Professor brain skills—facts and logic—to disarm the faulty associations and catastrophic conclusions. Even though your Professor brain has very little game in resisting the superpowers of emotion, when facts and logic are used correctly they are lethal. After all, these skills got us to the moon, helped David slay Goliath, and told you to walk away from David Lindhagen in the 10th grade.[14] Surely they can help you make reasonable decisions about your workouts. Facts and logic are some of the most omnipotent psychological weapons that you possess, but you have to learn how to use them properly if you want them to be effective. Think of it like Obi-Wan Kenobi's training of Luke Skywalker, but with facts as the Force and logic as your light saber. Trouble is, at the moment it's dark, and you're just swiping and stabbing like a 5-year-old with a Nutella buzz.

14 Ah, Crazy, Stupid Love.

Doing something about it—the self-imposed time-out

Time-outs are used in parenting, teaching, sports, and relationships to help defuse emotion and let your Professor regain control. Time-outs help slow down the Chimp. When the brain slows down, your Professor has a fighting chance to use its skills because you get a chance to reflect and confront what's being recommended for you at Computer and Chimp speeds. A self-imposed time-out is simply the act of setting a predefined period in which you don't let yourself act on your feelings or impressions. You use a time-out during the critical moment when the urge to train or work out is at its highest. During your time-out, you're using Professor brain skills (facts and logic) to answer two questions:

Do I need to be doing this now?

What will happen if I don't exercise now?

Spend five minutes (or however long your time-out is) thinking about these questions before making a decision.

Facts and logic can't instantly or automatically overpower emotion-based urges but, with practice, you can make it much easier to win brain battles. If you recall, the sole purpose of emotion is to drive decision-making. The trick is to recognize that your Computer and Chimp brain can never force you to act but can only offer up extremely attractive, emotionally charged suggestions. Step one in winning this fight is to know what emotionally charged and attractive suggestions we're talking about. Here are some automatic thoughts that athletes with excessive exercise habits have told us they have noticed:

Everything will be fine if I can just get through this session.

To be the best, I must do as much training as I can handle.

I can't think clearly until I know I've done it.

Feeling exhausted from training is the only way I can eat guilt-free.

When I train hard, it purges all the negativity I have.

You can spot the handiwork of the Computer-Chimp team in words like "must," "can't," "need," and "feel." The Professor brain is more likely to use words like "should," "prefer," and "wish." Use the Force during your time-out to counter

MORE! MORE! MORE!
MEMORIES
GO!
LET'S MOVE!
NOW! NOW! NOW!

automatic thoughts. The Jedi skills come in when you learn the counterarguments by heart, reciting them whenever the urge to exercise feels overwhelming. Now it's your turn. (See Exercise 2, pp. 204–5.)

Reward your good behavior

When you do manage to control your exercise habits (cut down, lessen, or replace), your brain needs to be rewarded for doing so. In psychological terms, this is known as "contingency management," but you can think of it sparking motivation to keep up good habits. Remember, the brain's natural reward system relies on feeling successful, experiencing satisfaction or pleasure, and having a sense of accomplishment to strengthen the likelihood that you will keep it up. Even if your "win" is small, such as deciding to stay home instead of doing a gym session, taking a rest day, or listening to your body before committing to a run session, know that it counts in Brainworld. If the natural reward of accomplishment or satisfaction isn't sufficient, try rewarding yourself with actual stuff (healthy treats or indulgences) or create milestones (such as three consecutive days of reduced exercise) that have increasingly powerful incentives.

Other strategies from the trenches.

I've (Simon) worked with many exercise-dependent athletes, and they all have a unique story to tell in terms of what it felt like to have exercise control their lives. The strategies that helped them recover may not appear in conventional treatment guidance. Here's a pick of a few of our favorites:

Focus on your why. When the urge to exercise becomes excessive, think about your "why"—why you got into the sport, why you like to race, what your driving force behind the passion started as. Keep trying to connect your current motivation—even if it is now out of control—to these original motives and focus on the discrepancy between your current why and your original "pure" why.

Focus on performance goals. When the need to exercise is taking over, go back to focusing on performance goals: What type of session or recovery is going to best impact my performance as an athlete?

EXERCISE 2

CONFRONTING YOUR AUTOMATIC THOUGHTS

Write down five automatic or instinctive thoughts you have about your urge, compulsion, or drive to exercise. Avoid trying to rationalize them or trying to filter them for judgmental humans (which are Professor brain filters). Just blurt them out.

My automatic thoughts about exercise:

1

2

3

4

5

Now, read back over these statements and check to make sure they have not been contaminated by your Professor brain. This list is likely to be very personal, probably a bit embarrassing, and may even give you some anxiety just writing or reading it (after all, it's your Professor brain that has to write it and read it). If this is the case, practice the exercise of detachment, "Watching the Suck," in Chapter 2 for getting used to *seeing* rather than *feeling* your crazy. Now just sit with these statements for a while. Stare at them. Look at the words on the page. If it helps, repeat them back to yourself in a funny accent or as song. Yes, we know this sounds ludicrous, but it's a remarkably effective tool to help increase the detachment from your thoughts from feelings.

COUNTERING

For each automatic thought you listed, develop a factually accurate counter-statement of what your Professor brain wants you to think instead. Your Chimp probably doesn't want to do these things, but go through the motions of thinking about it anyway and writing it down. Try to specifically address the faulty logic of the automatic thought, but make sure your counter statements are accurate and plausible. For example, if your automatic thought is "I feel anxious and irritable when I don't work out," you might counter it with "Exercise isn't the only thing that helps me feel less anxious and irritable."

Counter-thought to number 1:

Counter-thought to number 2:

Counter-thought to number 3:

Counter-thought to number 4:

Counter-thought to number 5:

Fill your time by substituting. Replace the time spent exercising with another highly valued activity. When you've chosen not to train, don't just try and gut it out by sitting there or doing a boring task—find something fun or pleasurable to do instead. Watch a movie, meet a friend for coffee, or spend time doing another hobby.

Find a "sponsor" to keep you honest. Just as some 12-step programs use a "sponsor" to listen, help support, and guide the recovering addict, you can find someone you trust to help you manage your exercise dependency. A sponsor should be someone who inspires you, is trustworthy, and does not need emotional support in return. It can be a close friend, but ideally it should be someone who has successful recovered from exercise dependency.

Read about or interact with other people who are also struggling with exercise dependence. It can also help to connect with other people who are struggling with exercise dependence. Storytelling and sharing experiences can be remarkably therapeutic because they increase empathy, reduce feelings of loneliness, and provide hope for recovery. Listening to the experiences of others, especially if they are similar to you, can have a remarkable effect on your ability and confidence to tackle your own challenges with exercise dependence. You can search online for blogs or magazine articles that describe very personal stories of dealing with exercise dependence.[15] We also recommend looking for online support groups that focus on exercise "addiction." One of our favorites is here: https://exercise-addiction.supportgroups.com. It's free and anonymous, but you should be aware that it's not moderated by experts and doesn't offer professional treatment advice—it's simply a place to interact with other people who are also struggling with exercise habits.

15 For example: http://www.shape.com/lifestyle/mind-and-body/how-one-woman-overcame-her-exercise-addiction.

It's not me, it's you.

Exercise dependency is a sensitive subject. It can be extremely awkward and difficult to confront and discuss this rationally with someone, let alone intervene. If this someone is you, then just reading this chapter might be sufficient to create awareness and motivation for change. In Chapter 6, "I Feel Fat," we introduced a few strategies to help you talk to someone who you suspect might have an eating disorder. In many ways, talking to someone with exercise dependence is similar. The goal is to build awareness and help motivate them to change their behavior. You do that by being empathic, honest but nonjudgmental, and, importantly, directing them to resources or professional help so that they can recover. Unfortunately, many people might notice a friend or family member's excessive exercise habits but never mention it directly to them for fear of causing offense or embarrassment. This is something you need to get over. This isn't a license to issue a condescending lecture but an opportunity to try to understand what's behind the behavior. If you want to see what an actual conversation looks like, we've added a sample dialogue later in this chapter. Remember, exercise dependence has biological (tolerance, withdrawal) and psychological (anxiety, need for control) components. Trying to convince someone to do less exercise because it's making an injury worse is about as effective as telling someone to stop smoking because it causes lung cancer (every smoker already knows this). The first step is to change the way you talk and listen to them. Although you can't force someone to change or get help, you can share your honest concerns, provide support, and tell them where they can get proper help. As with all sensitive topics, the language you use is *really* important. See the chart on the following page for a few ways to stop you from sounding like a sanctimonious douchebag.

It's never easy to talk about awkward or personal stuff. Here's one example of how you might have that conversation with your friend, Matt, an ultrarunner you suspect might be suffering from exercise dependence.

You: Hey, Matt, is it okay if I ask you about something that's a bit personal?

Matt: Sure. What is it?

You: I'm getting a bit worried about you . . . well, about your training. I know that ultras require lots of discipline and big mileage, but I sense that there's something more going on with you. It seems that you're always looking for ways to do more

HOW TO TALK ABOUT EXERCISE DEPENDENCE

THINGS TO SAY OR DO	THINGS *NOT* TO SAY OR DO
Use "I" statements when sharing your concerns. "I care about you" or "I'm worried about you."	Don't focus on the exercise itself. Don't say "You train too hard" or "You don't need to run that long." You might talk about the behaviors you notice, but then try to focus on the feelings.
Let them know that it's safe to talk to you and that you won't judge or criticize them. "As your friend, I really care about you. I won't judge or criticize you, I just want to know how I can help."	Don't use language that implies that the person is doing something wrong. We know that they probably are doing something wrong, but pointing out the obvious forces them to be defensive.
Encourage them to express how they feel; remember, it is important to understand how they feel, rather than just state how you feel. "I know this stuff is really hard to talk about, but can you help me understand what it feels like for you?"	Don't assume the role of a therapist or try to fix things. You don't need to have all the answers; it's more important that you listen and help them feel comfortable opening up to you.
If the person isn't very talkative, try to let silences linger longer than normal to give them more opportunity to speak. People don't like awkward silences. They will usually fill them if you can fight your urge to talk.	Don't use manipulative statements or phrases that focus on the impact it's having on other people. This can make things worse or increase the person's level of denial. "If you wanted this to work, you'd stop training as much."
Encourage them to seek help and explain that you will be there with them if they need you. "If you want, we can go and see someone together. Just to chat through some of this stuff."	Don't use threats, especially if you have some control or authority over the person as a parent or coach. Threats heighten an already stressful experience for the person and can make the behavior worse. "Unless you cut down your training, you can't [join in], [attend], [use x] anymore."

and more. It's not just the racing, but the ways you find creative opportunities to just hammer yourself. The self-organized runs for charity, the running in remembrance, the running-your-age each year. I know these causes are important to you, but I wonder if that's the only reason you're doing them. What's your take on this?

Matt: Hey, man, you know I love running. True, from the outside it might seem like I'm some sort of headbanger, but these people's stories really get to me. Take Stevey. He has these huge medical bills. It's just awful. I've got to do something to help . . .

You: I totally get that. It's awful what happened to Steve, and I think you wanting to help is great. But I'm not talking about Steve here. I'm talking about you . . . the potential damage you're doing to yourself and other reasons why you might be doing it. What's your take on that part?

Matt: What do you mean?

You: I guess I'm asking what's behind your need to do this much. Like what it feels like if you can't run, or if you don't run.

Matt: I feel crappy. Running is such a huge part of who I am. It helps me cope with life. It's my therapy, man.

You: So the big volume is a way to help you feel less anxious or to think through stuff? Can you help me understand that a bit more?

Matt: I suppose. I think if I didn't have running, I'd probably be off the rails, you know? An alcoholic or just eating way too much shit.

You: It feels good when you can channel certain urges into something healthy, right? I can certainly relate to that.

Matt: Exactly.

You: Except I don't see your running as particularly healthy at the moment. Your personality has changed a bit over the past year. I know Margie wants to spend more time with you, and I know the boys miss seeing you at our weekend sessions. And you've still got that calf problem, right?

Matt: [Thinking].

You: What about talking to someone about it? About sorting through some of the stuff behind the running and perhaps getting some balance back without compromising all the charity stuff?

Matt: You mean see a shrink?

You: [Laughs.] I don't know if you need a shrink. I just think that talking to someone about what's behind it all might help get some perspective. You know, help you feel less alone about it all or get a better understanding of why you want to run so much?

Matt: Hmm. Maybe.

You: Well, have a think about it. It's okay to be struggling with stuff. I'm really struggling not to drink as much. Perhaps we can ask for a two-for-one special? [Laughs.]

Matt: Ha, ha. Okay, I will.

You: You're one of my best friends, and I've got your back. You know me, I'm a stubborn f*cker and I won't let this go. Let's chat about it again next week when you've had more time to think about it.

Matt: Ok. Hey, thanks, man. I know you care about me.

If you think that nothing you say is getting through, you could even have this same conversation, but confidentially, with the athlete's spouse or partner. Sometimes it can help just to corroborate your concern.

General resources

Currently, there are no evidence-based programs or even standardized treatment protocols for people who suffer from exercise dependence. We hope this changes in the near future. However, approaches that do hold promise are based on treatments for behavioral addictions in general, such as gambling, gaming, and so on. While treatment approaches are varied, most are based on cognitive behavior therapy (CBT)—trying to change the way you think and act in order to change how you feel. Treatment options and resources come mostly from private groups, but there should be therapists near you that focus on behavioral addictions.[16] You might start by searching web-based directories like https://therapists.psychologytoday.com.

16 For examples, see: https://www.addiction.com/addiction-a-to-z/exercise-addiction/exercise-addiction-treatment/, https://www.eatingdisorderhope.com/information/orthorexia-excessive-exercise, http://www.rehabs.com/about/exercise-addiction-rehabs/.

TRAINING AND THE TAPER TANTRUMS: A SPECIAL CASE OF EXERCISE WITHDRAWAL

IF YOU'RE AN ENDURANCE ATHLETE who competes, then chances are you're intimately familiar with tapering. Technically speaking, a taper is a progressive nonlinear reduction of the training load during a variable period of time, in an attempt to reduce the physiological and psychological stress of daily training and optimize sports performance.* Virtually every athlete benefits from a taper, and the science is extremely strong on why it works.†

So that's the science part. The reality of how an endurance athlete experiences a taper often looks more like this: A week from its start, you look forward to it with a crazed longing—it's like a vacation just around the corner. You dream of all the things you're going to do in your spare time, and it makes the grueling slog of your final big training block more manageable. When taper day 1 arrives, you love the extra hour in bed, the feeling of staying up past 8 p.m., and getting some balance back in your life. Your partner probably loves this part of your taper as much as you do. He or she finally has you back, not the comatose adult-child barely able to do basic chores or walk upstairs without moaning about it. Then phase 2 begins. More time on your hands equals more time to worry that you have a big race very soon, more time to worry if you got your taper right, more time to worry about losing fitness, more time to worry about gaining weight. And that's before you get hit by weird physical and emotional sensations. You feel strangely sluggish and achy, and odd phantom pains start to appear. "Why does my knee hurt?" "Shit, my ribs ache. Have I broken something in my sleep?" The doubt and over-analysis set in, and you find yourself feeling crabby, frustrated, or lethargic—even depressed and panicky—anything *but* the light, zippy, and refreshed version of yourself that you need to be in 10 days. WTF? Welcome to the taper tantrums. >

---

* I. Mujika and S. Padilla, "Scientific Bases for Precompetition Tapering Strategies," *Medicine and Science in Sports and Exercise* 35, no. 7 (2003): 1182–1187.

† L. Bosquet et al., "Effects of Tapering on Performance: A Meta-Analysis," *Medicine and Science in Sports and Exercise* 39, no. 8 (2007): 1358–1165.

Continued

No one really talks about the dark side of tapering, but chances are you've experienced some degree of a taper tantrum if you're coming off a sizeable chronic training load. Many of the psychological feelings you experience are akin to those from a drug withdrawal because, well, that's partly what's happening in your brain and body.[‡] It might not be a seizure-inducing *Trainspotting* experience, but you have fed yourself a behavioral drug for months on end that floods your Chimp brain with neurotransmitters. When the neurotransmitter taps turn off (or to be more precise, down regulate), he's pissed! Combine that with the musculoskeletal adaptations during rest, and your cognitive appraisal system starts to work double overtime—"Oh no, I feel like crap!" "Am I losing fitness?" "Did I get my taper right?" It's a spiral that you need to intercept if you want to grow out of the taper tantrums.

★ **What you can do about it:** First, recognize and accept what's happening in your body. Just as you get grumpy and irritable if you don't have coffee (assuming you're coffee-dependent), your body also rebels when deprived of its regular training stimulus. This is a normal psychophysiological reaction that doesn't mean you've lost fitness, have new injuries, or are destined for a terrible race. As soon as the stimulus returns, you'll be firing on all cylinders again. In fact, start to see this withdrawal as increasing your sensitivity to the training stimulus. When you race or resume full training, you'll feel newly energized and focused. Second, use training sessions during your taper week very deliberately. Try to find sessions that keep you "open" but do not put your different energy systems in the red for too long. For example, if you're a runner, you might include short recovery runs that include two to three 10- to 20-second "pickups" (gradually increasing speed, ending in a full sprint).

---

‡ A. A. Berlin, W. J. Kop, and P. A. Deuster, "Depressive Mood Symptoms and Fatigue After Exercise Withdrawal: The Potential Role of Decreased Fitness," *Psychosomatic Medicine* 68, no. 2 (2006): 224–230.

FIGHT

GET STUCK IN WITH NEW BATTLE SKILLS

9

I DON'T LIKE LEAVING MY COMFORT ZONE

HOW TO CROSS THE FEAR BARRIER

I'm not going to call an ambulance this time because if I do you won't learn anything.

—BRIAN GRIFFIN, *FAMILY GUY*

It sucks to suck at things. It sucks even more if people are watching you suck. The suck is worse still if other people are doing the exact same activity as you and they are clearly *not* sucking. Welcome to the world of running, cycling, and swimming in public. The truth is, most people would prefer to suck at stuff in private. Even the thought of not being very good at something is enough for many to avoid situations entirely in which they will be watched, evaluated, and judged. Take racing. And by racing, we don't mean the local bike club ride with a sprint for a road sign; we mean formal races. You pay an entry, you pin on a number, and you compete against other people. Results get posted and it's there for all to see. Gulp. How can the exact same situation be exciting and invigorating to some, yet invoke sheer terror and avoidance in others?

It's a fact of life that virtually all of us avoid certain activities that make us feel apprehensive about our ability to be successful and the likelihood that a calamitous failure will get noticed. This is, of course, partly about confidence, but not entirely. I might have zero confidence that I can juggle oranges for one minute, but I'll still give it a go. So what's the difference? How much I care about the outcome? The presence of an audience? What's at stake? What I think my lack of this skill reveals about me as a person? Take the following comments from athletes we've helped (we've changed their names to protect the innocent!):

> I've now done six 70.3s and think I've got a good handle on how to race them. I really want to have a crack at an Ironman, but I'm a bit scared to. I mean, they're so f*cking long! I find an [Ironman] event that I think would be a good first race, but then I chicken out. I even registered for Arizona but just bailed. I made up some story about an injury, but there was nothing wrong with me! I just chickened out. Oh my God, you're the only person I've actually told that to.
>
> —DAN, 32, TRIATHLETE

> I know we're supposed to have training races, but I find it so hard to not feel 100 percent prepared for a race. My coach wants me to train through it, but racing on tired legs is tough when you're trying to actually compete! I know what people will probably say . . . "Oh, she's not as fast as I thought she was." That just really gets to me.
>
> —JANINE, 27, 10K AND HALF-MARATHONER

> Everyone tells me I need to get my pro license. I've been doing really well in the overall amateur and my times are in the mix of the pro field. I know I probably should, but it's a big step up. I'm not sure I'm ready for it, mentally. You know, getting pummeled every race.
>
> —ANTONIO, 26, TRIATHLETE

> I get called a sandbagger all the time but what people don't realize is that racing Cat. I/II is a completely different animal. Racing masters is fine for me. I'm old!
>
> —BEV, 40, CYCLIST

We're not suggesting that all of these athletes are simply scared of putting themselves out there, but when we learned more about their background and performance data we noticed a common theme. They are all physically ready or have the ability to become ready to step up to the challenge in front of them, but they have chosen not to.

To get to the bottom of this psychological conundrum and to teach your brain to enjoy, rather than fear, a new challenge, we need to talk about comfort zones. Yours, in particular. This chapter is designed to help you clamber over the comfort barrier and into the world of the scary unknown. If you have no problem entering the unknown but regularly shit yourself immediately beforehand, read Chapter 13, "I Don't Handle Pressure Well: How to cope with stress, anxiety, and expectations on race day."

The psychology of comfort zones.

We've all seen the motivational memes extolling the virtues of living outside some metaphysical comfort zone. I don't know about you, but trite and dangerously vague advice to "do something daily that scares you" isn't exactly a life lesson I'm keen to follow. Running across the road without looking scares me, as does diving into water without knowing how deep it is, but these are hardly inviting strategies to feel alive, let alone stay alive. Nope, we feel scared for a reason, and that reason is D-A-N-G-E-R. The problem is that your Chimp defines danger in quite a different way than your Professor brain (your frontal cortex, or the real you). If you recall from Chapter 1 ("Hello, Brain!"), your Chimp brain runs on emotion alone and has been designed to keep you out of harm's way or, if absolutely necessary, turn you into a fighting machine to make sure you still wake up tomorrow. When we know we will be physically and psychologically safe, scary can become exciting. Think roller coasters, haunted houses, and horror movies.

It's worth pointing out there are some people who crave and seek out sensory experiences so intense that only life-threatening situations will do. In sport, we know them as base jumpers, free climbers, skydivers, extreme skiers, wingsuit flyers, and so on. Cognitive neuroscientists have found compelling evidence that thrill seekers' brain chemistry is fundamentally different from yours and mine (assuming you're not one), partly because of their faulty controls on dopamine release and reuptake—the brain's chemical messenger for reward and pleasure.[1] It is perhaps unsurprising that sensation seeking is also

1 D. H. Zald et al., "Midbrain Dopamine Autoreceptor Availability Is Inversely Associated with Novelty Seeking Traits in Humans," *Journal of Neuroscience* 28 (2008): 14372–14378.

associated with other behaviors that sprout from a wonky dopaminergic system, such as addiction to drugs, alcohol, and sex.[2] So think twice before marrying a base jumper. (Only partly kidding.)

When a "normal" brain thinks about an intimidating situation, the primitive factions (limbic system) send strong chemical messages to the modern bits (your frontal cortex, or Professor brain) that try to convince it to join forces and keep you the hell away. Why? Because the Chimp brain thinks that [insert your own intimidating situation here] is nothing more than a cesspool of physical and psychological risk. Your Professor brain knows that death or physical harm is pretty unlikely (for example, athletes tend not to drown, have their organs explode, or lose limbs while racing), but it could be persuaded that psychological damage is a distinct possibility. Three of the most feared psychological and emotional daggers that your Chimp brain is especially keen to avoid getting stabbed by are humiliation (*Will I look stupid?*), embarrassment (*Am I doing it right?*), and inadequacy (*Am I good enough?*). Of course, not all of us feel this way. You've only got to go to a karaoke bar or participatory theater or watch "Wheel of Fortune" to see that some people simply don't give a shit about looking like an idiot. We'll come to those people in a moment. In the meantime, it's a statistically solid bet to say that most of us don't like the thought of being laughed at in public.

To avoid feeling embarrassed, humiliated, and inadequate, we create comfort zones. A comfort zone is simply a psychological fence that we erect around ourselves to protect something that we feel vulnerable about. The psychological fence emerges as a behavioral habit—actions we take to avoid the confrontation. You probably experience a lukewarm version of this on a regular basis: procrastination. Staying inside the fence gives us a sense of security and comfort—a predictableness that is calming. Beyond the fence lies the unknown—which we assume is discomfort, fear, failure, and judgment. Under these circumstances, it's no wonder that many people choose to avoid competing at all, or upgrading to a new performance category, trying a new distance, or entering a race they don't feel fully prepared for.

---

2 K. Blum et al., "The Addictive Brain: All Roads Lead to Dopamine," *Journal of Psychoactive Drugs* 44, no. 2 (April–June 2012): 134–143.

Comfort zones are a normal adaptive response to keep the inner peace. We all do it. It's as human as office gossip. Most comfort zones are very helpful; they materialize as habits or routines that take the thinking (and therefore stress) out of daily tasks. Usually we prefer to keep our underlying vulnerability very private, and for good reason. Admitting that we're flawed and then showing the entire world what that flaw is scares the hell out of us.

But make no mistake about it, COMFORT ZONES are entirely imaginary. Like an emotional plaster cast for a leg that's not broken.

They are made up by you, figments of your imagination—an imagination that has become hijacked by your Chimp brain and is motivated solely by keeping you alive, minimizing discomfort, increasing pleasure, and . . . drumroll . . . protecting your ego. And your brain has a Nobel Prize in protecting your ego and self-image—the perceptions you have about who you think you should be. Your Chimp brain will lie, cheat, and steal to keep up appearances. At least on the outside.

Many comfort zones are relatively trivial and easy to live with, such as continuing to swim on your own because the thought of joining a masters swim group fills you with fear about being too slow, not being able to do flip turns, only being able to do breaststroke, or simply being exposed as someone who clearly has no clue as to what's actually going on. Some comfort zones are trivial and just plain funny—like the inability to take a dump in front of your spouse. Some comfort zones are tolerable but frustrating—like always having to wait for a shower until you get home from the gym because the thought of being naked in a YMCA locker room gives you the cold sweats. Some are mildly irritating—often to others too—like your tendency to avoid anything with the word "race" in it because the thought of head-to-head competition creates a cascade of anxiety about aggression, embarrassment, and failure. Perhaps your comfort zone stops you from pushing really hard in a race because of a fear of the pain, or of "blowing up." Or worst of all, not finishing. **After all, if you lay it all out there and it's *still* not enough, what does that say about you?** Other comfort zones are more sinister and a recipe for long-term misery, like avoiding long-term relationships for fear of being rejected, or staying in a job you hate because you don't know what else you could do and you've got bills to pay.

Living in mental cruise control and making nothing but safe choices leads to boredom and complacency. A breakthrough in happiness, self-awareness, and mental toughness requires new experience. And the best experiences for your brain lie out yonder where the goblins live. Before we get to practical strategies, we need some ground rules.

Ground rules to make you more comfortable with feeling uncomfortable.

Recognize that actions can fail, but people cannot. One of the biggest misjudgments that people make is equating a failed plan with a failed person. Plans fail. Actions fail. People are not failures. The critical point is what we do with our failed actions and plans (or the thought of failure). Do we learn from them? Do we ignore them? The Ebola of failure is giving up when the consequences are not physically threatening. If the consequences are not life-threatening (or injury-threatening), in virtually all situations the best option for your brain is to *keep going*. Increasing scientific evidence suggests that enduring in the face of adversity and failure is likely to create neural, molecular, and hormonal changes in the brain that help you become better prepared, more adaptable, and more resistant in the future.[3] Scientists refer to the capacity of the brain to physically change in response to new experience as "neuroplasticity."

Learn to reframe your goals. In a comfort zone–busting new experience, force your goal to be something you are always in control of. When the goal is under your control, you always get to define success and failure on your own terms. If your goal requires other people to comply, you're already in trouble. The best goal is based on the effort you plan to give, not the time it takes you, where you finish, or how others see you. Start every new, intimidating situation with this simple pledge: *No matter what happens today, I agree to give it everything I've got, given the circumstances.* You might be unfit or underprepared, or the slowest

3 S. J. Russo et al., "Neurobiology of Resilience," *Nature Neuroscience* 15, no. 11 (2012): 1475–1484.

COMFORT
ZONE

person in your category—these are all your circumstances—but they have no bearing on the effort you give or the attitude you have during the experience.

Snap decisions are good for you, even if they turn out to be wrong. Yup, you heard it right. If we let our fears and concerns linger long enough, we can become paralyzed by them, unable to make a decision. Sometimes, it's good to be impulsive. Go on, I dare you, make a quick decision about something scary in the future. The "in the future" part is important because it gives us time to figure out the plan of how we're going to execute it. Don't confuse this with snap decisions about actions that also occur at the same time (like getting a tattoo while drunk, or buying something you can't afford). By quickly committing to a goal in advance, we overcome decision anxiety but still have time to think about careful execution. It's a win-win for your brain.

5 STEPS TO ESCAPE YOUR COMFORT ZONE

Step 1: Choose the comfort zones you want to bust out of

If you have no desire to leave a comfort zone because it's trivial or it doesn't prevent you from reaching a goal that's important to you, then my advice is to just leave it the hell alone. A mild case of illogicitis or harmless hypocrisy won't kill you. It's the comfort zones that stop us from enjoying life to the fullest that need to be confronted. Think about all the situations you currently avoid and why. If your denial runs so deep that you've justified everything, ask yourself this question instead: In 10 years' time, what things in my athletic life will I wish I had done differently? Perhaps it's joining a masters swim group? Trying to qualify for Kona? Running the Boston Marathon? Seeing how hard you can push your body in a race? So go ahead, peer over the edge for a while. (See Exercise 1.)

Step 2: Start by just watching

It's really helpful to reduce the stress of an intimidating situation by first being an observer, not a participant. It's like a behavioral toe-dip. You get to see what it's all about before actually risking any embarrassment. It also helps to challenge any false expectations or stereotypes you might have about the challenge

IDENTIFYING THE GOBLINS

Three comfort zones I secretly wish I could break free from:

1

2

3

Now circle one of the three that you think is having the most impact on your happiness, enjoyment, or potential as an athlete.

ahead. Of course this doesn't work for all comfort zone busts, but it does help when you're trying to start a new routine or action. Perhaps you want to join a new group, try a new distance, or participate in an entirely new sport. A great first step is to simply go along and watch. Anyone can do that! Sit in the bleachers, volunteer at an event, be at the finish line, or whatever. Experience it without experiencing it. Seeing others similar to you succeed is one of the most effective strategies to build confidence.

Step 3: Pre-create the fear

When you start thinking about leaving the comfort zone and having to face the goblins, instead of trying to control these thoughts and feelings, we're going to first really wallow in them. That's right, let's jump right in to the imaginary scenario and really f*ck up. This might seem crazy, but it works. Research in stress desensitization (a technique to help manage anxiety) and feedforward (a technique to cope with the future by thinking about and planning for it) tells us that some mental time travel to worst-case scenarios actually helps us now by confronting the irrationality of our fears and developing contingency plans for shit that could go down. (See Exercise 2.)

Step 4: Deconstruct the scenario

With the scenario firmly imagined and the mental movie played out a few times, now complete the Comfort Buster worksheet in Exercise 3 (p. 226) to create a playbook for how you can get through the experience.

GET TO KNOW THE FEAR EXPERIENCE

It's time to target the comfort zone you identified as the biggest threat to your happiness, enjoyment, or potential as an athlete in Exercise 1. When you have completed this exercise, you can repeat it for the other two comfort zones, but we strongly recommend that you tackle only one at a time.

In a quiet and comfortable position, close your eyes and visualize the intimidating scenario. Imagine all the aspects of the situation that you worry about the most. Really try to recreate them—the sounds, the smells, the sights, the people present, the thoughts, and emotions. Watch events unfold that match your fears. See it happening. Perhaps it's walking on the pool deck to your first masters swim session with no idea what the hell is going on, clueless about which lane you should swim in. You hear the splashing and smell the chlorine. You see the people staring at you. Secretly, you wish for your own lane. Perhaps your fear is getting dropped in your first Category I/II bike race, or finishing last in your first race as a pro.

Now repeat the visualization but this time picture yourself as an experienced outsider, as though you're watching someone else go through the exact same experience. Focus on the thoughts and feelings you have about them as you watch them do the same thing you did. How do your thoughts and feelings change as you witness someone else making the same "mistakes"? Do you find that you are more compassionate and supportive? Indifferent? You've now learned what actually goes through the minds of the people you were so worried about.

Use this knowledge to make your playbook for surviving the experience in Exercise 3 (p. 226).

EXERCISE 3

MAKE YOUR COMFORT-BUSTER PLAYBOOK

Now it's time to develop a plan to combat a few worst-case scenarios. In the left column, write down all the things that you are worried might happen. In response to each of these scenarios, write down two positive things to say and one positive thing you can do if this does happen.

Your comfort buster:

Think	Talk	Act
Things I'm secretly worried about happening	Two positive things I will say to myself if it does happen	One positive thing I will do if it does happen

Now go back to seeing yourself in the same situation that you visualized in Exercise 2, but this time focus on controlling your thoughts and actions using the strategies you mapped out in your playbook.

After seeing yourself survive the ordeal, take 30 seconds to focus on the feeling of accomplishment that comes with facing your fears and surviving.

Each time you find yourself worrying about the intimidating situation, re-run the mental image of yourself in the situation but this time coping with it using your positive thoughts and actions.

Step 5: Take the plunge

No more explanation needed.

Breaking through the fear barrier is a big deal. The dopamine hit that comes with completing a previously insurmountable goal or getting through a shit-scary challenge is indescribable. Aside from the neurological benefits, you walk a little taller immediately. Confidence grows, and you redraw the boundary of what you think you can do in the future. We've seen it over and over again with our own athletes. We walk them to the edge of scary sessions, events, or experiences, constantly reminding them of the comfort zone mantra: "Let's earn this one." They've anticipated the fear, considered all outcomes, and convinced their Chimp that the world is not ending. And then they jump. At times it does actually feel like we're the instructor for a tandem parachute jump. Most athletes can get themselves to the edge, but some still need a nudge to leave the plane. Some need to be talked into it quietly and calmly, whereas others need shouting at. To our surprise, many athletes are not even relieved that it's over but are energized and motivated. Some are tearful, some are grateful, but all are changed in some small way. Their athletic identity has matured. It can be such a transformative experience for athletes that we now routinely design our training programs with comfort-leaving experiences programmed in on a regular basis.

HELL NO! I WON'T GO . . .

Overcoming the fear of masters swim class

ANNA IS A 41-YEAR OLD runner, triathlete, and reluctant swimmer who lives in Phoenix, Arizona, with her husband and two dogs. She's completed 15 marathons, but she only started doing triathlon two years ago. She has a great run group she trains with twice per week ("They're like family now," she says), she does a spin class at her local YMCA twice per week, and she rides with her local tri club on Saturday. However, she always swims alone. Swimming is her weakest of the three sports, and it's her most frequently missed session. It seemed like she was always looking for a reason to bail on her swim workouts. It was clear that swimming left Anna uninspired, bored, and unmotivated. We recommended she join a masters swim group. Anna came up with a dozen reasons why this was not a good idea. "Oh, I need to swim at different times," "I plan to, but I really need to get my technique better first," "I'm too slow—I mean, I'm a 2:10/100 swimmer." It soon became clear that the real reason she didn't want to swim with the group was that the thought of training with "real" swimmers scared her. She couldn't do flip turns and had never done circle swim before (swimming in loops when there are three or more people in a lane). She had made her mind up: Swimming on her own was the safer and more comfortable option. It's just that it bored her senseless and threatened her enjoyment of triathlon.

I (Simon) asked her if she would let me help her think it through some more. Reluctantly, she agreed. I found a local masters group that met on Monday/Wednesday/Friday at 6:30 a.m., 12 p.m., and 6 p.m. I told her that I wanted her to go and watch two sessions the following week. The observation was to be part of her "training," and we added it to her Training Peaks calendar. While there, she was instructed to make a mental note of the structure of each session and whether she noticed anything surprising. We talked about her experiences at the end of the week. She noticed that there were lots of different abilities present, about five or six swimmers who didn't flip turn, and some who just "sat on the wall" if they wanted to miss an interval.

I took her through a guided imagery exercise in which she would attend the session she had just observed and she was encouraged to see herself messing up. Anna then completed her Comfort-Buster Playbook (see p. 230). As you can see, she had a lot more worries than she was letting on!

After reviewing her log, she agreed to repeat the imagery exercise on her own but see herself watching another rookie join the session and think about her thoughts of that person, while still having to focus on her own swim. She was surprised at how little time she had to actually notice her or care how she was doing. After all, she was trying to think about her own swim too. Finally, Anna completed the imagery exercise a third time but now visualized using some of the strategies she had developed from her log.

Within two weeks, Anna had attended her first masters swim workout, and after four sessions she moved up a lane. She looks forward to masters swim and has been amazed at how it sets her mood up for the day. She now swims with the masters group three times a week.

ANNA'S COMFORT-BUSTER PLAYBOOK

Your comfort buster: *Joining a masters swim class*

Think	Talk	Act
Things I'm secretly worried about happening	Two positive things I will say to myself if it does happen	One positive thing I will do if it does happen
Not being quick enough for circle swim	This is what I need! It's good to be pushed. I am developing mental toughness.	Slip to the back of the rotation. If lane swimmers are still going too fast, switch to a slower lane.
Feeling self-conscious in my swimsuit	No one cares what I look like. Everyone else probably feels the same!	Fake confidence by pretending I don't give a shit! Shoulders back, head up. Own it!
Swimming into people	Split the black line. Sight the lane rope, sight the lane rope!	Apologize and ask for tips to swim straight from my lane mates.
Not understanding what the coach is saying	Don't sweat it—just follow everyone else! I'll get better at this!	Ask my lane mate.
Not knowing what lane to swim in	Calculate my base and add 10 seconds to be sure. I can always move lanes.	I will ask the coach for the base pace of the slowest lane and count up from there.
Other swimmers getting frustrated with me for being too slow	Most swimmers remember how this feels. Focus on catch and pull. Smooth is fast.	Sit on the wall for a rep or move to slower lane.
Not being able to get up at 5:30 a.m.!	Count to 30 as soon as I wake up.	At count of 30, get straight out of bed.
Feeling awkward or like a loser in the locker room	Everyone is there to swim. I've done this a million times before.	Strike up a conversation with another gal getting ready.
Not having the right equipment with me (should I bring fins? A pull buoy?)	I can borrow most things from the box on the pool deck.	Ask the coach what I need.

10

WHEN THE GOING GETS TOUGH, THE TOUGH LEAVE ME BEHIND

RESISTING THE URGE TO QUIT

Character cannot be developed in ease and quiet. Only through experience of trial and suffering can the soul be strengthened, ambition inspired, and success achieved.

—HELEN KELLER

We've all been there. You've started a new training routine, or an exercise class, or just something that is uncharted and challenging. Buoyed by adrenaline, motivation, and pride, everything seems to be going fine; perhaps you're even enjoying things. And then without much warning, things start heading south. The discomfort feels worse than normal, or perhaps the motivation to keep getting up early begins to wane. For some, it's just the boredom of doing the same thing over and over again. Perhaps you don't actually stop but you mentally throw in the towel—you ease up or let the other runner or cyclist go because it just feels too hard to stay with them. You go into coast mode, even though you've got more in the tank. Before long you just want it all to stop. The argument in your head gets louder and louder as parts of your brain frantically try to cut deals with other parts of your brain to avoid bailing or permitting your body to ease up or come to a grinding halt.

First, the short-term focus appears: *Just get to the feed zone and then you can walk* or *Just 5 more reps and it will be over.* This works for a while. Then come the thoughts of escape and decisional regret: *How can I get out of this? Perhaps I could let my own tire down and fake a flat?* or *Why did I decide to do this? I'm never f*cking doing this again!* This may soon give way to a groundswell of anger: *Where the f*ck is the mile marker?* or *The instructor is meant to be counting to 1 minute, but he's not even looking at his watch, for f*ck's sake!!* For the record, these are all perfectly normal reactions to a brain in conflict.

The psychology of resisting the urge to quit is a bit more complicated than the motivational memes would have us believe, even though the choice itself is alarmingly simple. For years, scientists have been baffled by this little humdinger because your brain's decision to stop doing something that hurts or generally sucks is affected by its ability to process and filter large amounts of neurological, chemical, mechanical, emotional, and psychological data. All of the *what ifs* and *maybes* make for massive variability in your tendency to quit. When the scientists look beyond a study of one, it's even more complicated. It's important to note that quitting also refers to those instances in which you mentally throw in the towel—meaning you ease up, stop trying, or otherwise reduce the effort despite having the physical capacity to continue at the higher effort level.

To be a brave athlete, you have to determine the type of quit at stake and then make use of a toolbox of strategies to win the brain battle of stick-to-it-ness. We call this approach quitonomics—the practical science of not quitting stuff that sucks.

Quitonomics 101.

As we learned in Chapter 1, one of the primary jobs of your brain is to keep the inner peace. When opposing or conflicting thoughts live in the same brain (e.g., *I need to keep going, but I don't want to*), your brain freaks out and uses a variety of strategies to get back to harmony. Psychologists call this state of brain-in-conflict "cognitive dissonance" because your thoughts, attitudes, or beliefs are in opposition to each other, or "dissonant."

Cognitive dissonance usually takes the form of *I know this is bad for me, but I like it,* or its bedfellow, *I know this is good for me, but I don't like it.* Your brain is wired to always confront the mental debate, so it uses three strategies to restore the peace:

1. Simply change the thought or action so there's no more conflict. How very grown-up, right? So you resist the urge to quit the session, you stop a bad behavior or start a healthy one, etc.
2. Add a new thought or belief to prove you were justified. For example, you come up with an excuse such as *I didn't have the time, I got a flat tire,* or *I didn't feel good.*
3. Downplay the importance of one side of the argument so there's less conflict. You tell yourself, *Oh, it was only a training race,* or that quitting doesn't matter because *I'm only doing this for fun; I'm not exactly a pro athlete!*

The first strategy is the only one that doesn't require some self-deception. As you can see, the myriad excuses that some athletes roll out when they DNF is nothing more than a window display of their preferred dissonance-reducing strategy.

The legit quit versus the shit quit.

Not all quits are the same. Sometimes quitting is your best option. Quitting a bad relationship, quitting a job that makes you miserable, quitting midway through a training run because of injury pain. These are times when quitting is your brain's way of saying, "I care about you. You deserve better." We call them legit quits. In the world of the athlete, a legit quit is usually limited to the risk of real physical, emotional, financial, or social harm that would ensue if you were to continue. Only you can make this call and judge the actual risk of harm. Feeling injury pain is the most obvious, but other subjective and highly individual legit quit circumstances including meeting your other responsibilities in life and not pissing people off because you're being selfish.

We love legit quits because they're a sign that your physical, psychological, and emotional compass is well-calibrated. Your brain rapidly calculates what's at stake: *How much do I already have invested in this?* (known as "sunk costs" in behavioral science nerd speak). *What are the consequences of bailing right now? What are my alternatives, and how attractive are they?* On it goes.[1]

When it comes to exercise habits, we estimate that about 10 percent of all quits are LEGIT QUITS, but it's almost impossible to know, given the human brain's tendency to bullshit when asked to explain itself.

Now let's look at a different kind of quit, the shit quit. You know you've experienced a shit quit because it comes with a very deep-seated and private regret after you've bailed. Only you know which quit just happened. The trouble is, your brain desperately tries to rationalize both kinds of quitting because your brain's priority is to reduce the dissonance and restore the comfort and contentment that comes from knowing that your thoughts match your actions. And there's nothing comforting about knowing that you gave up when you secretly know that you shouldn't have. It's bad for calmness and contentment and forces your brain to resort to its dissonant-reducing contortions (and remember, two of the three strategies require self-deception).

Newsflash: If you're a chronic shit quitter, it's usually obvious to everyone except you. Before long, you've turned into that guy or that girl. The one who has a million excuses for why it didn't happen. The one who somehow never manages to get the session done or complete the challenge.

The more you quit, the more your ever-faithful brain tries to restore calm and reduce dissonance. Your brain spins more wild tales about why your actions were justified. Heck, you even start believing it! If you get into a habit, your brain becomes weaker and weaker at resisting it, quite literally. Neural circuits associated with the negative sensations and memories of the quit get strengthened; over time, these messages are transmitted faster and faster and a habit is born. Oh dear, you've essentially practiced quitting. Meanwhile, your frontal cortex has to dig deeper and deeper to rationalize why the quit was justified. The

1 For a great toe-dip into the contemporary science of decision-making, read Daniel Kahneman's *Thinking, Fast and Slow*.

"reasons" (excuses) become more and more elaborate. *I'm tired. The traffic was bad. Work got so busy. I just didn't have the time today.* We call bullshit on 90 percent of these reasons. If there's one behavioral trait of highly successful people, it's that they find a way to get it done.

HOW TO QUIT QUITTING

Endurance training is the perfect environment in which to confront this problem. For what it's worth, we all suffer from the occasional shit quit. After all, we're human. We're all flawed, irrational, dissonance-reducing people trying our best. However, if your shit quitting has become a habit, we need to intervene because it's only going to get worse, and you're teaching yourself that it's okay to walk away when things get uncomfortable.

It's worth saying that you don't need to worry about the occasional shit quit. Think of these like a Get-Out-of-Jail-Free card. Used sparingly (e.g., once a month), they provide a guilt-free "phew." Just don't make it a habit because shit quitting is a gateway drug. Chronic shit quitters need some help recognizing how to wrangle the part of the brain that wants to throw in the towel. Learning to avoid shit quitting is a skill that will help you reach your potential.

The first strategy requires you to engage in a bit of metacognition—thinking about how you think. You can also impress people at a party by saying "metacognitive."

Strategy 1: Perform a self-audit of your quitting

Regardless of whether you think you are in danger of using a shit quit in your current training, start by performing a self-audit of your quitting. As any behavioral science expert will tell you, a task that makes you aware of a problem is half the battle of solving it. Even if you think you're not a quitter, perform the audit because of what scientists call the Dunning-Kruger effect: the bizarre finding that illusory superiority is inversely correlated with actual superiority. In normal language, this means that people who most need the help are often the least likely to know it.

Once the worksheet in Exercise 1 is completed, look through each example and reflect on any patterns you notice. If your physical discomfort ratings are

AUDIT YOUR QUITTING

How the Quit Went Down: Recall up to four examples in which you stopped or eased up on a task prematurely. You could consider only your athletic world or life in general. Try to use examples that are important to you or particularly memorable. Because human memory is wonderfully biased, really take the time to think before you write. It might even take a few days to stew on this question before committing pen to paper. If you have trouble recalling previous quits, then use this worksheet to document your quits as you experience them.

Discomfort Ratings: Rate the reason for the quit based on your physical and mental discomfort at the time of the quit. The 0–5 scale for physical discomfort refers to the severity of bodily sensations you felt just prior to quitting (e.g., heart rate, breathing, discomfort in muscles), with 0 = no/minimal discomfort and 5 = worst possible discomfort. The 0–5 scale for mental discomfort refers to the severity of the psychological or emotional discomfort you were experiencing at the time. For example, if you recall feeling extremely angry, frustrated, or bored with the task, you might rate your mental discomfort as 4 or 5 out of 5. Alternatively, if you recall feeling unmotivated to cope with the physical discomfort or just "not up for it," you might rate the mental discomfort as a 3 out of 5.

Official Reason for Quit: Write down what you would say to people if they asked why you quit. And be honest, you lying turd. You don't actually need to have told people this; it's simply to get at your surface-level, dissonance-reducing strategies.

My Dark Thoughts: Write in a few things that only you will ever know or think about the quit. This is where you would list things that you might not be comfortable sharing with others.

Legit-Shit Rating: Finally, for each quit, rate it on the Legit-or-Shit scale, with 10 being absolute certainty of a Shit Quit, and 0 being absolute certainty it was a Legit Quit. Make sure you rate each quit after completing the other columns.

Continued

SELF-AUDIT

How It Went Down	Official Reason	My Dark Thoughts
DISCOMFORT Physical 0 1 2 3 4 5 Mental 0 1 2 3 4 5		LEGIT-SHIT RATING ______
DISCOMFORT Physical 0 1 2 3 4 5 Mental 0 1 2 3 4 5		LEGIT-SHIT RATING ______
DISCOMFORT Physical 0 1 2 3 4 5 Mental 0 1 2 3 4 5		LEGIT-SHIT RATING ______
DISCOMFORT Physical 0 1 2 3 4 5 Mental 0 1 2 3 4 5		LEGIT-SHIT RATING ______

higher than your mental discomfort ratings, then you probably need more exposure to physical discomfort to improve your tolerance. If your mental discomfort ratings are mostly higher than your physical discomfort ratings and your average legit-or-shit ratings are over 5, you need to learn more mental strategies to resist the urge to quit. Proceed to Strategy 2.

If you responded that your most common reason for quitting was the pain and discomfort caused by the exercise itself (not injury pain), then Chapter 11 is designed to help you through this—helping you to harden the f*ck up.

Strategy 2: Use cognitive priming to reduce your quit risk

Cognitive priming is the brain's equivalent of foreplay. Your brain likes it best when you warm it up and arouse it prior to a difficult challenge. In short, give yourself a brain-boner if you want it do something that's gonna hurt. Exposing our brains to thoughts and feelings about a specific task helps guide our behavior later in the same task. So, before every challenge, help your brain squirt dopamine. Dopamine is motivation's Sriracha sauce. A great way to open the dopamine floodgate is to watch and listen to inspirational stuff about the activity you are prone to quitting at. Unlike meme-turds, videos are a more immersive sensory experience, and virtually all capitalize on the dopaminergic power of music. Music has the ability to not just arouse pleasurable feelings but also increase craving or wanting—two critical elements of sports motivation.[2]

Strategy 3: Leverage biology to boost your brain's quit resistance

Early morning is almost always a better time to take on a challenging task. We're all busy people, and we sometimes don't have much choice about when we can fit exercise in. Jobs, kids, traffic, daylight—you name it—we live in a world of external restrictions. Throw in factors related to our own circadian rhythm (preferred sleep/wake cycle) and creating a sustainable exercise habit can be a battle. That said, neuroscientists and cognitive psychologists have discovered that we find it harder to take on a challenge later in the day.[3] The

---

2 V. N. Salimpoor et al., "Anatomically Distinct Dopamine Release During Anticipation and Experience of Peak Emotion to Music," *Nature Neuroscience* 14, no. 2 (2011): 257–262.

3 R. F. Baumeister, "Ego Depletion: Is the Active Self a Limited Resource?" *Journal of Personality and Social Psychology* 74 (1998): 1252–1265.

part of your brain responsible for self-control—the dorsolateral prefrontal cortex (DLPFC)—tires just like a muscle. It activates with less intensity if it's been used prior to being needed again. This is why your emotional reserves to tackle a challenge and tolerate discomfort get eroded throughout the day. As the day progresses, you are constantly resisting temptation, stifling emotion, and otherwise exerting self-restraint. You may not even realize that you're doing it. When evening arrives, most of us have simply become too tired to put up a fight. We default to the easiest option. This is why thinking about the large glass of wine at home becomes much more appealing than the thought of being shouted at by a personal trainer or swimming in a cold pool. So if you're lucky enough to have a choice, hit the gym or take on the quit-risk when your DLPFC is refreshed, happy, and raring to go.

Strategy 4: Cut a deal with your brain by issuing Get-Out-of-Jail-Free cards

Your brain has a built-in "pacing and bracing" mechanism called "anticipatory regulation." The level of suffering you feel at any particular time is based partly on what you think is still to come. If you get the shit quits, your brain may be quitting in anticipation of what's ahead. Because the thought of having to start something that's hard when you already feel crappy is a tough sell for your brain. In fact, the thought of having to endure something when you are already suffering, bored, or unmotivated can be far worse than actually doing it. By cutting a deal with your brain, you give yourself limited permission to quit—an "out." One of our Braveheart athletes, Elaine Morison, cuts a deal with herself to never quit on an uphill. When the thoughts of escape start piling on, Elaine puts off decisions about quitting until she gets to an easy part of the course.

This simple strategy is a remarkably effective way to keep your brain from giving into the quit. When we use this strategy for pain tolerance based on time or distance, we called it "segmentation." (In Chapter 11 you'll find a detailed description of how to use segmentation to harden the f*ck up.)

For shit quits, this can also be framed as a Get-Out-of-Jail-Free card—an option to cut and run any time you want. It works like a mental comfort blanket. It's important to note that this strategy can have the opposite effect on some people. For some, knowing that you can quit makes it easier to quit. Despite our years of experience, we've been unable to predict who this will work for and who it won't. The best recommendation is to try it out for yourself. Here's an example of what it looks like with a real athlete.

Tanja Fichera is a sprint-distance triathlete. Tanja used to have a tendency to quit mid-interval during high-intensity swim sets in an endless pool (a pool in which you swim in place against a current. It's like a treadmill for swimmers). It was a debacle that came to be known as the Tanja Tapout. Here's how it usually went down:

Tanja: But it's so hard to breathe! I feel like I might drown! I can't do it!

Coach: You won't drown, and yes, you can do it! Your brain won't let you drown!

[repeat]

Here's how we put an end to Tanja's shit quit. At the start of each 45-minute session, Tanja would place three yellow rubber ducks on the pool deck. Each duck represented a Get-Out-of-Jail-Free card. At any point during the session, she could stop mid-interval, and not have to worry about defending her quit to herself or her coach. However, every time she stopped, she used up one of her rubber ducks. She would pick up the duck and hurl it across the yard. Knowing the ducks were there helped Tanja reduce her anxiety about whether she could make it through the anxiety about drowning. This "out" helped her feel more relaxed about the session, which in turn improved her breathing. The challenge became how far she could get through the session before running out of ducks. Once she was able to complete the session, her next goal was to finish and still have at least one rubber duck left on deck. Within weeks she was completing the full session with all her ducks. Yes, still in a row.

Strategy 5: Request a nudge

Our brains hate being judged for not being good enough. Fear of embarrassment, humiliation, inadequacy, and failure kill motivation and happiness. What our brains love, however, is social support. Being encouraged, praised, and recognized is like dirty talking your amygdala—ground zero in the brain for drives, instincts, and rewards. Why do you think Facebook is so popular? It's amygdala porn.

When it comes to fitness, friends don't let friends exercise alone. Group exercise is motivating because it reduces our perception of effort, creates accountability, and offers loads of opportunity to give and receive praise. Plus, we can silently judge people (chill out; it's perfectly natural). The problem is getting your ass there in the first place. A great strategy is to extend the group's power to influence us. Next time you're at a group exercise session, ask someone to be your Thunder Buddy. Okay, maybe you don't actually ask them that, but do find one or two people willing to swap numbers with you (or ask instructors to recommend it) and text each other the day of the session with a nudge to attend: "Don't you dare bail on the class tonight! See you @5:45." Take turns being the nudger and the nudged. Try it—this strategy is gold.

I'VE GIVEN UP ON BEING FAST

Tackling the problem of shit quittery

DAPHNE IS A 28-YEAR-OLD legal assistant and age-group triathlete. She's been competing for three years and trains 10 hours per week. She mainly does sprint (1:26 PR) and Olympic-distance (3:02 PR) events, but last year she successfully completed her first half-Ironman. Daphne wants to focus mainly on longer-distance triathlons because she's a self-confessed "plodder" and insists that she's not fast enough to be competitive at the shorter distances. She has a tendency to not complete sessions, or she mentally gives up when it gets super-competitive. When asked about it, Daphne always has a compelling reason why things didn't go as planned.

After going through her self-audit (see p. 244), she sees that all of her quits rank 5 or higher on the Legit-Shit rating scale and that a clear pattern was evident:

1. She's more likely to quit sessions when she's training on her own,
2. She gets really down on herself for not hitting the goal of the session (and then having to explain it to her coach), and

3. The mental discomfort was generally higher than the physical discomfort, meaning that her head was usually quitting before her body.

Daphne sends her quit log to her coach, and they agree to continue using the quit log for the next month. Their thinking is that if she knows she will have to write down each quit, she's more motivated not to quit. Before each session that she knows is a quit risk, she watches a short motivational video on YouTube on her cell phone about the importance of never giving up. She contacts a triathlete friend and they commit to being accountability buddies for each other for afternoon and evening sessions when their tendency to quit is higher. Finally, for interval training sessions, she records her lap times but puts electrical tape over the screen so she can't see the times during the session. This forces her to run based on feel and stops her from getting discouraged when she doesn't hit the target times. After four weeks, Daphne has quit only two training sessions, down from the four she recorded in the week before entering quit therapy.

DAPHNE'S QUIT SELF-AUDIT

How It Went Down	Official Reason	My Dark Thoughts
Supposed to do 6 × 400 repeats on track. Only did 4. DISCOMFORT Physical 0 1 2 3 (4) 5 Mental 0 1 2 3 4 (5)	Needed to get to work by 8:30 a.m. and couldn't find a parking space so started later than normal.	I just got down on myself. My times were crap but instead of pushing on, I ended up discouraged and stopped at 4. No one around to know. Urgh, dreaded the questions from my coach. I feel like such a failure. LEGIT-SHIT RATING 8
Easy 90 min. run on schedule. Did 60 min. Like pulling teeth to get me that far! DISCOMFORT Physical 0 1 2 (3) 4 5 Mental 0 1 2 3 4 (5)	Still feeling tired from last week, plus a crap load to do for work tomorrow.	Simply couldn't be bothered. Part boredom, part worry about work stuff. Legs were feeling a bit heavy but certainly could have done an extra 30 min. LEGIT-SHIT RATING 5
Bailed on 6 a.m. swim twice. Woke up but just groaned when alarm went off. Told myself I would do lunch swim instead. Never happened. DISCOMFORT Physical (0) 1 2 3 4 5 Mental 0 1 (2) 3 4 5	Needed the extra sleep and pool is less busy at lunchtime.	I'm lazy. A real athlete would have sucked it up. FAIL! LEGIT-SHIT RATING 9
Did Olympic distance tri last weekend. Good swim, decent bike, but just let two gals run away from me. I just sort of gave up. DISCOMFORT Physical 0 1 2 3 (4) 5 Mental 0 1 2 3 4 (5)	Ran at my own pace. They were going too quick for me. Would have blown up if I followed.	I'm so mad because I can usually run with them. I'm the only athelte who's actually getting slower. Heart rate seemed OK, but didn't want to hurt any more. LEGIT-SHIT RATING 5

11

I NEED TO HARDEN THE F*CK UP

LEARNING TO EMBRACE THE SUCK

I wanted to quit because I was suffering. That was not a good enough reason.

—TED CORBITT

Eskimos might have 50 words for snow, but endurance athletes have 51 words for suffering. One thing that sets most endurance sports apart from other sports is that your success depends in large part on your ability to tolerate *exertional discomfort*—a rather posh way of describing the personal sufferfest that comes from increasing the exercise intensity. The harder you push, the more it hurts. All other factors being equal, the one who can suffer the most will rise through the ranks of competition. If you're new to endurance sports, you need to know the suffer lingo: in the hurt locker, on the rivet, in the pain cave, in a world of hurt, on the pain train, at a sufferfest, and—an all-time favorite for suffering on a bicycle—sitting on the sea cucumber (don't ask).

Pain versus suffering.

When we talk about exertional discomfort, we mean specifically the feelings caused by the intensity itself and not pain caused by actual tissue damage: a stress fracture, a pulled muscle, joint pain, angina, or whatever. If you are in any doubt about the difference between exertional discomfort and injury/illness pain, ask your doctor or physical therapist this one simple question about the type of pain you experience: "Could I make things worse by ignoring it?" Hopefully we don't need to explain what to do with the answer.

The bottom line is that you need to know the difference between hurting yourself and *hurting* yourself. If you are prone to succumb to the compulsion to exercise when you clearly shouldn't, please read Chapter 7 for help on coping with the mental turmoil of injury and how to resist the temptation to exercise with injury pain. While you're at it, you might also want to reread the Chapter 10 discussion about the concept of cognitive dissonance and the strategies your brain uses to justify bad decisions.

Science tells us that our brains will not let us die from exertional discomfort. In exercise physiology, this is known as the "central governor model of fatigue" and although somewhat controversial, it suggests that the only negative side effect of extreme exertional discomfort is that it simply feels so bloody awful.[1] Your heart won't burst, your lungs won't explode, and your muscle cells won't die of acidosis (all things we've been asked by athletes). That said, there are shitty outcomes related to Operation Suck-It-Up, such as blisters, sunburn, dehydration, and chafing, but they are preventable and not caused by the exertion itself.

So what *is* the difference between pain and suffering? Pain is an unpleasant sensory and emotional experience associated with tissue damage (actual or potential), which affects different levels of the nervous system.[2] As athletes, we often think of "good pain" as coming from the exertion itself or as an acute symptom of normal training adaptation (e.g., delayed onset muscle soreness, fatigue). In contrast, we think of "bad pain" as being from injuries to muscles, tendons, ligaments, cartilage, or bones. Your pain threshold is the point at which you start to feel the pain, and your pain tolerance refers to the maximum amount of pain you can handle. Pain threshold and pain tolerance relate to the next concept on the suck-experience ladder: suffering. **Suffering occurs in the**

---

1 J. P. Weir et al., "Is Fatigue All in Your Head? A Critical Review of the Central Governor Model," *British Journal of Sports Medicine* 40, no. 7 (2006): 586.

2 "Part III: Pain Terms: A Current List with Definitions and Notes on Usage," in *Classification of Chronic Pain*, 2nd ed., edited by H. Merskey and N. Bogduk (Seattle: IASP Press, 1994), 209–214.

prefrontal cortex of your brain and is defined by your experience and interpretation of the pain: what it means, why it's there, how important it is, your history with it, and how long you think it can be endured. Suffering is also affected by your mood and your coping skills, so it's no wonder that some people are better at it than others. Predictably, endurance athletes and coaches are very interested in pain thresholds and pain tolerance because of their critical role in an athlete's ability to suffer (cope with exertional pain) and therefore perform better (or worse).

Okay, let's get back to exertional discomfort, which we will hereafter refer to as ED. Let's just smile about that one for a moment.

The science of pain and suffering.

Before we tackle the job of hardening you the f*ck up, or more accurately, improving your ability to tolerate exertional discomfort, let's look at what the science tells us. The following is the only meta-analytic evidence-based statement we can make about pain and suffering among athletes. (If you're curious to know what "meta-analytic" means and why it's important in science, read the nerd alert, p. 248.) An evidence-based statement:

Athletes tend to have a higher threshold and tolerance for pain compared to normally active individuals and there is evidence that it is the exercise training that makes them like this, rather than them simply being attracted to sport because they're already tough.[3]

★ **What this means for you:** You're probably already better at suffering than you think, at least compared to nonathletes, and one of the best ways to get better at coping with ED is to force yourself to experience lots of it. Yes, you need to practice embracing the suck.

Findings from other studies suggest that your brain doesn't just come along for the ride when you're in the hurt locker, but is actively filtering how it wants you to feel—your perception of effort. For example, your ability to suffer is known to depend on your awareness of when it will come to an end. When athletes

3 J. Tesarz et al., "Pain Perception in Athletes Compared to Normally Active Controls: A Systematic Review with Meta-Analysis," *Pain* 153, no. 6 (June 2012): 1253–1262.

NERD ALERT!

The problem with cherry-picking: Meta-analysis and why it matters in sports science

WHEN SCIENTISTS SUMMARIZE what we know about a well-researched topic, they often use a special method called a "meta-analysis." A meta-analysis is simply a statistical compilation of the best studies on a topic—it's considered the most objective way to summarize the scientific knowledge. Here's an analogy: Let's say we wanted to know how good a specific age-group triathlete was. You could look at a single race result, but it's hard to know what to make of this because the competition may have been weak, everyone could have drafted on the bike, there could have been a monster headwind, or maybe the run course was measured 0.5 km short. Looking at a single result to judge an athlete is akin to reading a single scientific study and proclaiming that the finding is the new truth. What's even harder is if we want to compare two athletes (or scientific studies) who have never raced against each other. How do we know whether a win at Race X is as impressive as a 5th place at Race Y? Well, if you compiled all of the results from that one athlete and weighted each of the results by factors important to the outcome (e.g., the actual measured distance, the conditions, the strength of competition), you'd have a much better idea of who the shining star was. That's sort of what a meta-analysis does for individual scientific studies. So next time you hear of a single scientific study proclaiming that an ice bath improves recovery and performance or that visualizing a race makes you physically faster, quietly ask for a look at the bigger picture—the meta-analytic evidence on the subject.

are deceived about the amount of suffering that remains, perceived effort and exercise tolerance change. Psychologists refer to this as *anticipatory regulation*, and one way that you experience it is as pacing ability—the skill of being able to meter out your effort based on what you know you still have to complete.[4] When

4 Jos J. de Koning et al., "Regulation of Pacing Strategy During Athletic Competition," *PLoS One* 6, no. 1 (2011): e15863.

you don't know how much is left, perceived effort increases even when there's no change in actual workload.[5] Your brain's anticipatory regulation also helps you feel less pain if you plan for it in advance (feedforward) and then try to accept it rather than fight it when it arrives.[6]

★ **What this means for you:** When you know a sufferfest is in the cards, do the exact opposite of trying not to think about it—develop a pre-suffer ritual that welcomes it. Think of this as putting on suffer armor. When the suffering does come (and it will), we need to use mindfulness techniques (nonjudgmental awareness) to cope with it.[7] When we say "cope" we mean using thoughts, feelings, and behavior to reduce our perception of the discomfort. New research suggests that we can train our brains to actually do this. Okay, enough science! Time to learn how to harden the f*ck up and learn to suffer like a champ!

AN ACTION PLAN FOR SUFFERING BETTER

Suffering is a skill that needs to be learned the hard way. However, you can fast-track your ability to cope by having a plan. We use a two-pronged attack. First, we will improve your ability to be prepared to suffer. Then we will give you strategies to cope with the suffering as it happens.

Strategies that help you *prepare* for suffering.

Get experience of suffering

Think about the kind of suffering you're not very good at and then force yourself to experience it more often in training. This doesn't mean that every session needs to put you in the pain cave, but you should expose yourself to physical and mental discomfort fairly often, certainly every week. Remember, suffering can take many forms, such as:

---

5 H. S. Jones et al., "Physiological and Psychological Effects of Deception on Pacing Strategy and Performance: A Review," *Sports Medicine* 43, no. 12 (2013): 1243–1257.

6 Mark. A. Lumley et al., "Pain and Emotion: A Biopsychosocial Review of Recent Research," *Journal of Clinical Psychology* 67, no. 9 (2011): 942–968.

7 Alister McCormick et al., "Psychological Determinants of Whole-Body Endurance Performance," *Sports Medicine* 45, no. 7 (July 2015): 997–1015.

1. Enduring "the burn" of anaerobic activity (caused by a release of hydrogen ions that makes your blood more acidic and aggravates nearby nerve cells);
2. Coping with general fatigue from training sessions or races that just drag on and on;
3. Managing an increased perception of effort caused by frustration and disappointment at not hitting target times or getting dropped by faster training partners or competitors; or
4. Feeling unmotivated or unprepared for tough sessions but doing them anyway.

There are plenty more, but these are the most common. Biologically speaking, when we practice suffering we are reinforcing neural pathways associated with discomfort and behavioral persistence. Give it a try in Exercise 1.

Use feedforward to build your acceptance of pain

Feedforward is akin to mental time travel to think about the pain before it occurs. It helps build the expectation of suffering. This might sound counterintuitive. Why would you want to dwell on suffering? Unlike feedback, feedforward helps us improve future behavior by training the brain's love of anticipatory regulation. It's a form of advanced planning, except with feedforward you also try to immerse yourself in the experience as though you were actually there.[8] It's akin to bracing yourself for the future by thinking about it. This is also why when a nurse or doctor tells you that "this won't hurt" or "you'll just feel a little prick" they might be trying to calm your nerves but it's actually bad advice. It undermines your brain's ability to brace for pain. Cognitive neuroscientists have revealed that feedforward is a very effective tool for learning to cope with adversity because it helps us plan for all possible outcomes, rather than just hope everything turns out well. It's also useful as a cognitive priming strategy, as we discussed in Chapter 10. Critically, feedforward, as in Exercise 2 (p. 252), helps us develop pain acceptance skills, which are much more effective for pain management than pain suppression skills.

8 J. A. Walker and I. Daum, "Mental Time Travel: The Neurocognitive Basis of Future Thinking," *Fortschritte der Neurologie-Psychiatrie* 76, no. 9 (September 2008): 539–548.

YOUR SUFFER SHEET

Take a moment to recall up to three examples of when you last suffered and why. When you have completed your list, describe a training session that would force you to encounter it more often, an "Engineered Suffer Session." Try to make the training session match the type of suffering listed. For example, you might schedule a long brick to force you to cope with general fatigue, or you could deliberately schedule a hard session when you know motivation is low. You might do an interval session in which you attempt to hold PR-level splits or meet wattage goals to increase the likelihood of failure. We call these mental toughness sessions because the goal is simply to cope. Nothing else matters except getting through the session.

How It Went Down	Engineered Suffer Session
1	
2	
3	

EXERCISE 2

YOUR 5-MINUTE FEEDFORWARD AND SUFFER PLEDGE

Before a sufferfest, take 5 minutes to sit or lie quietly with your eyes closed and think only about the pain and suffering. You might have an upcoming 10K race or an Ironman, and you really want to do well. In your mind's eye, create the exact moments of the suffering. Immerse yourself in what you see, hear, smell, taste, and touch as it gets harder and harder. Pay attention to what the suffering actually feels like, and then imagine it ratcheting up and culminating in the worst possible pain and suffering—more than you have ever experienced. Really take time to imagine what this feels like, what's going through your head, and what you can see and hear. Even though you are sitting or lying comfortably, you will notice your heart rate and breathing rate start to increase.

After 5 minutes, open your eyes and think logically about whether you are prepared to take this on—to suffer more than you have ever suffered before. If you are, make a personal pledge (or a pain prayer, if that helps) to the suffering. Some athletes even find it helps to ask their body and brain's permission to let them experience the worst possible suffering. The important point here is that we are creating an expectation. And remember, expectation drives anticipatory regulation—the brain's ability to brace itself for what lies ahead. It's science, folks.

Strategies that help you cope *during* the suffering.

Segmentation

How do you eat an elephant? One bite at a time. Your brain likes things in manageable chunks. Whether it's solving problems, running a marathon, or dealing with life's shit balls—it's evolution's way of helping us persist through hard times. When the suffering begins, our brain pleads with us to not think too far into the future. *I can't endure 60 minutes of this, but I can do 10 minutes. I can't get through 8 weeks of solid exercise, but I can get through today.* The neurological beauty of segmentation is that once the segment is completed, you get a mini-squirt of dopamine (pleasure juice) that resets the coping clock. Use this principle to your advantage by exploiting how your brain reacts to completion and accomplishment. Running 2 × 5 km is easier than running 10 km. Swimming to a single buoy three times is far easier than swimming around three buoys. Never think about all that you still have to do because your brain hates you for it. Think only about what the next few minutes hold. The more intense the suffer-challenge, the shorter the segments need to be. The Ironman bike leg is not really 112 miles; it's 11 time trials of 10 miles each plus 2 miles of celebrating that it's almost over. The final 4 miles of a marathon on rapidly failing legs are

not another 30 minutes of torture, but just 16 laps of the track, or running to a series of landmarks on the course 200 meters apart. Segmentation also works for tasks that seem almost impossible to complete before you've even started. If you've ever started a session by thinking, *I honestly don't know if I can get through this*, then simply commit to doing 25 percent before making a decision whether to continue. See what happens.

Counting

And we mean counting like an obsessive crazy person. Good suffer-management skills rely on a profound and prodigious capacity for rhythmic repetition. This is one reason why music works to reduce perceived exertion. One of the best pain-busting strategies is to count to 4, 6, or 8, over and over again while in the hurt locker. If you're already doing a rhythmic activity (running, swimming, cycling), you can count in time with arm or leg turnover. Counting helps improve pain tolerance by controlling your attention. It fills your working memory (in the prefrontal cortex) with a task that is usually left to your procedural (automatic) memory. This uses valuable brain bandwidth that would otherwise be spent on wishing the effort was over and thinking about why you won't be coming back. Luckily, your brain finds counting easy, but not so easy that it can switch off completely. If you find that your head still wanders during counting, the task is not complicated enough for your brain. In this case, skip count by twos or threes or count in a different language. If none of this works, then count in prime numbers (smartypants). The sweet spot is a counting task that is easy enough to do while suffering but not so complicated that it makes your working memory heat up and start to smoke. Scientific studies show that when you force your prefrontal cortex (effort perception HQ) to work too hard while exercising, the perception of effort goes up, not down. Let's not do that.

There's more good news about counting. When you count, there's also an explicit sense of progress because numbers go up. For some, the rhythmic repetition can also help induce an auto-hypnotic state. Counting arm turnover on the swim is especially helpful because it can be used to gauge swim distance. However, this takes practice. First, calibrate your race-intensity stroke count against a set distance, say 100 meters. Test your stroke count at least three times to make sure you have a reliable estimate, preferably in the same type of water you will actually be racing in. For example, at race pace, you might take about 80 strokes in open water over 100 meters. By counting to 80 during the race, you knock out the distance as a series of 100m efforts, using both counting and segmentation to your advantage.

Thumb tapping

Most people have never heard of thumb tapping, let alone tried it. This is not to be confused with the pseudo-scientific nonsense that is *meridian tapping* (sometimes also called finger tapping). In pain management land, thumb tapping is simply a behavioral strategy to control attention and occupy working memory. If you've ever given birth, your midwife may have taught you a variation of this technique to cope with labor and birthing pain. For all its simplicity, it's remarkably effective at helping to cope with short periods of intense discomfort.

★ **How to do it.** First, make two relaxed clenched fists, as though you were holding a pen in each hand. With your thumb, gently tap the side of your index finger as though you were pressing the "clicker" on a pen. This technique is best for running because thumb tapping during a swim isn't practical and it's a bit awkward to do while holding the handlebars of a bike.

As you run, tap both thumbs in time with your leg turnover or tap your left thumb in time with your left leg and your right thumb in time with your right leg—whatever feels the least cognitively demanding to manage when you're hurting. You can also use it to set your cadence, not just mirror it. The rhythmic repetition also provides a metronomic cue for the legs or arms to keep moving. There's nothing special about the thumb, the clenched fist, or how you tap. If you had opposable ears with mini-claws attached, we'd recommend using those too. Thumb tapping is best used to get you through short bursts of hell—a hill repeat, the last mile of a race, or moments when it's really hurting. We don't recommend thumb tapping for longer periods (e.g., an entire race) because even though it's simple to do, it's still a superfluous physical movement that takes concentration and coordination.

Mindfulness

The final strategy is a bundle of techniques you can develop to better address issues such as coping with anxiety and stress and improving sleep. Mindfulness fosters a nonjudgmental acceptance of discomfort or distress (a here-and-now focus) in order to reduce the inclination to think about how bad everything feels and to "awfulize" the consequences. The central feature of mindfulness is paying conscious attention to the distress itself while resisting the temptation to judge it. In other words, no more "This sucks! I'm so miserable right now! I'm not sure how much more I can take." There is growing scientific evidence that mindfulness strategies work well for athletes.[9] However, athletes often find this challenging because they tend to get impatient at being told to just sit still with their own thoughts. So instead of trying to beat or suppress pain or discomfort, you are simply curious about it. Mindfulness works in a similar way to counting and thumb tapping—you crowd out thoughts of distress and doom in your prefrontal cortex by focusing attention on other things. Some common elements of mindfulness training are passive attention, curiosity, and acceptance.

Passive attention is likened to noticing without watching. This means that while the feelings of suffering (e.g., burning muscles, frantic breathing, thoughts of escape, anger) are demanding your full attention, you recognize that they are there, but you don't linger on them. Instead, you let your focus wander around your body and your environment. Here's an analogy to help explain how it works: Imagine you are standing on a bridge looking down on a fast-moving stream. There are leaves floating by with writing on them. Just as you finish reading what's written on one leaf, it's gone, disappearing under the bridge beneath you. You don't get time to think about the statement's meaning because you're too busy trying to read the next leaf, and so on. That's the essence of passive attention. Before you attempt passive attention during suffering, try it out in a quiet room. As things grab your attention (e.g., noises outside, the pressure on your glutes from sitting, the blister on your right toe), focus intently on them for 10–15 seconds before moving on to the next sensation. When you get good at this, you can start labeling each sensation based on categories of Emotion, Thought, Body Sensation, Judgment, Urge, and Memory. Preface each label before putting it in its respective cubbyhole. For example, if you first feel an ach-

9 D. Birrer and G. Morgan, "Psychological Skills Training as a Way to Enhance an Athlete's Performance in High-Intensity Sports," *Scandinavian Journal of Medicine and Science in Sports*, supplement 2 (October 20, 2010): 78–87.

ing in your feet and begin to worry about it getting worse, you might say, "That's a body sensation" [the ache], "That's an emotion" [the worry], and so on. You can do this out loud or in your own head.

Curiosity is simply the process by which you let your attention poke around without looking for anything in particular. For example, while swimming you might do a body scan in which you go from head to toe, thinking about how each part of your body feels at that particular time. It's like you're checking in with different parts of your body before moving on. Unlike passive attention, you deliberately target certain areas of your body or the feelings the discomfort generates. When you're suffering, use curiosity to mentally examine as many features of the suffering as possible. For example, you might zero in on your muscle burn, the anger, the boredom, and so on. Try turning each sensation into a color and shape. For example, the sharp pain in your quads might appear as jagged and red, but your waning motivation after two hours of running might feel like a dimming yellow light.

Acceptance involves zeroing in on an unpleasant or painful sensation, but rather than fighting it, you welcome it. For example, when you're suffering, you might see this as an opportunity to harden up. Congratulations, you're now officially on the clock for training mental toughness. Alternatively, you might look to mentally change the shape and color of the pain sensation. Lesley often sees her pain during a race as a card game in which she raises the stakes on her body and how much it can handle. The goal in all of these acceptance strategies is to become invested in the sensation itself rather than simply wishing it would go away.

Mindfulness is really just a special kind of meditation—a word we avoid using with athletes because it's laden with preconceived judgment. There are plenty of great resources for mindfulness training available online. With our athletes, we use a free app called Headspace (www.headspace.com). It provides a really easy and engaging way to learn the basics.

CASE STUDY

I'M SICK OF SETTLING FOR *JUST FINISH*

A game plan for embracing the suck

NICK IS A 43-YEAR-OLD competitive runner. He ran cross-country in high school and the occasional 5K and 10K in college for fun. After graduating, work and family commitments took over, and he became a self-confessed couch potato. He started running again at age 35 as a way to get back in shape, lose his growing beer gut, and cope with work stress. He's not looked back since.

Nick now runs 30–40 miles per week and focuses on full and half-marathons. He reports a history of cramping in longer runs but feels like he's getting over that after modifying his training and race nutrition. When asked what he wants to focus on mentally, Nick explains that he wants to be more competitive: "I want to ratchet up the pain and suffering at the race because I enter with a just-finish mindset instead of going balls out and attacking the course." Nick thinks he mentally gives in when it gets hard, switching to a survival mindset. He goes on to say, "I start running very reactively rather than constantly pushing." He also talks about his fear of cramping: "It's always in the back of my mind when I am at these races, which is another reason I pull back. When training, I'm like, 'You cramp you stop. No big deal.' But racing, not so much."

When we look at Nick's training data, it's clear he has the physical capacity to hold a faster pace in racing. The first thing we do is get Nick to do more short-distance racing (mile, 5K, 10K) and high-intensity interval training. We don't adapt his training for this because the goal is simply to force him to face his suffering. We give him race goals of being tactically aggressive, even if that means a high risk of blowing up. Once he is able to easily recognize the "go, no-go" decision point for pushing or easing back (the suffer versus no-suffer pivot point), we teach him to use thumb tapping for one minute, followed immediately by four minutes of counting to 6, over and over again. This gives him a 5-minute window to focus on a specific mental goal that changes his focus of attention away from backing down to embracing the opportunity to suffer. He now has a special game plan to deal with "the suck" when he has to face it. (And he will!)

12

I KEEP SCREWING UP

DEVELOPING JEDI CONCENTRATION SKILLS TO BECOME A BETTER ATHLETE

Everyone has a plan until they get punched in the mouth. —MIKE TYSON

If I could single out a phrase that's been yelled at me by teachers, parents, coaches, and my wife, it's this: "For God's sake, Simon, pay attention!" If staring at strangers or daydreaming were Olympic sports, I'd be podium material. I get distracted really easily, I get bored quickly, and I'm a terrible multitasker. It turns out that these are a lethal combination when it comes to endurance sports. Qualities like single-mindedness and being in the zone are hallmarks of great athletes, not qualities like "in his own world" or "gets bored and stops halfway through intervals." However, I can happily sit down reading or writing for hours on end, often forgetting to eat. Lesley is the exact opposite. When it comes to training and racing, she's like a laser-guided missile. She's on focus rails. But put her on a cognitive task or one that she has zero interest in, and she's like a Jack Russell terrier trapped in a sack.

How can we be so different on the things that keep us focused, yet so similar in that each of us has a strong preference for how we use our concentration? It turns out that many athletes are just like us, or at least some combination.

Some of the athletes we've coached have no trouble staying focused. They plan and execute as if it's a military operation. However, some athletes just get bored and stop training. Others always seem to be surrounded by drama on race day (a mechanical problem, forgotten kit, lost license, or something else), and their crisis somehow becomes your crisis. It can get to the point at which other athletes don't want to share a ride or go to races with this person because they know there will inevitably be something that threatens to derail their own plans. For other athletes, there is a specific issue that they never seem to get right, like pacing or race nutrition. All of these things are mental mistakes caused by poor attentional control. Assuming you show up physically prepared, mental errors are the biggest cause of bad races, and they are self-inflicted.

Let's clarify that when we use the terms *concentration* or *focus* we don't actually mean that. Psychologists prefer the term *attention* because it more accurately describes what's going on in the brain. Attention is a much broader concept that refers to the brain's job of selecting what is and isn't relevant in any given situation and allocating brain resources and processes accordingly. The subtle and important distinction being made here is that the brain's challenge is not just to stay locked in on something (i.e., concentration or focus), but to sift, organize, and select what to pay attention to, when, and for how long and, critically, how to switch attention quickly and effortlessly while also stopping stuff that's irrelevant from grabbing your attention. Consider how this plays out in competition. To avoid a drafting penalty, triathletes are required to:

1. Know the rules about the draft zone,
2. Control their pace and position relative to others so draft zones don't overlap,
3. Know where the drafting referees are, and
4. Make on-the-fly tactical decisions that comply with the rules but also result in a physical or psychological advantage over others in the "group."

That's a lot to pay attention to! If we reduced this problem to just "concentration" you would simply need to accomplish the first two tasks. But as you might expect, if you want to optimize your performance, that's only half the story.

Let's add a few more brain concepts into the mix. We'll call the things that compete for our attention *cues*. The universe of cues at any particular time is our *attentional field*. Your attentional field is made up of cues in your own head (thoughts, feelings, perceptions), as well as those outside (sights, sounds, smells, etc.). These cues can also be classified as *performance-relevant* (things that you need to pay attention to in order to complete the race as fast as possible), or *performance irrelevant* (things that have no bearing on your ability to complete the race as fast as possible). Got it? Ok, let's now turn to screwing up.

Attentional issues lead to mental mistakes.

In almost all cases, endurance athletes make mistakes because they're paying attention to the wrong things (cues) at the wrong time, most likely because their attentional field is the wrong size. As we'll learn later, stress and anxiety do weird things to our attentional field. It's like an involuntary response that helps us up to a point, but then becomes attentional kryptonite. Here are some examples of the mental errors or screwups that endurance athletes make because of poor attentional control:

- Always noticing who looks fitter, leaner, and stronger.
- Regularly showing up late.
- Going off like a banshee, only to hyperventilate two minutes later.
- Forgetting to eat or drink during training or racing.
- Not able to pace very well.
- Forgetting where their bike is racked in the transition area.
- Keeping pace with a stronger athlete even though it's not sustainable.
- Forgetting essential race gear—shoes, helmet, goggles, wetsuit, and so on.
- Being unable to suffer or having poor pain-management skills.
- Staying at the race expo way too long.
- Swimming off-course, biking off-course, running off-course.
  Getting lost, period.
- Wasting time in transition or leaving transition without a race belt.

- Missing their start time.
- Getting a drafting penalty.
- Having thoughts of escape, such as *Why do I do this to myself? I'm never f*cking doing this again!*
- Crashing a lot on the bike.

There are literally hundreds more, including some of our favorites in triathlon, like leaving T1 still wearing a wetsuit or putting on an aero helmet backward like a bird beak that snaps the athlete's head back as it catches the first wind. In cycling and running events, we've seen many athletes celebrate a win too early and get passed on the line. Some of these errors result from lack of knowledge (e.g., knowing when your helmet must be buckled up in a triathlon) or lack of a physical skill to help cope with adversity (e.g., lacking the balance on a bike to remain upright after being bumped or knocked). However, in most cases, mental slipups are due to attentional problems. These are problems that can be mostly trained away. Unless you've been trained in attentional control, most of us suffer from attentional blindness if the conditions are right. If you stayed awake in Psych 101, you may have already seen this famous experiment, but if not, try it again.[1] It's fab.

Beware—your Chimp wants to control your attention, too.

Your Chimp gives you urges, instincts, feelings, and impressions that will beg and plead with you to pay attention to certain things. These "certain things" are almost always irrelevant to your performance. In fact, Chimp talk is hardly ever relevant to performance because its focus is on instincts and drives to keep you alive, keep your ego intact, and prevent you from humiliation, embarrassment, and inadequacy at all costs. Remember, these things are rarely in real jeopardy on the days that you squish yourself into Lycra.

There are select occasions when Chimp talk is helpful. For example, it may save your body from the medical tent by giving you an overwhelming instinct

1 https://goo.gl/qst3wE.

to sit or lie on the side of the road when you're suffering from dehydration on a hot run. Your Professor brain knows you need to keep moving, but it's no match for the survival instinct of the Chimp. This type of brain-body battle is seen in endurance sports fairly frequently. Sometimes the Chimp brain wins—as was the case when Melanie McQuaid passed out 400 yards from the finish line in the 2011 XTERRA World Championship. Sometimes the Professor brain wins, as was the case when Sian Welch and Wendy Ingraham crawled to the legendary "sprint" finish at the 1997 Ironman World Championships. Sometimes, it takes someone else's Professor brain to help you, as was the case when Alistair Brownlee helped his delirious and dehydrated brother, Jonny Brownlee, get across the line at the final of the ITU World Series in 2016. On some occasions, your Chimp talk may be welcomed by your Professor brain, who gives it full permission to take over. For example, have you ever sped up because you are pissed off that you flatted? Maybe you discovered the ability to dig deeper than ever before because someone you wanted to impress was watching? Both are examples of a good Chimp-in-charge situation. When attention is channeled in certain ways, you can unleash Chimp strength.

As athletes, our ultimate goal is to be able to recognize when we are vulnerable to making mental errors given our own attentional strengths and weakness, and then be able to TRAIN OUR ATTENTION so we can make great decisions under pressure or when stressed.

This is the secret to becoming a consistent athlete. To understand why we make attentional errors and what to do about it, we need to understand how attention works. After all, if you don't know how a car engine works, how the heck are you supposed to fix it when it mucks up? Science nerds, start your engines.

What does the science tell us?

Attention is one of the most researched topics in psychology and cognitive neuroscience. With the advent of sophisticated methods of measurement, like functional magnetic resonance imaging (fMRI) and eye tracking, brain scientists are making new discoveries every year. Here are robust findings that are relevant to athletes:

The prefrontal cortex does most of the heavy lifting when it comes to attentional processing. Yup, your Professor brain is doing the work or, more specifically, a region just above your eyes in the prefrontal cortex that controls executive function.[2] This part acts like an orchestra conductor, telling parts of your brain to step it up a notch and other parts to quiet down. This is important because an unwelcome Chimp-in-charge can spell danger for great attentional control. Conversely, Chimp management improves attentional control and decision-making.

The human brain can't actually multitask when it comes to thinking.[3] You can perform multiple behaviors at once (e.g., singing while driving), but that doesn't mean you're thinking about both. When you think you're multitasking, your brain is actually switching from one type of attentional focus to another with lightning speed. A good analogy is watching TV. Our brains do not have picture-in-picture capability; you can watch only one station at a time. If you're easily distracted, then you have the opposite problem—you channel surf without being able to stay on the correct channel long enough. So, if you're a poor multitasker like me, whether it's because you get stuck on one channel for too long or you channel surf too much, you need to work on improving your attentional flexibility instead of just throwing more balls in the air. This translates to improving your channel changing skills and/or the ability to tune into the correct channel when it's needed. This requires that you know what is important and unimportant at key moments, access memories that help you determine what's likely to be successful, and shift your attention between the relevant information quickly and effortlessly. We'll get to some strategies on how to do so shortly.

---

2 E. E. Smith and J. Jonides, "Storage and Executive Processes in the Frontal Lobes," *Science* 283, no. 5408 (March 12, 1999): 1657–1661.

3 M. I. Posner, "Attention: The Mechanisms of Consciousness," *Proceedings of the National Academy of Sciences* 91, no. 16 (August 2, 1994): 7398–7403.

How to conceptualize attention.

An old-but-good theory about attention that has been used extensively in sports is called Attentional Style Theory (AST).[4] Although AST doesn't incorporate all of the latest neuroscience research on attention, it's remarkably consistent with most of it. It remains a valid and highly relevant approach for athletes because the fundamental principles are solid, and it provides a working model that is both easy to understand and helps us develop strategies to improve our attentional skills. Your attention is comprised of two dimensions, width and direction.

The first dimension, **attentional width**, ranges from very narrow to very broad. When your attention is narrow, you are focused on specific things or tasks. For example, when you are trying to sight the buoy in an open water swim or you are focused on holding someone's wheel, your attention is narrow. When your attention is broad, you are paying attention to many things (or trying to). For example, when you walk through the race expo, you might be scanning the area for things that interest you, or you are looking for the packet pickup tent. In a race you might be trying to avoid a drafting penalty, so you are scanning for other riders around you before deciding when to pass. Most situations in endurance sport require attention somewhere in between narrow and broad.

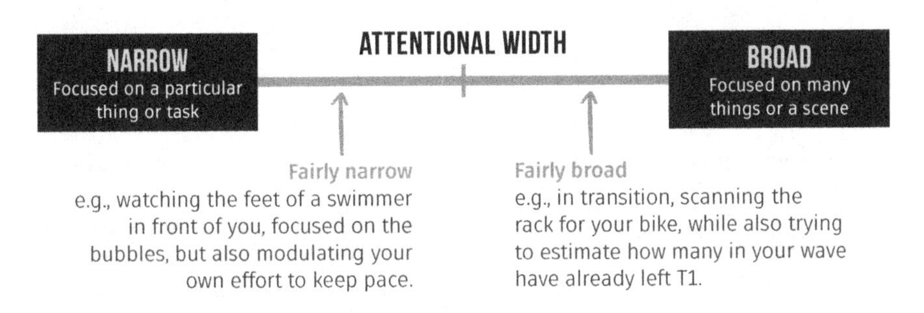

The second dimension is **attentional direction**, and it is either internal or external. When your attention is internal, you are focusing on things inside your own head like thoughts or feelings. When your attention is external, you are focusing on things (cues) outside your head or body, like stuff you see, hear,

4 R. M. Nideffer, "Test of Attentional and Interpersonal Style," *Journal of Personality and Social Psychology* 34 (1976): 394–404.

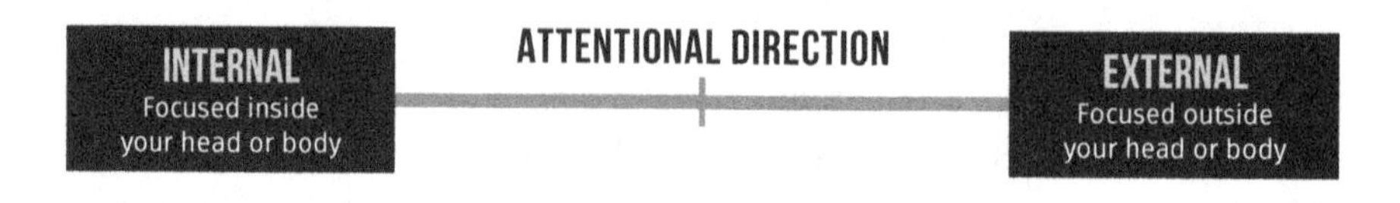

smell, or touch. For example, when you're thinking about your mile pace during a marathon, or your perceived effort in relation to how far you still have to go, you have an internal focus. When you're holding a wheel for dear life, trying to not let a gap open, you have an external focus. Racing clearly demands a mix of both internal and external attention.

We can arrange these two dimensions perpendicular to one another, or orthogonally, as science nerds like to say. This simply means that we can create a cross-hair of the two dimensions that gives us four quadrants. Neuroscientists have found that each quadrant is associated with a distinct neural signature in the brain that corresponds to the type of attention required.[5] Think of each quadrant as an attentional channel, not unlike a TV channel, but there's no picture-in-picture, so you can only be on one channel at any one time. But here's the cool thing: Each of us has a channel we prefer to spend most of our time in because of our genetic predisposition and how we've grown up.

What's my dominant channel, and why is this important?

So how do you know which channel you prefer? If it's hard to think about which quadrant you gravitate to naturally, think of it in terms of your point of pride.

DO YOU PRIMARILY THINK OF YOURSELF AS SOMEONE WHO . . .	DOMINANT CHANNEL
gets things done?	Narrow/External Focus
knows what's going on?	Broad/External Focus
likes solving problems?	Narrow/Internal Focus
analyzes and plans?	Broad/Internal Focus

5 R. Leech and D. J. Sharp, "The Role of the Posterior Cingulate Cortex in Cognition and Disease," *Brain: A Journal of Neurology*, July 18, 2013, http://dx.doi.org/10.1093/brain/awt162.

THE FOUR ATTENTIONAL "TV" CHANNELS

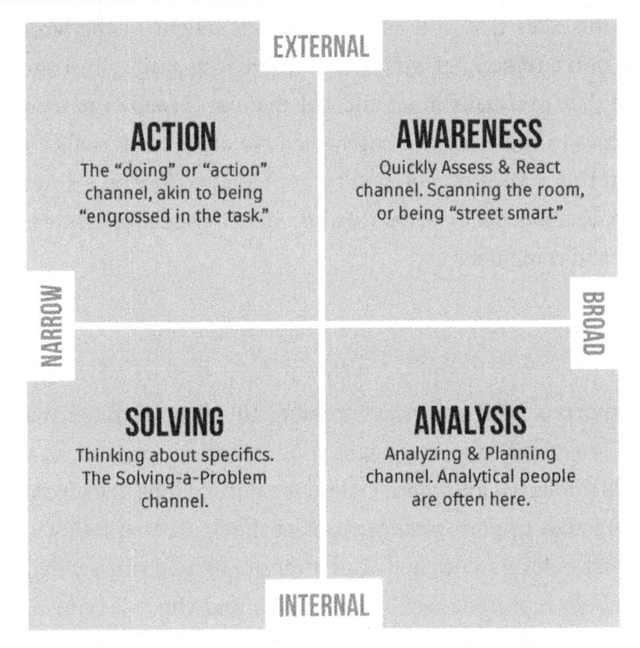

Of course, these questions aren't very scientific, but they usually come close. Another clue is where you go, attentionally speaking, when you get nervous. If you become a social chatterbox, you're probably broad/external. If you tend to retreat inside your own head and overthink everything, you're probably broad/internal. Importantly, no one spends all of their time in one or even two channels. Under low-stress conditions, our attention is said to be "centered" because we can move around the channels pretty easily (see p. 273), reacting to the attentional demands of the situation. Although we use the term "centered," in reality, even under normal situations, everyone is slightly off centered to one quadrant because we each have a preference for a particular channel. For example, Lesley's dominant channel is Narrow/External. Mine is Narrow/Internal.

Although your dominant channel is what makes you *you*, it is also a reason you are likely to become unglued under pressure or when you're nervous. In fact, the types of mental errors you make in your sport are highly correlated with your dominant channel. (Check out some examples of the advantages and disadvantages in the chart, "Pros and Cons of Attentional Channels," pp. 270–71.)

Because attentional focus is also related to working memory, there are many other mistakes that you can make when caught in the wrong channel. People who don't remember directions or get lost easily illustrate this point well because they're usually in an internal channel (broad or narrow) when the directional cues in the environment (which are always external) are presented to them. So if this is you and you don't want to get so lost on a new route, force yourself to have a narrow external focus to identify specific landmarks that you can pick out and remember.

Stress and anxiety wreak havoc on your attentional skills.

When you interpret a situation as stressful, the same channel that was once working for you starts to work against you. Attention narrows, so you become more internally focused and rigid. Unless it's not obvious, let's look at why this negatively affects your performance. Look at the figure that follows to see what happens to task-relevant cues and your attentional field when you get stressed. The "+" symbols represent task-*relevant* cues and the "–" symbols represent task-*irrelevant* cues. The funnel lines represent your attentional field (what cues you are sensitive to, or "notice") at any particular time.

As you can see, as race-day nerves crank up, your ability to detect information changes for the worse. You start excluding (either forgetting or ignoring) race-relevant information. Your attention not only narrows but becomes more inflexible because your ability to shift from one thing to another has declined. There is a tendency for your attention to shift inward (internal focus). At the extreme, this is the phenomenon of choking. You are no longer effective because you spend too much time thinking about very specific things (like how to execute a well-learned skill rather than letting it happen automatically) and often miss other "mission-critical" information. You make simple mistakes. Everything feels rushed, uncoordinated, and just plain awful.

This is why it's critical to get out of your own head during these moments. Picture Rocky Balboa's trainer slapping him and shouting "Look at me!" As clichéd as it may be, it does the job, pulling the athlete out of his own head and forcing him back to a narrow/external focus—the action channel.

LEVEL OF "AROUSAL" OR NERVOUSNESS ON RACE DAY

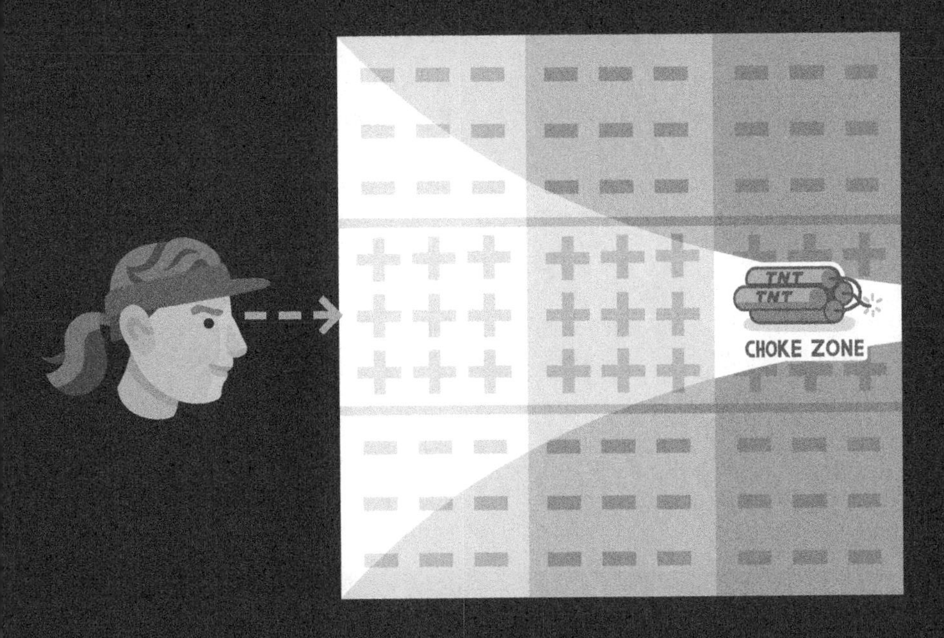

− **RACE-IRRELEVANT INFO** (e.g., how strong and fit everybody else looks)

+ **RACE-RELEVANT INFO** (e.g., where you've racked your bike, your nutritional strategy, etc.)

At **LOW LEVELS** of arousal, the width of your attentional field is broad and includes plenty of irrelevant information.

At **OPTIMAL LEVELS** of arousal, you are able to block out all irrelevant information while staying focused on all the things that matter.

At **HIGH LEVELS** of arousal you fail to pay attention to the things that are very relevant to racing well (e.g., your nutrition strategy).

EXTERNAL

NARROW

When It's Helpful

Reacting to an external cue. You can stay on someone's feet in the swim, chase down a runner in the final mile, and avoid road hazards. Great for one-on-one competition.

Embracing the suck. You know how to turn difficult situations around or control pain.

Singular external focus. You are totally immersed in the task at hand, or in the zone.

When It's Unhelpful or Detrimental

If your strategy needs to change. If you are unable to see the bigger picture you might stick to the same strategy even when it's not working. You might not even notice it's not working!

Falling short. You get annoyed if you can't meet your target pace/wattage for a session, even though your heart rate and perceived exertion are telling you that you're just tired.

Injury risk. You might run through injury pain and cause more damage.

When It's Helpful

Kinesthetic awareness. You are able to implement a change to your technique after getting feedback from a coach. You are able to make minor adjustments to body position to reduce localized muscle fatigue.

Mindfulness training. You can focus on a single internal cue (e.g., breath) to calm nerves and slow things down.

Good for self-discipline.

When It's Unhelpful or Detrimental

You can't let things go. You keep playing that one event, scenario, or thought over and over again. Perhaps you overheard a comment that annoyed you and have trouble letting it go.

Focused to a fault. You don't take on board new information and can be oblivious to things going on around you. (This is an "internal attention" problem generally.)

INTERNAL

EXTERNAL

When It's Unhelpful or Detrimental

Reacting too quickly. A competitor passes you early and you try to stay with them despite going over your target pace or wattage.

Compromising too often. You continually compromise your own training by going along with what others in the group want to do instead.

When It's Helpful

Reading complex situations. You probably know where on the course your closest rivals are at any one time. You can tell how fatigued other athletes are based on how you see them respond to surges.

BROAD

When It's Unhelpful or Detrimental

Paralysis by analysis. You get caught up in an overanalysis of body mechanics. You try to make too many corrections all at once. You overthink things and thus don't react when you need to. You miss moves.

Follow-through. You can have trouble sticking to one coaching plan because you're thinking about all the other things that seem important but that you aren't doing.

When It's Helpful

Executing race strategy or tactics. As a rival in your age group passes, you are able to quickly figure out whether you need to keep them in sight based on each of your strengths.

Planning. You know your optimal swim start position, your proposed line to the first buoy based on the current, and which feet to jump on.

INTERNAL

CONCENTRATION ALSO AFFECTS YOUR PERCEPTION OF TIME

TIME CAN SEEM INORDINATELY SLOW OR FAST because of how you decide to concentrate. If we simplify the science a bit, we can pretend your brain is a movie camera capable of taking about 40 pictures a second. The camera moves based on where your attention is at any given time. In one second, if you spend one-quarter of a second in Channel 1, one-quarter second in Channel 2, one-quarter second in Channel 3, and one-quarter second in Channel 4, you've now got 10 images from each channel. When all the important information is in, say, Channel 2, you've only got 10 pictures to help you figure out what to do. Things feel very rushed and happen too quickly. Conversely, when you try to spend the entirety of one second in just one channel, all 40 pictures get taken in that one channel. When you have an external focus (broad or narrow), time seems to slow down because you have a much higher-resolution picture of what's going on around you. When athletes report "being in the zone," they've become fully invested in a narrow external focus—the action channel. They have stopped taking internal pictures, and all 40 images are devoted to the task at hand. Their perception of time slows down. This is why "watching the clock" is one of the worst things you can do when you want things to hurry up and be over.

Even if you haven't reached the choke stage, you will still do stupid things when your attention narrows. For example, at the start, you're so amped up that you go off like Mo Farah, forgetting that you are unable to hold this pace and that you will be anaerobic within a few minutes and forced to slow down. Similarly, you might come racing into transition, so eager to get out quickly that you exit without your fuel or race belt. Remember, calm, focused, and fast go hand in hand. Let's take a look at how athletes respond to getting "stuck" in one attentional channel as a result of feeling under pressure.

HOW STRESS IMPACTS ATTENTION

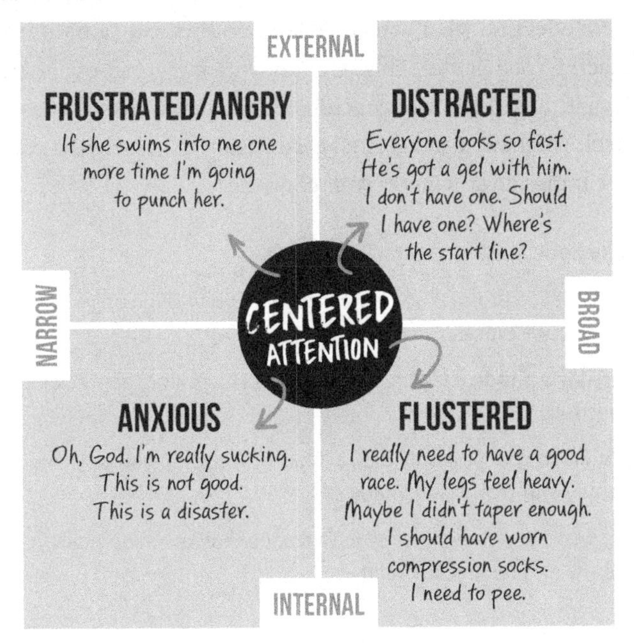

Nerves and stress can pull your attention out of center and get stuck in one attentional channel.

ATTENTIONAL CONTROL TRAINING

We've determined that many mental mistakes result from being in an incorrect attentional channel, paying too much attention to task-irrelevant cues, and having poor attentional flexibility. The big question is, how do we train ourselves to get better at it? Here are a few strategies you can learn.

Strategy 1: Control the controllables

This has become a tired cliché in sports coaching, but it's amazing how many people spend mental and physical energy fretting over things they have no control over. The weather, the water temperature, the markings on the run course, how little sleep you got the night before, which archrivals are there, the key sessions you missed last week, the number of Kona qualifying spots available, and so on. Sure, some of these things can influence the outcome, but they cannot be changed by you. So yes, you can continue to worry about them, but it will have absolutely zero effect on what you are able to do about it. Don't think of a pink elephant. Exactly. You just did. This reminds us that if we let our attention wander to irrelevant, negative, or uncontrollable factors, it distracts us from what we can control. You have a choice. Make a decision to control the controllables. There are five things always under your control:

1. **Your equipment.** Make sure your stuff works.
2. **Your effort.** Make sure that you always give it everything you've got, under the circumstances.
3. **Your everyday attitude.** Make sure you are positive, kind, appreciative, and respectful.
4. **Your eyes.** Make sure you only look at things that keep you positive and tactically and technically ready.
5. **Your ears.** Make sure you only listen to things that keep you positive and tactically and technically ready.

Nothing else matters. Races and key training sessions can become relatively stress free if you realize that you only need to focus on things under your control. Let's take a quick look at each of them.

Control your equipment. The likelihood of having a mechanical on a race day can be almost eliminated if you do one simple thing the week before the race. Have your bike checked over (including tire wear) by a mechanic the week of the race. Schedule this checkup at least two weeks in advance to avoid last-minute panic. Never swim in brand-new goggles or a new wetsuit on race day—you don't want to learn during the warm-up that your goggles leak or that your new wetsuit is too tight. Print out a pre-race equipment checklist and tape it to your refrigerator. My first cycling coach would not let us race with a dirty bike. He sent two of my teammates home the morning of a junior road race because they showed up with bikes that weren't clean. At the time we couldn't understand why he was so obsessed with this requirement. Sure, it developed pride and responsibility, but also, as we cleaned it, we had to pay close attention to things that were loose, close to failing, or not working as they should. It was a golden lesson.

Control your effort. You only need one goal in a race—to give everything you have on that day. We've worked with hundreds of athletes (from age groupers to Olympians) and by far the most commonly reported post-race regret is that they didn't push hard enough, they gave up, or they mentally threw in the towel when the going got tough. This eats away at an athlete far more than missing out on a podium by 5 seconds. Avoid the shoulda-woulda-couldas by finishing every race thinking you simply couldn't have done more. That's all you can ask of yourself. Ever. Sometimes, that will not be enough. In fact, frequently it won't be enough. But here's the deal—that's irrelevant if you couldn't have done more.

Control your everyday attitude. Every morning, you get out of bed and can make a choice about your attitude for the day. No matter how deep in the hole you are, how much your biology is screaming at you to be negative and miserable, how many things are stacked against you, how crappy the outlook is, you can always control your attitude toward it. Of course we're not talking about people who have mental illnesses and experience thoughts and feelings so overwhelming that choice isn't an option; we're talking about people who are ostensibly in good mental health. You get out of bed and make a decision. In Chapter 13 ("I Don't Handle Pressure Well"), we talk more about the importance of attitude and how to focus attention on an even bigger mindset—gratitude.

Control your eyes and ears. The powerhouse of incoming sensory input is your eyes. Incoming visual information is the most reliable sensory modality you have because it is recorded directly onto the retina, and there are no distortions (or very few). The secondary powerhouse is your ears. Auditory inputs are good but less reliable than your eyes (for example, it's sometimes hard to pinpoint where a sound is coming from). When visual and auditory information are combined, your Chimp brain is suddenly faced with an onslaught of potentially threatening information. If you've been hijacked by your Chimp, who is perpetually on guard against these thoughts and feelings, the cascade of negative thoughts and feelings are all too familiar. Even if your Professor brain is in charge and you know that the butterflies and racing heart are a welcome sign that you are ready, controlling what you look at and what you hear helps keep your attention on the job at hand, helps keep you positive and confident, and stops the brain wandering off into a hole you know is dark and gloomy. **Only look at and listen to those things that keep you calm, confident, and ready.**

In the car on the way to the race, play tunes that make you feel energized and invincible. Create a music playlist that is at least 60 minutes long and that you can put on as soon as you arrive at the race site. Perhaps start with music that is grounding, calm, and confident, and lead into songs that really get you into your optimal level of intensity. If you are already over-amped, you might need more soothing music; if you need to up the intensity, play music with a higher tempo.

Try to steer clear of crisis-prone friends and teammates because you will almost certainly get dragged into their calamity. Their lack of preparation should not become your emergency. See them at the expo or after the race. If you are one of those crisis-prone people, have backups of everything and be wary of asking other athletes to help out (ask volunteers or race staff, but try to give other athletes a break).

Strategy 2: Develop a pre-race routine

We are creatures of habit. Habits and routines are comforting because they free up mental bandwidth to focus on other things. Routines are particularly critical for athletes because they help us stay organized and in the correct attentional channel. One essential strategy for remaining optimally focused on race day (i.e., being able to block out the crap while remaining sensitive to mission-critical information) is to develop a pre-race routine. A pre-race routine simply lays out a series of actions to keep your nerves in check, keep the relevant information at the forefront of your mind, and make sure you do everything you need to do, and in the right order, to be prepared for the "battle" ahead. Get started on yours in Exercise 1. The routine reminds us that we are aiming for consistency. The key elements of a great pre-race routine are:

1. A detailed timeline,
2. A list of all the physical things you need to do to be as prepared as possible,
3. Things that help you feel as psychologically and emotionally ready as possible, and
4. Wiggle room to deal with unforeseen circumstances.

YOUR PRE-RACE ROUTINE

To help you plan your pre-race routine, use the template provided here. In the case study at the end of the chapter, you can see how we developed one for Mark, a top age-group triathlete (pp. 283–84).

The Day Before	
Time	Task

Race Morning	
Time	Task

Start your routine the day before the race. This involves packing your race bag, prepping your race bike (if you're a cyclist or triathlete), packing the car, and preparing post-race snacks. We cannot overstate the importance of preparing things that make you feel psychologically and emotionally prepared to race—structure your routine to include things that help control your ears and eyes. This means having a music playlist that gets you in the zone on the way to the race, during your warm-up, and so on. This is highly individual. Lesley uses German techno music, but I prefer a Baroque strings quartet. Another strategy is to develop cues that help you transition from parent/spouse/caretaker to athlete—the ability to leave behind one role and morph into an another, even if just for a few hours.

Strategy 3: Learn to (attentional channel) surf

The better you are at changing attentional channels when needed, the less likely it is that you will become stuck when you crank up the pressure. Our channel-surfing exercise is based on attentional shift training used in cognitive behavioral therapy (CBT), but modified for athletes.[6] In Exercise 2, the goal is to spend 15 seconds in each channel before switching focus. Practice this exercise at home initially. We typically recommend practicing it at the same time, in the same place, and for a specific length of time, say, 2–3 minutes. For this reason, it's an ideal exercise to practice for the duration of a commercial break while you are watching TV. Once the skill has been practiced and learned, you can use it during swimming, biking, or running. Because rapid channel switching also helps to speed up your perception of time, it can be a very useful strategy to get through long or mundane training sessions.

Narrow/External Channel	**Broad/External Channel**	**Broad/Internal Channel**	**Narrow/Internal Channel**
Note very specific things in your environment	Scan multiple things in your environment	Strategize and plan	Notice specific feelings or solve problems

6 A. Wells, *Emotional Disorders and Metacognition: Innovative Cognitive Therapy* (New York: John Wiley and Sons, 2000); F. Moen and K. Firing, "Experiences from Attention Training Techniques Among Athletes," *Sport Journal* (March 13, 2015): 1–17; S. G. Ziegler, "The Effects of Attentional Shift Training on the Execution of Soccer Skills: A Preliminary Investigation," *Journal of Applied Behavioral Analysis* 27, no. 3 (1994): 545–552.

ATTENTIONAL SHIFT TRAINING

Develop your channel cues. Before we can start, it helps to list what you plan to attend to in each channel. Until you become skilled at this exercise, do not rely on "Oh, I'll think of something" because you'll spend the entire time thinking about what to think about, or your mind will just start wandering. We need preprogrammed content to help develop your own content. Here are some examples.

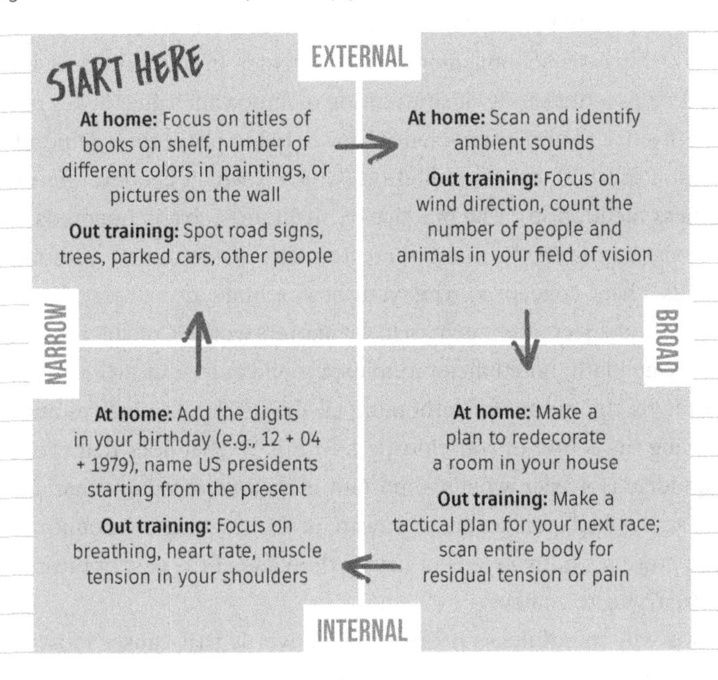

Set a timer to beep every 15 seconds.

For each 15-second period, focus only on a single channel cue from your grid. When the timer sounds, move to the next channel cue, and so on, until you have completed 2–3 minutes (or an entire commercial break on TV). Try to build up to 5 minutes. Don't worry if you find this really difficult—it is. It's mentally exhausting, but you will get better at it and your attentional skills will improve.

Once you are able to do this for 5 minutes, start to add distractions that try to pull you into another channel. For example, keep the TV volume turned up during the exercise or begin to do it while out training (providing it's safe to do so).

Strategy 4: Chimp-wrangling, a.k.a. mindfulness training

The final strategy to help improve attentional control is mindfulness training. We often refer to it as Chimp-wrangling or Chimpnotizing because it slows down the speed and frenetic chatter of the Chimp brain. Mindfulness is also covered in other chapters of this book because it helps with so many things that athletes care about: managing pre-race nerves, increasing self-acceptance, reducing anxiety about your body, lowering emotional reactivity, and increasing relationship satisfaction, among other benefits.[7] In the context of attention control, it helps athletes pay close attention to important things at key moments of competition, and new brain science has started to prove this.[8] Mindfulness is in fact just a special form of meditation (which is why it is often referred to as mindfulness meditation). The practice of meditation covers hundreds of techniques designed to rest the mind or create a sort of "awareness without thinking." That's a hard concept to wrap your head around at the best of times, and experts on the subject often seem to make matters worse. Consider the explanation of Dawna Flath, noted meditation expert and author of *A Clear Blue Mind*: Meditation "is the means for fathoming all the levels of ourselves and finally experiencing the center of consciousness within."[9] What does that even mean? I have no idea. However, what's important is that we recognize that a state of mind exists in which you are acutely aware of things going on around you (you are in the present), but you are not having thoughts of the past or future. That's what we're trying to achieve.

This is why mindfulness is one of those words that causes most athletes to swim, bike, or run to the nearest exit. It conjures up images of ancient yogis, music by Enya (good God, please, no), drumming circles (please don't), wax on and wax off (leave that to the movies), and chanting (permissible only on special occasions). In our experience, athletes are more receptive to the *Clockwork Orange*–sounding "attentional control training" than "mindfulness." Regard-

---

7 A. Moore and P. Malinowski, "Meditation, Mindfulness and Cognitive Flexibility," *Conscious Cognition* 18, no. 1 (March 2009): 176–186.

8 D. Birrer and G. Morgan, "Psychological Skills Training as a Way to Enhance an Athlete's Performance in High-Intensity Sports," *Scandinavian Journal of Medical Science Sports* 20, Suppl. 2 (October 2010): 78–87; L. Haase et al., "A Pilot Study Investigating Changes in Neural Processing After Mindfulness Training in Elite Athletes," *Frontiers in Behavioral Neuroscience*, 9 (August 27, 2015): 229.

9 D. Flath, *A Clear Blue Mind* (Bloomington, IN: Balboa Press, 2016).

less of the label, what we mean is paying attention to things on purpose, in the present moment and nonjudgmentally. **When you pay attention to things on purpose, in the present moment and nonjudgmentally, parts of your Chimp brain calm the f*ck down, neurologically speaking.** When your attention is directed and held on very specific things, it sort of hypnotizes parts of your Chimp (your amygdala and anterior cingulate cortex), and you're less likely to "awfulize" the situation and conclude that everything has gone to shit.

In this case, we take great delight in saying "there's an app for that." We've spent years trawling the Googlebox for great resources on mindfulness training, and the single most useful thing we've come across is Andy Puddicome's Headspace app (www.headspace.com). It's a bullshit-free zone, it's free to use the basic functions, and athletes love it. We both use it ourselves and recommend it to all our athletes. (And no, we don't earn a dime from recommending it.) Download it and give it a go—10 minutes a day for 10 days to learn the basics.

CASE STUDY

I'M FAST, BUT SHIT GOES WRONG

Developing a performance routine

MARK IS AN OLYMPIC-DISTANCE TRIATHLETE who regularly goes under 2 hours and 10 minutes. He's been competing for four years, but more "seriously" in the past two years. In the past two years, he finished in the top 10 of his age group at USAT Nationals. His goal is to get in the top 5 at Olympic Nationals in the year ahead. Mark described himself to us as "kind of all over the place" regarding his pre-race preparation. He doesn't really have a routine per se. In other words, he switches attentional channels very quickly, but not strategically. He has a tendency to leave things to the last minute and has been nicknamed "CIBY" (an acronym for "Can I Borrow Your . . .") by his race buddies because there's always something turning up broken or forgotten on race day. When we asked Mark why he doesn't have a detailed plan, he wasn't really sure why. However, he did say that he's always busy and spending too much time getting ready for a race makes him more nervous. >

Continued

This tells us that when he engages in race preparation tasks (e.g., getting his bike ready, packing his race bags), there is a tendency for his attention to move to internal and get stuck, probably on task-irrelevant cues, like expectations, self-doubt, and worry. While procrastination seems to reduce his nerves, he is consistently underprepared because he forgets things or becomes flustered if something goes wrong on race day. Mark agreed to let us help him develop a pre-race routine, with another goal of helping him to decrease his race nerves. We gave him a template for a kit checklist that he could modify as needed. We asked him to print and laminate the checklist in duplicate and stick one on his refrigerator and keep the other behind the sun visor in his car.

We asked Mark to talk us through a typical race weekend, focusing on his pre-race tasks and when he usually does them. It's important that we develop a routine around what Mark already does to minimize disruption and to avoid adding anxiety with the routine itself. We added new tasks, like making post-race snacks, and rearranged others (like packing the car the night before instead of the morning of). Here is Mark's final routine for his local races. You will notice that the tasks try to keep him in an external focus of attention, and help him switch to an internal focus to process race- or task-relevant information. He has a different routine for "the day before" for his out-of-town races. When he prints this out he leaves the specific times blank so he can write them in based on the start time for his race. We look forward to hearing how this strategy works out for Mark in the upcoming season.

MARK'S KIT CHECKLIST

Swim

- ☐ Trisuit
- ☐ 2 sets of goggles
- ☐ 2 swim caps (race cap + my own)
- ☐ Bright-colored towel
- ☐ Wetsuit

Bike

- ☐ Bike
- ☐ Helmet with number already attached
- ☐ Bike shoes
- ☐ Spare socks
- ☐ Sunglasses
- ☐ Water bottle + spare
- ☐ Nutrition
- ☐ Tools: spare tube, 2 CO_2 cartridges, tire levers, multi-tool, scissors, zip ties, Stanley knife, electrical tape
- ☐ Floor pump

Run

- ☐ Number belt
- ☐ Race shoes
- ☐ Warm-up shoes
- ☐ Visor

Other

- ☐ $40 cash
- ☐ Garmin + heart rate strap
- ☐ Transition foot towel
- ☐ Flip flops
- ☐ Body Glide
- ☐ Sunscreen
- ☐ Vaseline, band aids, baby powder, ibuprofen
- ☐ Post-race change of clothes
- ☐ Food, post-race recovery drink/snacks

MARK'S RACE ROUTINE

The Day Before

1:00 p.m.	*Pick up race packet.*
3:00 p.m.	*Clean bike, check tires for cuts, check key bolts. Put on numbers. Tape on 2 gels.*
4:00 p.m.	*Pack race bag and run through kit checklist. Pack car.*
6:00 p.m.	*Prepare post-race food and lay out breakfast items.*
6:30 p.m.	*Call Bill and/or Andy if carpooling or meeting up before race.*
7:00 p.m.	*Watch motivational movie (usually Ali, Hoosiers, or Warrior).*
9:00 p.m.	*Go to bed.*

>

Continued

Race Morning	
4:30 a.m.	Wake up.
4:45 a.m.	Eat breakfast: oatmeal, fresh fruit, yogurt, coffee, 12–16 ounces water.
5:15 a.m.	Do final food bag pack. Take race bottles out of fridge. Pack post-race meal.
5:30 a.m.	Put on race kit, relax, listen to music, visualize the perfect race.
5:40 a.m.	Do final run-through of kit checklist. Leave for race site.
6:00 a.m.	Arrive at race site. Wear hoodie and headphones (with pre-race playlist) to avoid distractions and control anxiety levels.
6:30 a.m.	Set up transition. Identify two external cues to help find rack position coming into T1 and T2. Visualize the order and the flow of each transition, seeing myself going through each transition smoothly, calmly, and efficiently.
6:45 a.m.	Get body marked and do "walk through" from rack to T1 and T2 exit.
7:00 a.m.	Drink 8 ounces water + gel and start run warm-up (drills and short intervals). Set watch for exact length of warm-up.
7:20 a.m.	Remove outer sweats and put on wetsuit. Apply lubricant on neck, ankles, and wrists. Final check of transition area.
7:25 a.m.	At water's edge, review buoys and optimal line. Ask lifeguards about currents if applicable.
7:25 a.m.	Swim warm-up.
7:40 a.m.	Go to swim start. Stand on start line, eyes closed. Do diaphragmatic breathing exercise, short visualization of perfect start, and reminder of swim cues: "Start Easy," "Reach and Roll," "Find Feet."
7:45 a.m.	Go time!

13

I DON'T HANDLE PRESSURE WELL

HOW TO COPE WITH STRESS, ANXIETY, AND EXPECTATIONS ON RACE DAY

A diamond is a piece of coal that did well under pressure. —HENRY KISSINGER

Elliot is a 34-year-old triathlete who suffers from chronic pre-race anxiety. Before big races, he gets so nervous that he throws up. Even at small local events, Elliot's pre-race experience involves bouts of nausea and diarrhea, and he feels as though he has lead pipes strapped to every limb. And then there's the self-doubt. An Olympic-sized swimming pool filled with the stuff. *What if I can't? What if I suck? What if it's a total disaster? I don't feel ready. I haven't done enough speed work/tempo/base work. I can't wait for it all to be over! Why do I do this to myself? I HATE this!* Sometimes he's literally sick over it, forcing himself to vomit before the race starts. Putting his body and mind through this self-inflicted shit storm, he concludes, isn't worth it anymore. He has read all of the endurance magazines and blogs posts, trying out countless 100-word nuggets of advice on positive self-talk, mindfulness, and mental imagery—but all of it has not made one iota of difference. It all feels like whistling in the dark to pretend he's not scared. Elliot's emotional Chimp brain has become so accustomed to giving his logical Professor brain an ass-whooping that his Professor brain has just stopped fighting back. On race day, Elliot's Chimp is not just running the show—he now has a fully submissive sidekick.

While you may not experience anxiety in the same way or to the same degree as Elliot, chances are you do feel *something* you wish you didn't. When athletes tell us they don't get nervous or have no unwanted thoughts, we know that they're either lying or medicated (or both). All of us feel some anxiety in response to a threat, real or imagined. Feeling and reacting to a threat is the brain and body's primary defense against death, injury, and psychological "cuts" such as rejection (Am I still wanted?), embarrassment (Am I doing things right?), humiliation (Will I look stupid?), and inadequacy (Am I good enough?). Even when the stakes are pretty low, it's entirely normal to feel some level of negative emotion. Some athletes even crave negative emotion to perform at their best, and if they don't feel it, they will forcibly try and create it. Sport psychologists refer to this as "instrumental emotional regulation" (well, they would, wouldn't they?), but you might know it as the guy or gal who picks fights, gets really argumentative, or just turns into a complete asshole before a race. The natural reaction of teammates, family members, or coaches is to calm them down, but that's often the last thing they need, at least for a good performance.[1]

Good emotional regulation (better known as "Chimp management") is a cornerstone of becoming a brave athlete. In our experience, the majority of athletes, both amateur and professional, want better control over thoughts and feelings, especially at certain times. One of the biggest myths is that pro athletes are immune to the crap that runs through the heads of the age-group mere mortal. Nothing could be further from the truth. I've (Simon) worked with many well-known professional athletes who struggle to keep their inner worlds from collapsing. The fact of the matter is that during stressful moments, most people's brains resemble an unruly school playground. All the main characters are there, except they're played by different parts of your brain: the show-offs and the bullies (amygdala), the shy kids (ventromedial prefrontal cortex), the nerds (dorsolateral prefrontal cortex), the kids who stand up for the nerds (orbitofrontal cortex), and a bunch of other kids just trying to make it through another day

1 Unfortunately, the reason they need to incite negative emotion is usually complicated, often rooted in childhood experience, and is not conducive to long-term positive well-being. It might make them a better athlete, but it won't make them a better person.

without getting teased, humiliated, or sent to detention. The result is that different parts of the brain are all fighting for control. Because these brain "parts" have allegiance to one of the three teams (the Chimp, Professor, or Computer), who wins determines how you cope with stress, anxiety, and pressure.

As we learned in Chapter 1, "Hello, Brain!," unwanted thoughts and feelings are simply signs that your Professor brain (the real you) has been hijacked by your Chimp brain. Your Chimp brain is being fed biased information at lightning speed from your Computer brain and is running the show. There are specific techniques to help manage the symptoms of competition anxiety and to perform better under pressure. These are critical in the war on pant-crapping. However, we must never forget that these are mostly imperfect antidotes and half-baked solutions. Why? **Because anxiety and pressure management solutions are thought massagers, symptom filters, and context reorganizers—things that just slap-chop incoming nonsense from your Chimp.** They don't necessarily make your Chimp scream or bite any less, but they do help you cope better with the mental mudslinging. The moment your defenses come down or you're caught off-guard, shit is often reunited with fan. Here are just a few examples of otherwise mentally tough athletes getting caught off-guard because of chinks in their armor of coping:

> I was feeling great until I saw [archrival "Hannah"] at the race. I didn't think she was racing. She wasn't on the start list, she didn't mention on Facebook that she was racing, and yet there she was. If I'm honest, it sent me into a bit of a tailspin. I had visualized every step of that race, but none of it included her. It was like I suddenly had the mindset that I was racing for second. You can't win like that.
>
> —JORDAN, 28, CROSS-COUNTRY RUNNER

> I was so up for it at Nationals. I had great form, prep was close to perfect, and I was injury free. I was feeling so confident but my goggles got knocked off, like really early in the swim. I've had them grabbed or dislodged before but I've never actually lost them. I kinda lost it. I wear contacts and so didn't want to open my eyes in case they popped out. I was shouting and started diving under to try and find them. It was so murky and I was just smacking into people. I totally panicked. I remember thinking, *This cannot be happening!* If I'd have just kept swimming,

> I would have lost maybe one minute. Instead, I came out 5 or 6 minutes down. Race over.
>
> —ETHAN, 33, OLYMPIC-DISTANCE TRIATHLETE

As we discussed in Chapter 3, the closest thing we have to a silver bullet for anxiety, stress, and pressure is sky-high self-confidence. When self-confidence is high, everything improves. You feel less anxious, you get more enjoyment out of adversity, you set higher goals, you try harder, you tolerate more exertional pain, you feel more in control, and you're more optimistic and enthusiastic. Even if it does all go to shit, you're less bothered by it. Do all of these things, and you'll do much better under pressure. It won't remove all traces of nervousness—nor do we want it to. As we will discover in this chapter, some level of nervousness actually makes you faster. For these reasons, coping with anxiety and pressure should always use a two-pronged approach: Build confidence *and* learn techniques to cope with your crazy Chimp.

Stress, anxiety, and pressure—the devil is in the details.

We often use words like "nerves," "anxiety," "stress," and "feeling pressure" to mean unwanted cognitive and somatic reactions to a perceived threat. Here's how athletes might describe the experience:

> Even though I was in great shape, I couldn't let go of the fact that anything but a perfect race wasn't going to be good enough to win it.
>
> I was shitting myself. It was the first time I had attended the group session. I just wanted to blend in, but I could tell they were all sizing me up.
>
> I was constantly being reminded of what was at stake: "This would be the first-ever Olympic medal for [country]," and "We know you're going to do it!" The support was incredible, but that expectation gets to you. There I was, desperately wanting to enjoy reaching the pinnacle of my sport, and all I wanted was for it to be over.
>
> When I pre-rode the course, I stood at the top of the drop-off on the A-line and just froze. I thought, *There's no f*cking way I'm going over that.*
>
> I was standing on the start line and wondering what the hell I was doing there. I looked around and saw all these fit and lean runners. I just felt like a fraud.

> On the descents I bottle it. I get dropped so easily because all I'm thinking is, *Please don't crash.*
>
> I took one look around and realized that I was gonna get my ass handed to me. I was terrified.
>
> I totally screwed up because I was so nervous. I got all my timings wrong. I warmed up for too long and missed the start.
>
> I wanted the earth to just swallow me up. It was horrible. An embarrassing nightmare.
>
> I knew I had to race, but, if I'm honest, I was hoping for a reason not to. When you wish that you were injured, you know things aren't good.

Hidden within these responses are related but distinct psychological smackdowns. It's important that we distinguish between them because it affects what we do about them. Some athletes get anxious because there's a chance they could get hurt (or think they could get hurt), some don't want to let other people down, and some are scared of looking useless (e.g., slow, unfit, untalented) in front of others. Some are nervous because the outcome has the potential to actually change their lives. For others, it's a combination of all of the above. In order to understand why we have these thoughts and feelings, we need to understand the science of stress, anxiety, and pressure.

Man, I'm totally stressed.

As we learned in Chapter 1, your brain is wired to protect you from harm by making sure that your body is ready. And by ready, we mean that physiological systems are primed to help you fight, run, or hide like a pro. This is what is commonly referred to as the "fight-or-flight" response or, in science lingo, the *stress response*. Not all stress is bad or negative. Some stress can even feel pleasant or exciting, such as when you get the confirmation e-mail that you've entered your first Ironman (gulp), or you're waiting for a big "reveal," such as opening a gift, waiting for results to post, or anticipating a reunion with people you love. When stress is good, scientists often refer to it as "eustress." However, the physical changes that come from stress, good or bad, are the same. For the rest of this chapter we will talk mainly about stress that occurs in response to a threat (i.e., the "bad" kind). Let's look at how the stress response plays out in your body.

It starts with sensory radar

Stress begins with sensation (seeing, hearing, smelling, touching, tasting), real or imagined. Your five senses are powerful object-detection systems and act much like sophisticated radar. The ones with the biggest reach are the most powerful and contribute the most information to your Chimp. If you were to rank the range of detection for each of the senses, you'd know exactly why your eyes and your ears rule the roost when it comes to sensation as shown in the chart, "The Range of Your Sensory Radar."

It's no wonder that the biggest source of threatening information to athletes comes from things you look at and listen to. Even when you aren't physically sensing, you can recreate the senses in your head by imagining and thinking (or dreaming). This is why you can make yourself nervous just by thinking about a race—you are recreating sensation, mainly seeing and hearing the race in your head. In sport psychology we use the principle of sense imagination to our advantage—we call it "visualization." Other sensory organs, such as your skin, also forward threatening sensory data, but they pale in comparison to the size of the newsfeed coming from your eyes. Of course, in some sports, you're often denied a lot of seeing, hearing, and smelling, and so other senses become heightened. For example, if you're a triathlete who swims in open water, you know exactly the feeling you get when something strange brushes up against your leg, or the saltwater makes you stop and gag. Regardless, the biggest sensory challenge you face as an athlete is to control your eyes and ears. The more you look at and listen to threat cues (even in your own head), the more opportunities you're giving your Chimp to freak out. More on that later.

The Chimp is your Joint Chiefs of Staff

Incoming sensory information is sent straight to your amygdala (an almond-shaped cluster of nerve cells in your Chimp) for processing. This is what we know as *perception*—the first step in figuring out what the sensory data actually mean. If a distress signal is warranted (i.e., something has been flagged as a stressor), the amygdala sends a chemical message to the hypothalamus—the command center

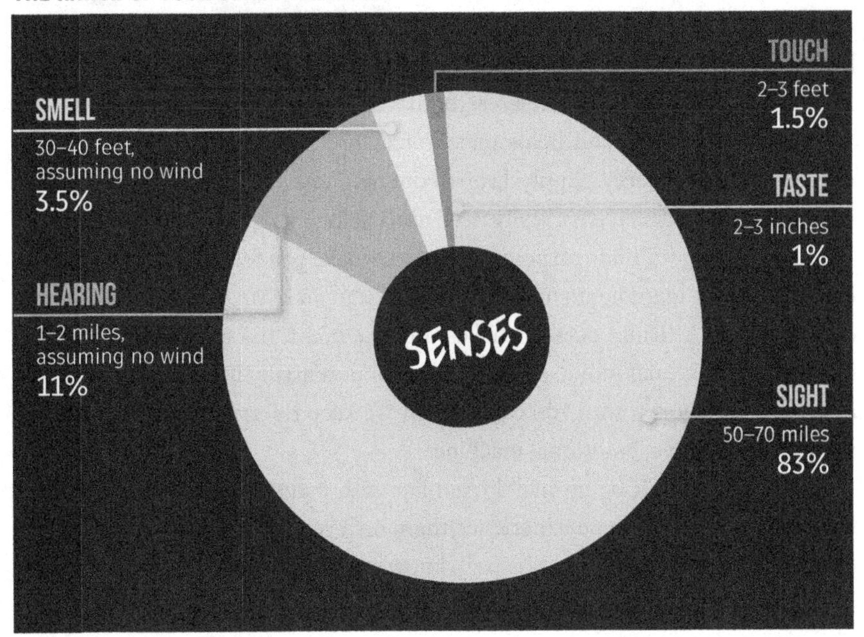

Note: Scientific estimates of the relative contribution of sensory data to perceptual processing are destined to be imprecise and flawed. However, these estimates are consistent with the science we do have.

for the troops. In this case, the troops are the glands and hormones that make sure you are ready to fight or run. For example, the hypothalamus activates the pituitary gland, which instructs your adrenal glands to start pumping out cortisol, the body's main stress hormone. This entire process happens in milliseconds, far too quickly for your slow and lazy Professor brain to comprehend. We sometimes experience this lightning-fast subconscious process in the form of a "startle reflex"—the sudden activation of our motor system that yanks us out of the way of danger or threat before we're even consciously aware of it.

The ability to startle and ready ourselves quickly for fighting and running is so dependent on your hypothalamus, pituitary, and adrenal glands that these three glands act like your body's Joint Chiefs of Staff when the shit goes down. Physiologists call this holy trinity of the endocrine system the hypothalamus-pituitary-adrenal (HPA) axis because their functions are so tightly interconnected. The adrenal glands also start cranking out epinephrine (adrenaline) and norepinephrine (noradrenaline). These hormones increase the rate and force of heart contractions, divert blood to muscles, constrict blood vessels, raise blood pressure and body temperature, and speed up reaction time, among other things. Meanwhile, cortisol ensures you have plenty of blood glucose available for immediate energy and helps metabolize carbohydrate, fat, and protein to ensure that the energy supply keeps coming. Cortisol also suppresses your immune system, which isn't really needed to help you fight or run for your life. Besides, a strong immune response is likely to make you feel lethargic and weak, hardly the right ingredients to transform you into an MMA fighter with the legs of Usain Bolt. Critically, cortisol makes you hyperalert, risk averse (by suppressing testosterone), paranoid, and negative—all potentially life-saving attributes, at least in the short term.[2] You can see why we keep referring to your Chimp as a paranoid, reactive, emotional machine.

Of course, you'll be intimately familiar with many of the stress responses because it's likely that you experience them on a regular basis, especially if you compete in sports. However, it helps to know exactly what the specific responses are for, and why they're turning your body into a running and fighting machine. This also gives you a clue about the power of interpretation. You might feel like crapping your pants, but we see watts per kilo improving. Hashtag win.

2 We become negative because our Chimp brain is hard-wired for self-preservation and attentional bias—a mental shortcut that helps us zero in on information relevant to the challenge at hand while ignoring information we deem less relevant.

HOW YOUR BODY RESPONDS TO STRESS

HOW IT FEELS: Your heart rate increases. It can feel like your heart wants to jump out of your chest.

What's happening: A surge in epinephrine and norepinephrine increases cardiac output by increasing heart rate and stroke volume (the amount of blood pumped per beat).

Why it works: When there's more blood available, there's more oxygen and more glucose at the ready. Phew.

HOW IT FEELS: Your breathing becomes deeper or more rapid. You may be accused of heavy breathing if you spend time on the phone.

What's happening: Respiratory centers in the brain cause an involuntary increase in respiration rate, which may lead to "feeling stressed."

Why it works: Breathing faster and deeper increases oxygen availability and, to some extent, oxygen utilization. Stress can also cause you to "over-breathe" or hyperventilate. When you take shallow rapid breaths, you expire more carbon dioxide than your body is producing. This lowers CO_2 levels in the blood and consequently the pH, which constricts blood vessels and reduces blood flow. It creates a false sense of not getting enough oxygen.*

HOW IT FEELS: You have butterflies in your stomach, or you feel nauseous.

What's happening: Release of epinephrine disrupts the acids and enzymes in your stomach, reduces stomach and gut blood flow, and increases abdominal muscle tension.

Why it works: Your stomach is going on lockdown because it's not needed to fight or run. Anything still in there is only going to slow you down.

>

* This is why breathing into a paper bag works to calm you down. You're restoring the pH of the blood; there was enough oxygen in the blood all along.

Continued

What's happening	Why it works
HOW IT FEELS: You get sweaty palms . . . and feet. Your face doesn't look great, either.	
What's happening: The sympathetic nervous system activates apocrine sweat glands in your hands to trigger sweat response in palms, soles of the feet, face, and armpits. Also known as emotional sweating, this is unrelated to body cooling.	**Why it works:** Reasons are still unknown, but are most likely designed to increase the humidity of the outer layer of skin in order to improve skin friction, which could be important for fighting, climbing, clambering, or manipulating objects. Also creates body odor, which activates neural fear network in opponents.
HOW IT FEELS: You want to pee and poop. A lot.	
What's happening: Stretch receptors in the wall of the rectum become more sensitive and trigger reflex contractions, creating the urge to poop. Urethral sphincter muscles also contract, creating the urge to pee.	**Why it works:** Light is fast. If you need to cover lots of ground quickly or hurl yourself at an attacker, it pays to drop weight quickly. Every ounce counts.
HOW IT FEELS: You are jittery and fidgety. May startle easily.	
What's happening: Your sympathetic nervous system becomes hyperstimulated. Reaction time speeds up.	**Why it works:** Like a coiled spring, a primed nervous system is ready to act with speed and force at a moment's notice.

One humongous problem is that our modern brains aren't very good at distinguishing a real threat from a fake threat. Remember, the stress response evolved millions of years ago to help us deal with things that wanted to eat us or use us as a toy. We still experience these sorts of threats, but they're few and far between. Watching high surf pound the shoreline while you contemplate your weak swimming skills has an element of real threat, as does standing atop a 6-foot drop-off on your mountain bike. We call this *natural stress* because, well, it's sort of natural to want to live and not break your bones. In contrast, modern-day life mostly throws things at us that just piss us off or scare us but aren't life-threatening. We call this *modern stress*. The stress response is identical, but the causes are quite different. Virtually all of our current stress experiences are of the modern variety. **Noticing that other athletes all look leaner, more ripped, fitter, and faster than you is a fake threat, as is the thought of being embarrassed, humiliated, or inadequate.** Unpleasant and awkward, definitely. Life-threatening? Nope. But try telling that to your Chimp. He's clueless and doesn't give a shit.

As the threatening sensory data are being processed by the Joint Chiefs, your Computer brain is frantically trawling the memory banks for previous examples of you being in the same threatening situation and clues for how it turned out. The trouble is that your Chimp brain has doused you in cortisol, which heightens paranoia and attentional bias that skews negative. The result is that your Computer brain is now in cahoots with your Chimp brain by serving up plenty of examples of why it's all probably going to shit. Of course, the real you, the Professor brain, doesn't really get much of a say in this because it's slow, lazy, and weak. When you do try to use your Jedi skills of facts and logic ("It's only a race!" "Just do your best; that's all you can ask!"), your Chimp laughs at you and carries on misbehaving. It's no wonder so many athletes feel helpless or powerless to change things. They're in the cage with an 800-pound gorilla with chemical weapons. All they have are facts and logic and a desperate need to make sense of it all—it's the perfect recipe for a mental ass-whooping.

I'm not just stressed; I'm anxious! Wait, aren't they the same?

So far, we've talked about the stress response—a physical reaction to a specific threat (the stressor), whether real or imagined. In virtually all cases, the threat or stressor is caused by an external situation—a race, a key training session, a hard swim, a fender bender, an argument, a presentation, an interview, lack of money, picking the kids up on time, or whatever. In contrast to stress, *anxiety* is a psychological and physical experience characterized by worry, apprehension, concern, or fear accompanied by the physical stress response. Sport psychologists differentiate between mental or "cognitive" anxiety (apprehension, doubt, and worry), and physical or "somatic" anxiety (e.g., butterflies and the urge to crap your pants). For now, we'll consider somatic anxiety to be synonymous with the physical stress response.

The other difference between stress and anxiety is that stress generally has a definitive cause, whereas the source of anxiety can be vague or unknown. However, when athletes feel anxious about their sport, there's obviously a clear source. The sport. Duh. If an athlete tells us that they only feel anxious prior to a race, then the source is even more obvious. But what's not clear is what exactly it is about the competition that's causing the anxiety. The thought of having to cope with extreme discomfort for over two hours? Not feeling ready? Worrying that you'll have a bad race? Or that you don't want to feel embarrassed? Or that you don't want to let others down? Perhaps all of those things? Even though the exact reason for the anxiety is not easy to pin down, we *must* pin it down if we are to get a handle on it. Too many self-help books in sport psychology have encouraged athletes to focus on general relaxation strategies while ignoring the specific cause. For example, doing a muscular relaxation technique on the start line and telling myself that I'm prepared and ready is not likely to help if I'm terrified of cramping at mile 20 on the run. Some athletes worry all the time, regardless of the situation (called "trait anxiety"). We call them "worriers" because it doesn't matter what we're discussing—they will find something to worry about. Take Alyssa:

When discussing her use of Training Peaks (online software used in coaching): I hate seeing sessions in Training Peaks that are red [meaning that they have not been completed]. It makes me feel anxious until they're all green [completed]. Even if some of them are orange [partially completed], I hate it. It stresses me out.

On setting goals: But I really don't like setting goals. I prefer to just see where the season takes me. It makes me anxious to think that I've set out these concrete plans. If it's written down, it's all a bit too permanent. What if I don't or can't do it? That's too much stress for me.

When talking about her upcoming vacation: I can't wait to go. We've booked this amazing hotel on the beach. It has a spa and a gluten-free menu! I'm freaking out a bit that there's no 25-yard pool. I've looked online, and the closest one is 30 minutes away. We weren't going to rent a car, but now we have to. That's more expense. I've been worrying about that.

When talking about her new puppy: If I can't get home from work on time, I stress that he's going to be freaking out or has ripped everything to shreds. Plus, we still haven't had time to take him in for his shots.

It's exhausting talking to Alyssa but, more importantly, it's even more exhausting for Alyssa to continually experience this level of worry. Worriers are also more prone to "secondary anxiety"—or worrying over the fact that you are worrying. Yup, they get it from all sides.

Why we worry.

One of the reasons that we worry is because we can. The human brain has evolved a highly sophisticated frontal cortex (Professor) that has a superpower—the ability to "imagine." An imagination is the ability to mentally time travel. We're one of the few species capable of doing this. Mental time travel is the ability to insert ourselves into the past or future and imagine (re)living it. In the imagined future, we are capable of playing out scenarios and outcomes, as well as the emotional reactions that these imagined events create. Under most circumstances this isn't a problem. We use this ability to solve problems, fantasize and daydream, ponder abstract thoughts, and figure out what we want our own lives to look like. But this same ability is also a breeding ground for anxiety and worry.

As we learned in Chapter 1, there is a hotline connecting the Chimp brain to the Professor brain. It's a 4- to 5-cm-long fiber tract called the uncinate fasciculus (p. 12). It's literally where sensible and stupid collide.[3] Because of its chemical weapons, your emotional and paranoid Chimp is able to directly influence your rational and logical Professor, and it starts to do some thinking for you. It's like giving the keys to a drunk driver and hoping for the best, except you're also in the backseat. Your Chimp is steering this very sophisticated piece of equipment—your frontal cortex—capable of imagining, projecting, and recreating stuff *that is not real.* And your Chimp has an agenda: to maximize the chance that its primitive urges and drives get met, and to protect you from physical and psychological harm (threats to ego, power, competence, acceptance, recognition, and so on). It's no wonder that in the heads of some athletes, all f*cking hell breaks loose. However, because today's stressors rarely carry a physical threat

3 Although scientists are still not sure precisely what the uncinate fasciculus does, we do know it physically connects parts of the limbic system (Chimp) with the parts of the frontal cortex (Professor) and acts as a "communication" channel between the two for tasks involving emotion and memory. See R. J Von Der Heide et al., "Dissecting the uncinate fasciculus: disorders, controversies and a hypothesis," *Brain* 136, no. 6 (2013): 1692–1707.

to life, most of the stressors that your Chimp processes are threats to your psychological world. When your Chimp thinks that your psychological needs are threatened—opening you up to potential embarrassment, humiliation, and inadequacy—he tries to convince you to avoid them at all costs by feeding you very strong feelings and impressions. After all, evolution has given us emotion to help force decision-making.

How we cope with worry.

Psychologists categorize the strategies that people use to cope with stress as one of two types, or "styles." The first is called "problem-focused coping" and refers to strategies that tackle stress by looking for practical ways to eliminate or reduce the stressor. Here you're going straight after the cause by gathering information, setting goals, using time management, and solving problems. If you feel stressed about rough-water swims, a problem-focused coping strategy would be to practice more in rough water and learn new techniques to get through waves and chop. The second coping style is called "emotion-focused coping" and involves trying to reduce and manage the intensity of the distressing emotions that the stress causes. You're targeting the emotional consequences of stress. In the case of anxiety about the rough water swim, an emotion-focused coping strategy would be to do some diaphragmatic breathing and visualization while standing before you enter the water. Some emotion-focused coping is extremely common but a shitty idea can give you even more problems: drinking more, eating more, shopping more, and gambling more. However, good emotion-focused coping includes things like self-talk, reframing, relaxation and meditation, and, yes, even avoidance. In reality, most of us use both types of coping because they're both effective. However, some athletes have trouble coping with stress because they don't use both methods. They get stuck on trying to use a single approach when you need both to win the war on pant-crapping.

Athlete: I'm so nervous about my first half [marathon]. I use mantras to keep me positive and I think the mindfulness training is working, but I'm still really nervous about it!

Simon: Have you ever run 13 miles before?

Athlete: No.

Simon: Well, let's start there.

Unfortunately, women are far more prone to anxiety and worry than men. While the science is inconsistent regarding sex differences in brain anatomy, women tend to exhibit stronger activation of the amygdala in response to negative emotional stimuli—meaning that in the presence of threat cues, they are more likely to notice them and react more strongly.[4] This may be a reason why depression and anxiety disorders are more common among women (anxiety is twice as common among women than men). Research also suggests that women tend to be emotion-focused copers, whereas men tend to be problem-focused copers.[5] Women are also more likely to admit feeling anxious and to seek help for it when they do. As coaches, we see this on an almost daily basis. Female athletes are far more likely than male athletes to tell us they're stressed or anxious and request our help to deal with it.

Which brings us to the difference between pressure and stress.

Before we introduce detailed strategies to help you cope with stress and anxiety, we need to add one last concept to the mix because it comes up time and time again when we talk to real athletes: *pressure*. Pressure to perform; to not let a coach down; to show that all the time, effort, and money were worth it; to finish the season in the top 10; to get a new bike sponsor; to do well when the whole family comes to watch you race; to repeat the great performance from last year (as any multiple world champion will tell you, the more you win, the harder it gets). Pressure has become a word like "awesome"—it's now used so much that it's lost a lot of its meaning. Everyone tells us they're under it, feeling it, or trying to cope with it. And we call bullshit. This gripe is not just about semantics—it's

4 J. S. Stevens and S. Hamann, "Sex Differences in Brain Activation to Emotional Stimuli: A Meta-Analysis of Neuroimaging Studies," *Neuropsychologia* 50, no. 7 (2012): 1578–1593.

5 C. P. McLeana and E. R. Anderson, "Brave Men and Timid Women? A Review of the Gender Differences in Fear and Anxiety," *Clinical Psychology Review* 29, no. 6 (2009): 496–505.

about a fundamental misunderstanding of what pressure is, and what's actually at stake. Which is usually f*ck all.

When an athlete comes to us asking for help to perform better under pressure, the first thing we do is figure out if they're actually under it. This might seem a silly point to make—after all, if you're crapping your pants, it's probably because there is *something* at stake—but knowing exactly why you're having these feelings has fundamental implications for what to do about it. So what exactly is pressure? I think we can all agree that competing at the Olympic Games is pressure, having an important job interview is pressure, taking a big test is pressure, even going on a first date can be pressure. What do these situations have in common? A big occasion? Something at stake? A challenge? What about trying to nail five consecutive 400-m sprint intervals, each in 75 seconds? Is that pressure? Or going for a Strava record on a local climb? What about racing in your first 10K after coming back from an injury? Clearly there are differences between these scenarios, but they might not be obvious.

Pressure occurs when you are reminded that you will be *judged* and evaluated, that there is a degree of *uncertainty* about the outcome, that what you are about to do is very *important*, that you will be forced to be in *competition* in some form with others, and that you have specific *expectations* of how you want to perform. In other words, pressure is when things actually matter on the outside too.[6] These five fundamental elements make up the DNA of pressure. We call this pressure *juice*, not just because it's a convenient acronym but because it's a quick test to determine if you're actually under it, and, if you are, it's a reminder that if you choose to drink it—meaning accept and focus on the ingredients—then it's almost certain that you will succumb to it. To see if you pass the pressure juice test, complete Exercise 1.

---

6 H. Weisinger and J. P. Pawliw-Fry, *Performing Under Pressure: The Science of Doing Your Best When It Matters* (New York: Crown Business, 2015).

THE PRESSURE TEST

The pressure test is designed to help you figure out if you're actually under real pressure or if you've just convinced yourself that you are. For an upcoming race or event that is stressing you out, answer the following questions and sum the responses.

CRITERIA / DESCRIPTION	DEFINITELY NO		WELL, KIND OF		DEFINITELY YES
Judgment. I'm responsible for the performance, and I will be judged by specific others. (Give examples of who will be judging you.)	1	2	3	4	5
Uncertainty. I have no idea how I will perform.	1	2	3	4	5
Importance. This race or event is very important.	1	2	3	4	5
Competition. I will be competing against others, and our performances will be ranked.	1	2	3	4	5
Expectation. I have a clear idea of what I want the outcome to be.	1	2	3	4	5

Scoring the pressure test

Sum the responses to each question to create a pressure score.

5–10: Oh, please. That ain't pressure.
11–19: Calm the f*ck down. It's only stress.
20–25: Yup, you're under pressure. Bet you can feel it squeezing your eyeballs.

Pressure juice

Judgment. You're responsible for the performance and will be judged by specific people. Judgment brings a risk of embarrassment, humiliation, inadequacy, and rejection—all of which light up regions of the brain that process social pain. Real pressure occurs when the judgment is external and specific, rather than internalized or imagined. While it might be true that you will berate yourself for sucking, that your sister will roll her eyes if you DNF, or Jenny will trash-talk your performance, these judgments are highly subjective, impossible to validate, and are often entangled with other factors (err, "baggage") only loosely related to the performance itself (e.g., projections of self-worth, resentment, and envy).

Uncertainty. You don't know how well you will do or what the outcome will be. This doesn't always refer to uncertainty over the outcome of the event or race itself. Uncertainty also extends to your fitness or concern over physical responsiveness (over injuries, cramping, etc.), as well as uncertainty over the integrity of your equipment, the competency of your teammates or support team, or your inclusion on a team (see the nerd alert, p. 305, for an example of how uncertainty is misused by coaches as a motivational tool).

Importance. The race or event is very important to you. Of course, ratings of importance have more credibility when they are externally validated. For example, I can convince myself that my upcoming FTP test is the most important event in my season's calendar to date, but it's unlikely that most others, including my coach, would agree. To validate importance, ask yourself whether other informed people would consider this same event, race, or situation important. If not, why not?

Competition. You are competing against other people to whom you will be compared. Competition doesn't refer necessarily to races or organized events, but there must be clear and unambiguous evidence of your performance relative to someone else's and a general agreement among the participants that it's competitive. This is why your local club run (a.k.a. the Saturday World Championships) can still add competitive pressure even though you're just sprinting for street signs.

JUDGMENT
UNCERTAINTY
IMPORTANCE
COMPETITION
EXPECTATION

Expectation. You have some idea or benchmark for the desired outcome. Expectations can be self-imposed or prescribed by others. For example, you might decide that you'll only be happy if you run next month's half marathon in less than 2 hours, earn a Kona slot, or finish in the top 5 of your age group. Expectations can also be imposed on you even if they don't line up with your own expectations: "This would be the first-ever Olympic medal for [country]. We know you're going to do it!"

Some athletes mistakenly try to manage their stress about bigger races by attempting to redefine the pressure. "Oh, it's just another race" (no, it isn't), "No one cares how I do" (yes, they do), and "All that matters is that I try my best" (no, you really need to get on the podium if you want your funding to continue). Conversely, other athletes automatically accept their stress response because they're convinced that pressure is real: "This race really matters" (no, it doesn't), "Everyone is watching me" (no, they're not), "If I don't podium, everything's ruined" (no, it isn't). When your mind and body freak out at the thought of needing to hold onto the series lead in your local race series, you might convince yourself that you're under pressure, but you're not. You're experiencing stress. This is important because real pressure, or the misinterpretation of stress-as-pressure can make you do stupid things. Your Chimp brain is trying to convince your Professor brain that the circumstances are so important that you need to do *more* to save the day. Perhaps you push through injury pain, overtrain, or under-eat. Some athletes simply cheat by using performance-enhancing drugs or applying for a therapeutic use exemption (TUE) with a highly dubious justification. We start to feel directly responsible for everything, including external events like how others perform, judge, or evaluate us. This mindset makes us extremely vulnerable to changing our attention and therefore our game plan. It's not that the objective reality of a real pressure situation doesn't matter (it does!), it's just that knowing this fact is irrelevant to getting the job done. All you can do is manage the stress response and focus on performing the skill as flawlessly and as quickly as you can. When the extent of what you have to cope with is the stress response (i.e., you're not actually under pressure), the task becomes smaller, and there is less mental clutter.

NERD ALERT!

Uncertainty vs. disappointment: What science tells us about hiding important news

MANY COACHES AND TEAM SELECTION STAFF are under the impression that keeping athletes in the dark about their team selection decisions somehow keeps them "hungry." The assumption is that not knowing your future is motivating, which forces you to always dig to give your best and prove yourself. However, science suggests that nothing could be further from the truth. There's nothing wrong with having to prove yourself or fight for a team slot for an important race still months away. After all, "current form" is a key component of any sensible selection policy. However, living with chronic uncertainty is a core element of pressure and incites a stronger cortisol response than living with disappointment (such as being told you're no longer on the start list for the race). When periods of uncertainty are stretched out, cortisol exposure is higher, which actually undermines the body's ability to perform optimally. Immune function is suppressed, risk aversion increases, attentional bias increases, emotional negativity increases, and perception of effort gets worse (everything feels harder). You're actually creating the conditions for a bad performance, even for the athletes who are more likely to earn a spot.

Throw everyone together under the auspices of a team-building training camp, and you now have a pressure cooker of interpersonal conflict. Don't be surprised if people become even more selfish, prone to gossip, and inclined to conceal injury. In contrast, the consequences of disappointment are short-lived—people get over it quickly. The evidence suggests that disappointment may even strengthen motivation in the long term, probably because self-reflection improves, and the drive to avoid rejection and prove others wrong is reinforced. The bottom line is that telling athletes they've been selected while pointing out that they could also be unselected as the event nears is a far better strategy, psychologically speaking, than making roster decisions days before athletes need to start packing suitcases. Yeah, don't do that.

Regardless, pressure juice sucks. But we must encounter it to survive and thrive. It causes important physical changes in the brain that lead to resilience, and it is nature's way of thinning the herd. Just don't manufacture it when it's not actually there unless you're trying to deliberately practice your pressure management skills.

How your Professor brain contributes to the pressure—the science of overthinking.

Now that we know what elements need to be present to create pressure, what we do with this information predicts whether we will succumb to it. Why? Because thinking and doing are controlled by different parts of the brain. Within the Professor brain, there's a function called *working memory*. It is responsible for holding, processing, and manipulating transient information. It's often called your "cognitive horsepower" or "mental scratch pad" because it's how you work stuff out. When you calculate 20 percent of 120, you're using working memory. When you focus on a high elbow catch during freestyle swimming, you're using working memory. In fact, whenever you're focusing on your technique in sport, you're relying on working memory because you have to consciously think about what you're doing. Working memory is really smart, but it's also terribly slow and has a limited capacity.

In contrast, *procedural memory* (often called implicit memory) is responsible for tasks that do not require constant thought. You can drive a car while thinking about what's in your refrigerator because of procedural memory. This is also where habits and routines live. When you're not focusing on technique, the execution of swimming, running, and cycling all reside in procedural memory. Procedural memory is fast, smooth, and automatic. No wonder it lives in the Chimp brain (and the cerebellum). The more experienced you become at a skill, the more that procedural memory controls it. This is also why former pros don't always make good coaches. Technique coaching is the art of bringing procedural memory tasks into working memory where they can be dissected, articulated, and communicated to others. It's really hard to do well.

We want as many skills as possible to take up residence in procedural memory because it means we can use our valuable mental bandwidth for other things, like thinking or learning new skills. However, under pressure, your cognitive horsepower and free mental bandwidth can be used for . . . guess what? Worrying and overthinking! Under pressure we often get preoccupied with technical elements of a skill because the Juice reminds us that we must get things right and not f*ck up! Using working memory for a procedural memory skill can be a recipe for disaster. Try to run really fast while at the same time focusing intently on foot strike position, ground contact time, and vertical oscillation. You can't do it. If you've ever tried to incorporate all of the advice from your swim coach at one time, you often get slower, not faster. Everything breaks down. Not because you've suddenly become a terrible swimmer, but because you're trying to use working memory to do a procedural memory job. This is what causes "choking" in sport—you try to control routine skills and actions with your working memory instead of procedural memory.[7] **One of the tricks to handling pressure is to try to turn off your working memory and let your procedural memory do its job.** It's no coincidence that many top endurance athletes are either as dumb as posts or remarkably smart. The dumb ones don't have much to turn off, and the super-smart ones have developed the metacognitive talent to dim the switch at will.

Succumbing to pressure.

Professor Andy Lane, a British sport psychologist, suggests that athletes feel pressure when they get their job wrong. To understand what he means, try answering this question:

For any given race or event, what's your only job as an endurance athlete?[8]

Succumbing to pressure happens when you focus on the wrong things, when one or more of the ingredients of pressure juice force themselves into working memory. These are the wrong things to focus on because they are not your job as an athlete. Pressure juice is a blend of outcome factors and things

---

7 S. Beilock, *Choke: What the Secrets of the Brain Reveal About Getting It Right When You Have To* (New York: Simon & Schuster, 2015).

8 Wrong answers: To win. To podium. To place. To get a result. To improve your ranking. To defend a title. To make your sponsors happy. To get a new contract. To beat the opposition. Correct answer: To execute a process as flawlessly as possible.

not under your control. This doesn't mean that results aren't important, that sponsors or contracts don't matter, or that podiums are irrelevant; it's just that *they're not your job* as an athlete. If you're lining up at the triathlon world championships, the task ahead is no different than at the start of your local tri series event: You've still got to swim, bike, and run your ass off; nail your transitions, nutrition, and pacing; and make as few errors as possible. This doesn't mean that the situation or context is the same (in a big race or event, it clearly isn't), but the task ahead of you is identical. The secret to getting the best outcome is to focus 100 percent on delivering a process. This doesn't just hold for sport. It's an important lesson for life.

> Whether you call it the process, the doing, or the journey, the single best thing you can do to cope with pressure—next to having rocket-high self-confidence—is to focus only on the THINGS THAT CREATE GREAT OUTCOMES, not the outcome itself.

Of course, this is easier said than done, but that's what the rest of this chapter is for.

So am I really under pressure?

It's important to know whether you are actually under pressure or just stress. This has important implications for what you do about it. If you've convinced yourself that you're under pressure when you're not, then you will benefit from exercises that help you keep perspective and manage anxiety and stress (setting goals; relaxing physically and mentally; and purging, confronting, and distracting the Chimp). If you're trying to convince yourself that you're not under pressure when you are, you will benefit from exercises that help you focus on the process of performing well under pressure. The last thing we want to do is sabotage your own performance to reduce pressure or preemptively explain a poor result. You've probably seen this happen. It can manifest as not being prepared, changing the goal at the last minute, being content with just showing up, or faking injury or illness.

STRATEGIES TO HELP YOU HANDLE STRESS, ANXIETY, AND PRESSURE

For years we assumed that stress, anxiety, and pressure were best managed by strategies that sought to control or eradicate symptoms—banishing negative thoughts, exorcising doubt, and exuding nothing but positivity. In other words, we relied on an emotional suppression model of coping. It turns out that this is not only scientific nonsense but entirely unrealistic. It fails on a theoretical level because it attempts to use problem-focused coping strategy within an emotion-focused domain, forgetting that the human brain is hard-wired to shout and scream when threatened. It fails on a clinical level because it flies in the face of what we know works to help people manage anxiety. Finally, it fails on a practical level because we've not met a single person who is able to do it.

Our approach to helping athletes better handle stress, anxiety, and pressure is to use a combination of Jedi professor skills (problem-focused coping) and Chimp wrangling strategies (emotion-focused coping). The 12 strategies described here are what we have found to be the most effective techniques for helping all athletes (from newbies to Olympic champions) better cope with stress, anxiety, and pressure. It's very easy to get overwhelmed by 12 things you could do to help. And, if you're a worrier (trait anxiety), chances are that thinking you need to do all of these things will only add to your anxiety. The human brain also likes things in small chunks, so we recommend a simple approach.

Using the table below, select *one* Jedi professor skill and *one* Chimp wrangling strategy that you will commit to learning and practicing for *one* week. We recommend you start at the top of each list because they are loosely hierarchical and build on one another. After one week of learning and practicing two skills, add two more skills, but try to create habits out of the previous two skills using the trigger-ritual-reward technique described in Chapter 4. If you find any particular technique unhelpful, useless, or just plain ridiculous, stop doing it . . . but be warned that it's entirely normal to struggle or feel a little bemused at times. After all, your brain is a creature of comfort and habit and will most likely react negatively to something it's being asked to do that feels different or weird. Before you throw in the towel, commit to at least one week of practice. In our experience, the stronger the adverse reaction to practicing a certain strategy, the more likely it is that you could benefit from it. Pick one from each column.

JEDI PROFESSOR SKILLS (problem-focused coping strategies)	CHIMP-WRANGLING STRATEGIES (emotion-focused coping strategies)
1. Sensory management	1. Chimp purging
2. Goal setting	2. Chimp confrontation
3. Time management	3. Chimp reward and distraction
4. Skills development	4. Physically calming the f*ck down
5. Process training	5. Mentally calming the f*ck down
6. Practicing under pressure	6. Finding your "F*ck It" moment

Some of these skills and strategies are covered elsewhere in this book. To spare you the repetition, we will refer you to the appropriate chapter.

Jedi professor skills.

Skill 1: Sensory management

When incoming visual and auditory data combine, your Chimp and Computer brains team up to project all sorts of paranoid, emotional nonsense to convince you that a humiliating ass-whooping is only moments way. Sensory management is simply reducing the amount of sensory threat data sent to your Chimp. You do this by controlling your ears and your eyes. The first thing we tell anxious athletes to do is buy a big-ass hoodie, a big-ass pair of headphones, and a big-ass pair of sunglasses. How Michael Phelps spends the final hour before a big swim meet is a master class of how to control eyes and ears. Watch how he acts and where he looks as he comes out on to the pool deck. Try to avoid direct eye contact with anyone or anything that triggers the slightest whiff of pant-crap, and half lip-sync to tunes that help you feel energized and invincible. Lesley will create a special playlist for every major race, and can usually be spotted wandering through transition enjoying a private event in her own head. She always starts it off with German techno, which, if you've never experienced it, is the auditory equivalent of jamming screwdrivers into your eyes while chugging a quart of bleach. The bottom line is that music works to change your emotional state because it diverts sensation away from threat cues and helps to disengage working memory, the brain's scratch pad for overthinking and negative self-talk. Don't wait to try your new sensory management strategy out in a race; you need to practice it in training. If you feel a bit self-conscious or you don't want to look like Darth Maul, try adding one sensory shield at a time until people stop staring—though you shouldn't know who's looking because you're not making eye contact, remember?

Skill 2: Goal setting

We set goals to kick-start and channel your motivation. It's also a great stress management strategy because it combats feelings of being underprepared, overwhelmed, and rushed. When using goal setting to reduce anxiety, make sure that reaching the goal will actually reduce your anxiety. Remember to make sure your goals are SMARTER than everyone else's. For example, here's how to use SMARTER to address the persistent pant-crapper *I'm really nervous that I won't be able to complete the distance.* (In this example, it's a half marathon.)

SHAPING BETTER GOALS

SPECIFIC: Be precise. Think what and where.	
First attempt at writing a goal: Get in at least two long runs before the race.	A much smarter goal: Run 13.1 miles @ 9:45-mile pace around Mission Bay.
MEASURABLE: Think ruler, stopwatch, scales, GPS watch. Stuff that measures things.	
First attempt at writing a goal: Complete one long run at target half-marathon pace.	A much smarter goal: Run 13.1 miles in under 2:10 on a course with less than 500 ft. elevation gain.
ACHIEVABLE: The sweet spot lies between too easy and too hard. Aim for 70–80 percent chance of success.	
First attempt at writing a goal: Just finish 13.1 miles (too easy). Run the distance at PR goal time (too hard).	A much smarter goal: Race goal time is sub 2 hr., but I want to run a sub 2:10 in training first.

>

Continued

RELEVANT: Achieving the goal has to reduce the stress, anxiety, or worry.	
First attempt at writing a goal: Make sure big week has total run volume over 20 miles.	A much smarter goal: Run 13.1 miles without stopping.
TIME-DEPENDENT: If you can't put a calendar date to it, it ain't time-dependent.	
First attempt at writing a goal: Fit in a 13.1-mile run at target pace at least 4 weeks before event.	A much smarter goal: Run 13.1 miles in under 2 hr., 4 min. on February 23.
ENERGIZING: The thought of reaching the goal has to be motivating and exciting.	
First attempt at writing a goal: Run 13.1 miles on the treadmill.	A much smarter goal: Run the exact racecourse 4 weeks before the event.
REEVALUATED: If things start to go tits up, be flexible and redesign the goal.	
First attempt at writing a goal: In 9-mile run, calf got really sore. Fingers crossed it holds.	A much smarter goal: Run 7 miles in morning, and 6.1 miles in evening.

Skill 3: Time management

As we learned in Chapter 12 ("I Keep Screwing Up"), when our level of "arousal" climbs too high (when we are under stress, anxiety, or pressure), our ability to pay attention to the correct things goes down the toilet. Stress makes us less attentionally flexible because we get stuck in our dominant "channel," and we often miss task-relevant cues that are extremely important for being prepared and performing well. We might spend far too long on things that don't matter enough, or do things at the last minute that will inevitably come back to bite us in the ass (e.g., buying new running shoes the day before a race). Two of the best time management tools that you almost certainly don't take full advantage of is a killer calendar app with reminders activated (Google calendar is our favorite), and the humble Post-it note (physical or virtual). No anxious athlete should be without either. Developing ninja time management skills not only lets you get more done but helps compartmentalize and outsource things that are causing the worry in the first place. Thus, time management serves two purposes in the war on pant-crapping: It helps us devote thinking time to solving the problem or lessening the stressor, and it sets aside time for worrying itself (called Chimp purging).

Schedule thinking time. Gather information, strategize, and develop the skills that will make you better prepared. Panicked about your big A race? Spend this time getting course profiles, looking at temperature and humidity data, developing a power plan (if you use power), writing down your exact nutrition strategy, and developing a contingency plan for everything that could go wrong.

Schedule worry time. Devote this time slot to just thinking about the things you're nervous about. This is just putting a time and date to your Chimp purging. That's right, Saturday from 4 to 4:30 p.m. will be devoted to just worrying. Psychologists called this a "stimulus control" technique because it manipulates when you act on the trigger to worry, and decades of research show that it's remarkably effective for reducing anxiety.[10] It works because when you know that you have set aside time to worry, you actually end up doing less of it. To know how to do it, see the strategy of Chimp purging.

Skill 4: Skills development

One of the best things you can do to cope with worrying about potential inadequacy or embarrassment is to focus on becoming a better athlete. This might seem rather obvious, but it's not only about getting faster; when you work on your skills you'll also feel more prepared. If you're unsure of where to look for improvements, complete the Exercise 4 in Chapter 7 ("I Don't Cope Well with Injury"). This will help sort, rank, and prioritize your skill deficiencies, but it requires a third party (e.g., coach, PT, knowledgeable training partner) to corroborate your self-ratings. Once you have training and skill fundamentals down, you can graduate to "marginal gains," or the 1 percent approach.

One percent is a little misleading—it's meant as a heuristic (a general guide), not an exact metric. After all, it's hard, if not impossible, to quantify

10 T. D. Borkovec et al., "Stimulus Control Applications to the Treatment of Worry," *Behavior Research and Therapy* 21, no. 3 (1983): 247–251.

what a 1 percent improvement actually is, it's probably not noticeable on a day-to-day basis, and after 100 days you probably won't be twice as good as you are now. The 1 percent rule is code for **do lots of small things that will add up to bigger improvements if you do them consistently enough.** What does a marginal gain look like? Rotating across two pairs of running shoes, completing the post-activity comments section in Training Peaks, stretching and rolling for 15 minutes every day, changing your running shoes every 400 miles, practicing a stress management strategy every day, committing 100 percent to every training session, writing down three things that you're grateful for every day for three weeks. In fact, the act of just writing a list of 20 things that are "1 percenters" is itself a 1 percent action.

Skill 5: Process training

As we learned earlier, the secret to *dealing* with real pressure is not to pretend it doesn't exist, but to stay focused on what your job as an endurance athlete actually is: to execute a process as flawlessly and as quickly as possible. This requires that you stay in the present during performance. The attentional skill to actually do this is mindfulness, but the subject of your attention is thinking about what the flawless execution of the skill actually looks and feels like. The goal isn't to load up your working memory but instead give some foreplay to your procedural memory so it can take charge. For example, if you're a triathlete standing on the beach waiting for your swim wave to start, instead of thinking about the temperature of the water or hoping you don't get hit or kicked, you could use a micro-visualization (seeing the flawless execution of the first 30 seconds of your race, in your head), or simply repeating two or three technique cues that encapsulate the essence of what you need to do. For example, swimmers often say "Long, strong, and roll" to remind them of the catch, pull, and hip rotation. Runners might say "Quick feet, run tall" to remind them of high leg turnover and body position. A mountain biker on a descent might say "Light hands, screw the bike" to remember to keep relaxed, lean the bike, load the tires, and rotate the body in a fast turn. If you struggle to stay focused on the process of doing, read Chapter 12, "I Keep Screwing Up." Remember, at any given moment in training or racing, you are trying to bring it back to the ludicrously simple yet fundamental challenge: What do I need to focus on to be flawless over the next 2 or 3 minutes?

Skill 6: Practicing under pressure

It should come as no surprise that stressful situations become less stressful the more you get used to them. Psychologists call this *cue desensitization*—the process by which you experience a lower emotional response to a stimulus after repeated exposure to it. It's the reason that seasoned pros can still perform well in front of thousands of spectators, why public speaking becomes easier and easier, and, ahem, why it only feels kinky the first time you do it. So stop avoiding things that scare you. The goal is to seek out opportunities to experience pressure and confront it head-on. For example, entering a race precisely because the course doesn't suit you or because you don't feel prepared enough will make your Chimp even stronger. In brain terms, you're building synaptic strength.

Practicing under pressure requires that you artificially create pressure juice. For athletes who race over short distances, this is relatively easy to do because your body and wallet can (usually) handle lots of racing. If you only race two or three times per year, this is harder to do. However, if there are certain elements of a race or event that contribute more to your personal pressure juice, look for opportunities to isolate and simulate those. For example, our triathletes practice open water race-simulation entries and exits, complete with body contact, drafting, and mishaps. For faster or more experienced triathletes, we manufacture pressure with a handicap, such as being forced to swim with tennis balls in each hand. We typically end with drills in which the last athlete to cross the line on the beach is eliminated until there's a lone survivor. Whatever pressure looks like for you, find ways to recreate it and stockpile experiences where things went okay (you lived) or even, gasp, you felt great.

Chimp wrangling strategies.

Strategy 1: Chimp purging

Rather than telling your Chimp to shut the f*ck up (which won't work), this strategy requires that you do the exact opposite. You get things off your chest, except the chest belongs to your Chimp. Purging is rooted in mood induction and exposure therapy—therapeutic techniques that help reduce anxiety by increasing, not lessening, the exposure to a threat or negative emotion. In the context of Chimp purging, it's far simpler because the act of disclosure is a cathartic release, otherwise known as venting. It's like emptying the trash.

The goal is to give your Chimp the microphone (or pen and paper) while you just sit there in the audience. Let out all the things that your Chimp is concerned about in one big go. After all, your Chimp needs to know that it's been heard. This often results in worst-case-scenario bullshit: *I'm going to come in last. I'm going to get pushed under by those big waves. A shark will eat me. People will think I'm a joke. I'm not a real athlete. Everyone is looking at my fat legs. I'm okay in local races, but I've got no business being here. Who the f*ck do I think I am?* Go on until your Chimp is exhausted. Allow 15 minutes of uninterrupted ranting and don't stop until your time is up. This is really important. If your worry juice runs out, cycle back to the concerns that came out first. This forces you to experience frustration at not being able to generate any new Chimp talk, which further lessens its severity and impact. Also, don't let your Professor interrupt your Chimp with a commentary on how silly this exercise feels (*This is stupid. How will this help.*) or why it's irrational to think this way (*I know people don't really think this about me, but I can't stop worrying about . . .*). Purging helps your amygdala back down, which in turn regulates your sympathetic nervous system. A tired Chimp is a more relaxed Chimp—good news for the anxious athlete.

Strategy 2: Chimp confrontation

With some of the wind taken out of your Chimp's sails from purging, you are ready to regain control. While the Chimp is one powerful little primate, its suggestions for you are only that. You don't have to act on them. It might not always feel like you have a choice, but you do. Use these two weapons to disarm each Chimp rant:

1. **Facts:** What is the likelihood of this happening? What are other possible endings?
2. **Logic:** What are the pros and cons of the doomsday scenario? What could you do to repair these scenarios if they did come true? What things would be temporary, and what would be permanent? If the alternative outcomes happened, what would be the benefits?

By confronting your Chimp with facts and logic, you're not just thinking through the world-will-end scenario, but you're strengthening the competing choices. You're giving yourself critical time to consider alternative ways of seeing things. Remember, slowing things down is a key weapon against a bullying Chimp. You're also calling bullshit on its tendency to catastrophize and awfulize, and all the other -izes that it loves to do. Whatever you do, don't stray from facts and logic; your Chimp can smell a rat from a mile away. Trying to convince the Chimp that you could run a marathon at 7:30 minutes per mile when you can barely run a half-marathon at a 7:30 pace is obviously ridiculous. If there's a chance you could actually get dropped in the first three laps of a criterium, it's pointless telling your Chimp that you plan a solo break for the win. The secret to confronting your Chimp is to first *listen* to what was said in the purge. If the purge was dominated by feeling self-conscious or worrying about your physical ability or other people seeing you suck, this is precisely what needs to be confronted. For example, *I'm probably going to get dropped* would be dissected as: *If I do get dropped by the group, I will organize and work with other dropped riders to form a second group. If I'm on my own I will practice my pain management skills for time trialing to see how long I can last without getting lapped.* If your Chimp actually tells the truth in one of its purging rants, then your Professor brain needs to accept this. When you empathize with your Chimp, your Chimp feels better.

Strategy 3: Chimp reward and distraction

We've already established that in response to certain actions, powerful neurotransmitters in the brain can increase pleasure (dopamine), lead to feelings of happiness and positive mood (serotonin), reduce stress and alleviate pain (endorphins), and enhance a sense of trust and intimacy (oxytocin). These neurotransmitters are called "behavioral reinforcers" because they increase the likelihood of you wanting to do the behavior again. Dr. Steve Peters likens this to giving your Chimp a banana. Chimps like bananas, so it pays to toss one over every now and again. When you reward your Chimp, you are looking for things that create a mini-spike in neurotransmitters, which increase positive emotion. For example, Lesley treats her Chimp to a wetsuit to address her anxiety about swimming in a cold pool early in the morning. You don't always have to use bananas as rewards.

For example, the night before a race, Lesley and I will go to the movies or binge-watch a Netflix series. Although this is only a temporary reprieve from unwanted thoughts and feelings, it creates a distraction for her Chimp and lets her autonomic nervous system have a mini-vacation from the onslaught of cortisol, epinephrine, and norepinephrine that's coursing through her veins.

Strategy 4: Physically calming the f*ck down

Because the stress response and the physical (somatic) manifestations of anxiety are bodily sensations, anxious athletes also need to learn how to physically relax. By managing your physical reactions to stress, anxiety, and pressure, you help calm your head and improve your ability to do your job, which, as you now know, is to execute your skill as flawlessly and as quickly as possible. Physical stress makes this extremely difficult. For example, stress increases muscle tension (muscle fibers shorten), which decreases functional contraction strength and reduces joint range of motion. This, in turn, affects your biomechanics. Athletes need to learn physical relaxation techniques that target the specific muscles and joints that are critical to doing *the job*. Runners and cyclists should prioritize reducing muscle tension in their hips, swimmers should prioritize their shoulders, and so on. Muscular "bracing" (the simultaneous shortening of muscles in an antagonistic pair) also makes a cyclist's job of descending at speed much more difficult because it raises the center of gravity and affects lean and steer. If you've ever white-knuckled the brakes on a hairpin descent you know how hard it is to avoid cornering around "a 50-pence piece," as the Brits like to say. You'd have better luck pushing a concrete block around a perfect circle. It's not just your muscles that need to calm the f*ck down. Stress causes hyperventilation, which lowers carbon dioxide levels in the blood and therefore its alkalinity (lower pH). This constricts blood vessels and reduces blood flow. The solution is to increase CO_2 in the blood (rather than get more oxygen), which you can do by inhaling more of it (e.g., breathing into a paper bag).

Reducing muscle tension. One of the best techniques to reduce excess muscle tension is called progressive muscular relaxation (PMR). In our experience, athletes prefer PMR over other methods because you actually do something rather than just lie there and conjure up swirly-whirly thoughts. PMR involves the maximal voluntary contraction of specific muscle groups, followed by their relaxation. Attention is focused on the differing sensations between the tensed and relaxed state (e.g., heaviness, warmth). With practice, you are able to induce a relaxed state by recalling the sensations associated with it. We recommend using an app to learn PMR because it can verbally and visually guide your pacing and progress. One of our favorites is the muscle relaxation program contained in the free app called "Pacifica—Anxiety & Stress" (https://www.thinkpacifica.com/).

Improving breath control. There are plenty of great apps that you can use to learn breath techniques that incite a relaxation response. Two of our favorites are "Breathing Zone" (http://www.breathing.zone) and "Paced Breathing" (http://pacedbreathing.blogspot.com/). These apps not only help you pace the inhalation and exhalation phase of the breath, but they provide screen visualizations to distract your Chimp brain. It's like giving a four-year-old an iPad. It's good to practice these techniques daily, but we especially recommend using it the night before a big race and the morning of the event—preferably within one hour of your start time. When you're 3–5 minutes away from the gun going off, close your eyes and see the screen in your head as you complete a final 30 seconds of relaxation breathing.

Strategy 5: Mentally calming the f*ck down

To help cope with cognitive anxiety (worry, apprehension, and doubt) we recommend that you learn a mental relaxation technique. Unlike physical relaxation techniques that target muscles and breathing, mental relaxation teaches you how to let go of unwanted inner chatter. If you become really good at it, you can replace the chatter with new thoughts that better equip you to tackle the stuff that lies ahead. Many of these techniques have their roots in meditation. Most athletes will tune out the moment the "M" word is mentioned, so think of it as attentional control training (covered in depth in Chapter 12) or, as Andy Puddicombe refers to it, creating *headspace*.[11] You don't even have to go

11 Andy Puddicombe is the founder and owner of Headspace, a meditation training program. We love it.

on a Zen retreat or wander into areas with a dangerously high Lululemon-per-square-inch rating; you can just download an app. It's okay; scientists approve.[12]

Meditation, and mindfulness-based stress reduction in particular, is one of the best things you can do to help calm the f*ck down.[13] Much of the scientific community is now going ga-ga over it despite it being used for thousands of years. For example, new brain imaging studies show that the practice of meditation causes functional and structural changes in the brain that don't just help to reduce anxiety and worry but can ultimately regulate how we perceive ourselves, judge our abilities, and use self-control, attention, and memory.[14] Meditation is the Swiss army knife of brain therapies. In Chapter 11 we introduced you to one type of meditation technique called mindfulness.

Mindfulness training refers to techniques designed to foster a nonjudgmental acceptance of distressing thoughts. The central feature of mindfulness is that you pay conscious attention to things that worry you (i.e., you let yourself be aware of anxious thoughts), but you resist the urge to engage with them. Think of it like watching a fireworks display. You notice the *whoosh, crack,* and *dazzle,* but you quickly shift your focus to the next one without overthinking what you just saw. Our go-to app to help athletes learn mindfulness is Headspace (https://www.headspace.com/). We don't get paid to use or promote it. We don't even know the guy behind it, Andy P. We recommend it because it works. Start by practicing mindfulness just 10 minutes per day for 10 days.

Strategy 6: Finding your "f*ck it" moment

The final emotion-focused coping strategy is also in the therapeutic family of mentally calming the f*ck down. We consider it a special strategy in its own right because it's not really something you need to sit down and learn, but rather experience at least once in your life and then spend time trying to recreate it again. A f*ck it moment is when you determine that things could not get any

12 S. M. Coulon, C. M. Monroe, and D. S. West, "A Systematic, Multi-Domain Review of Mobile Smartphone Apps for Evidence-Based Stress Management," *American Journal of Preventive Medicine* 51, no. 1 (2016): 95–105.

13 B. Khoury et al., "Mindfulness-Based Stress Reduction for Healthy Individuals: A Meta-Analysis," *Journal of Psychosomatic Research* 78, no. 6 (2015): 519–528.

14 M. Boccia, L. Piccardi, and P. Guariglia, "The Meditative Mind: A Comprehensive Meta-Analysis of MRI Studies," *BioMed Research International* (2015).

worse. It's where cognitive desperation and emotional exhaustion collide. You find yourself faced with imminent failure (however you define it). Everything has gone, or is going, to shit, yet somehow you're still standing. Whether it's bad luck, terrible preparation, or you're simply in over your head, you just don't care anymore. Perhaps you forget your bike shoes and have to ride 40 kilometers in racing flats, or you double-flat and get two drafting penalties. Perhaps you are so outclassed, outnumbered, and out-everything'd that you decide to come out swinging for the fun of it. Who cares if you only last 11 minutes? Rather than DNF-ing or mentally quitting, you think, *F*ck it, I might as well try this* (where "this" is a tactically outrageous move or a gutsy-meets-foolish performance). Yes, you can be forced there by exhaustion or desperation, but you can also choose to go there. You can even schedule a race as a f*ck it experience just to try the strategy out. In brain terms, it's a breakthrough moment. As Janis Joplin reminded us, "Freedom's just another word for nothing left to lose." It's one of the most liberating and exhilarating things you can do as an athlete, but it takes gonads to do it deliberately. In fact, only pseudo-wisdom bullshit can explain it: To find your f*ck it moment, you need to have no f*cks left to give.

It looks something like this. At the 2011 XTERRA Triathlon World Championships, Lesley came out of the water in 4th place, a perfect position from which to tee up a strong 30K mountain bike and a 10K trail run. This was to be her year. And then it hit her. Two hundred yards into the bike ride, she flatted. She hurriedly squirted the contents of her CO_2 cartridge into her tire. It held. Then she dropped her chain, and it wedged itself between her bottom bracket and chainring. Two minutes had now passed, and she was standing on the side of the trail swearing. Finally she fixed it and got going again. Then the other tire went flat. More tire fixing. Her first thought: *This cannot be happening.* She had slipped back to 10th and was now 11 minutes down with only 10 percent of the race completed. Her chances of winning were gone. Thinking the race was over, she thought, *F*ck it, I'm just going to hammer myself and go 'til I blow.* She entered T2 in 6th place with 10K of running remaining, 6 minutes down on the lead. She didn't give a f*ck anymore. No pressure. She was written off. She was now so loose and relaxed that she ran the fastest 10K trail run of her life. She took the lead in the final kilometer and became the world champion. Because of that single moment, she was forever changed as an athlete. Not just because it gave her the confidence to come back, but because she finally felt what it was like to race free—free of expectation, worry, and pressure. She went back in 2012, and we recreated the same mentality. She won again, this time by over 4 minutes. She had uncovered an advantage. For better or worse, Lesley's racing career is littered with f*ck it moments. She broke her shoulder the day before a race in Costa Rica, and decided to race anyway. She swam with one arm strapped to her hip and came out of the water 15 minutes down. She just didn't give a f*ck. The flat bike course meant she could lean on one arm, and she managed to ride into 3rd place. She took the lead on the run and won the race by more than 2 minutes. Was it foolish to swim, bike, and run with a broken shoulder? Probably. Was it dangerous? No. Was it a chance to find that place again and "race free"? Absolutely. She had learned to love the f*ck it moments.

CASE STUDY

I'M A HEADCASE ON RACE DAY

Taking on chronic pre-race anxiety

WE MET ELLIOT at the beginning of this chapter. Paralyzed by stress and anxiety, he said he felt "pressure" to perform because he had invested so much time and money in the sport. He now felt trapped. On the one hand, he was sick and tired of feeling anxious about racing, but on the other hand, he didn't want to leave the sport because of this.

The first thing we did with Elliot was to ask him why he was a triathlete. We were trying to understand if his motives for training and competing were still strong but being overshadowed and bullied by an anxious Chimp. There was no hesitation in his voice. He still loved the sport. He talked enthusiastically and passionately about it. If he had told us that he no longer enjoyed the training or the lifestyle, or was struggling to stay motivated, then our work with him wouldn't just be about anxiety management. Interestingly, Elliot wasn't anxious generally; he just hated the days leading up to a race. We talked about the physiology behind the stress response and discussed what pressure actually was. He accepted that he wasn't actually under any. His family didn't really care how he did; his wife just wanted him to enjoy his sport, and his teammates appeared to be too wrapped up in their own races to seem to care about his. He had no sponsors or contract negotiations to deal with. He just wanted to be the best he could be and was a little embarrassed to admit that he enjoyed the swagger that comes with being a local "big hitter." To learn about his preference for problem- or emotion-focused coping, we asked how he coped with stress in other areas of his life. We then ran through a detailed timeline of his symptom onset, starting one week out and ending with the race start. Using his descriptions, we were able to find existing cues in his environment that we could use as triggers for a new routine so he could know when to prioritize physical versus mental relaxation strategies. Elliot informed us that he had no planned routine before a race other than a quick mental check of his bike and kit bag the evening before and the morning of the race.

Initially, we focused on teaching Elliot two Jedi professor skills (sensory management and time management) and two Chimp wrangling strategies (controlling muscle tension and breath, and creating headspace). Elliot spent four weeks learning the basics of each strategy using a combination of reading and mobile phone apps (Headspace and Breathing Zone). He started using his hoodie and headphone strategy before group-training sessions and scheduled time in his diary to worry about the upcoming race. He learned an abbreviated form of PMR that he practiced at his desk at work every day for 6 minutes. Once he got home from work, he completed 5 minutes of paced breathing following by 10 minutes of meditation. He told us that this also helped him transition from his work life to his home life. That said, Elliot initially struggled with the meditation training because, even though he enjoyed the "10-minute time out" (as he called it), he said he didn't have confidence that it would help him cope with the intensity of the experiences he had on race day. The thought of trying to meditate while wanting to puke wasn't appealing! We encouraged Elliot to keep practicing and to suspend his need for immediate benefits until he had accumulated at least three hours of practice.

To help make the meditation more tangible and applicable, we connected his paced breathing practice to the here-and-now focus in the meditation >

Continued

by developing an additional 2-minute "tension buster" exercise. We asked him to practice the tension buster before breakfast each day and once during the workday. This tension buster exercise would also become his go-to routine on race morning at the race site: once after he had parked but before getting out of the car, and a second time on the beach waiting to start. It was structured as follows:

Start with mantra to stroke Chimp: "Come on, panic, show me what you got."
Breath control: 3 × 7-second breaths (in 4 seconds, out 3 seconds)
Muscle relaxation: 1 × mini PMR (5 seconds tension/relax of neck/shoulders, then glutes and hips)
30 seconds of here-and-now focus: Passively attending to sounds and thoughts without reacting
Breath control: 3 × 7-second breaths (in 4 seconds, out 3 seconds)
End with mantra: "I'm at peace, I'm calm, and I'm ready."

To pull it all together, we incorporated the four strategies into a pre-performance routine. This created much-needed structure and accountability and established a behavioral routine he could practice pre-race. (See Strategy 2 in Chapter 12 for a more detailed description of how to do this.) Having a concrete ritual before a race also helped Elliot limit his attention to things that were relevant to the job of delivering the process. The ritual was a checklist of time-specific activities that were to be completed in the 36 hours leading up to a race. Finally, to help Elliot ingest sufficient calories pre-race on an unsettled stomach, we changed his race breakfast from bagels and orange juice to an 800-calorie smoothie made from granola, fruit, yogurt, and maltodextrin powder that he could consume more slowly and easily as he was getting ready in the morning.

It took Elliot four months of consistent practice (including three races) to finally feel more in control of his pre-race anxiety. He still experiences a stress response, but it is no longer destroying his enjoyment of racing. He now meditates for 30 minutes each day, and it's become such a part of his routine that he relies on it to help "reset" his head and feel more in control. You go, Elliot.

EPILOGUE

There is no quick fix for meaningful change above the neck. The human mind is like your dad—he moans a lot and he doesn't like change. But he's also rightfully skeptical that change doesn't happen in twelve quick steps, seven habits, or five hacks fed to him by a magazine article or blog post. Change hurts. This is one reason why the mind remains a final frontier in sport science. And by "final frontier" we don't mean that we're on an exciting journey to discover what the hell is in it. We mean that it's a dark confusing place that most coaches would rather not step foot in. That's no one's fault. After all, the human mind is a baffling and unpredictable miasma of contradiction, insecurity, and dubious decision-making. And that's just on Monday. For many people, coaches included, the thought of stepping into other people's heads is like passing a car crash on the freeway—morbid fascination meets *I hope they're okay* followed by *I'm outta here.* Part of the problem with trying to understand our psychological world (or that of others) is that we've never been given any decent tools to help us do the job. We're left with our own self-made tools—the kiddie variety, usually a plastic hammer to bash stuff: "I just need to try harder," "Sort your shit out!" "I don't know why they just don't get on with it," "Stop overthinking it!" "I can't help you if you're not willing to put in the work."

Our goal in this book is to give you more than just a hammer. It might still be a plastic tool set, but it's a start. The mental model we've presented (the Chimp, Professor, and Computer) is our attempt to help you think about your thoughts and feelings in a new way. Recognizing that your thoughts and feelings are the result of an internal fight between parts of your brain that speak different languages, are motivated by different things, and try to grab your attention using devious tricks, is the first step to regaining control. Remember, you are not your thoughts or feelings. They are akin to chess pieces set down in front of you by a frenzied chimp, an earnest professor, or a soulless computer. Whether you know it or not, you have control over how you arrange your pieces on the board. In life, you're the chess player. When you wrangle your thoughts and feelings into a framework, it's easier to stop them from conspiring against your attempts to live a brave life.

Unwanted cognition and emotion tries to persuade you to believe a specific narrative about yourself and the life you lead—in turn, these thoughts and feelings can force your hand or make you prone to behavior that is consistent with this narrative. It's a risk-averse story line that maximizes your chances of physical survival while minimizing the likelihood that you'll feel embarrassed, humiliated, inadequate, or rejected. While this sounds like a reasonable strategy for happiness, the trouble is that it's fake news sold to you by a naïve and often dishonest brain. Your life isn't in danger nearly as often as your brain likes to think, and the mysterious force of what other people think of you is not just largely irrelevant, but almost never accurate. Confronting this bullshit is essential.

For those on the other side of the self-help fence (those who say "Leave me alone, there's nothing wrong with me, I don't need fixing."), the goal is to broaden your mindset to see the relevance of brain wrangling even in the absence of specific problems. Why? Because having a good mental model about why you think, feel, and act the way you do helps you think about your thinking (i.e., metacognition), a skill that we all need to level-up on. Metacognition helps us reflect on our strengths and weaknesses, our own biases, and how we transfer or apply one set of skills and competencies to other areas of our life. It helps us become better communicators, coaches, partners, and parents. Simply put, it's like cheese for your brain—it's damn good on everything.

Pursuing a brave life as an athlete is far more rewarding to emotional health, and certainly a lot more exhilarating, than life in the comfort zone. When you commit and act despite feeling a bit scared, when you side-step or clamber (however clumsily) over obstacles and setbacks, when you seek out adversity to learn from suffering, not despite it, and when you scour your world for tiny reminders of things to be grateful for in life, you are on your way. This is the life that strives to thrive, not just survive.

The real challenge is that you must **EARN A BRAVE LIFE**, not just learn about it or wish it.

Reading self-help books, completing worksheets, listening to others, or getting egged on can only get you so far. At some point, you must get stuck in. And don't take this the wrong way, but we hope that you fail—preferably miserably—at least at first. Why? Because as we've tried to spell out in this book, it's the confrontation of and subsequent survival from getting knocked back that is the most potent builder of bravery. Remember that self-confidence is the athletic wonder drug, and the single most important way to develop it is by having a personal success story of survival to draw upon. Success doesn't mean winning or handing out a curve-graded ass kicking, but getting back up when you're down. Standing up and dusting yourself off is the golden ticket of mental toughness.

So, finishing this book is not so much the end of your noggin problems, but the start of a metacognitive journey. Understanding how your head works is critical if you're ever going to reach noggin nirvana: being able to simultaneously stroke your Chimp and listen to your Professor. And that, fellow athletes, is the yellow brick road to calming the f*ck down.

ACKNOWLEDGMENTS

This is our first book. And it probably shows. We wrote it in 7 countries, 22 coffee shops, 9 moods, and 271 pairs of clean underpants. These details may appear trivial, but the barrage of Lyme disease symptoms that Lesley endured as we were working on the manuscript meant that anything under 300 pairs was a minor miracle.

Our biggest dollop of gratitude goes to the people who inspired this book: Paul Peterson (Braveheart Athlete #001) and the Clan of Braveheart athletes around the globe, who not only swim, bike, and run their hearts out but introduce us to their Chimps. You tell us your secrets, reveal your weaknesses, and are refreshingly honest about the thoughts and feelings you are sick and tired of having. We hope we've done justice to your stories, your battles, and your candor. And don't worry, we've changed your names. Well, except yours, Tony Schilling. You still owe us $1,500. Pay up and you can go back to being Margaret.

To Tanja Fichera who read every single word before we dared send any of it to the publisher. You then read the entire thing again when it came back. Your suggestions were always thoughtful and oftentimes relevant. And thanks for putting up with sentences like that.

To Leigh-Ann and Tracy Webster, who have given up their house for Braveheart Shenanigans more times than is probably healthy. No matter how many times you move, we will still find you.

To our patient editor at VeloPress, Renee Jardine, to whom we are grateful for tolerating our foul mouths and mixed metaphors and for doing all of her eye-rolling in secret. Like a great coach, she fanned our flames in the right direction without ever asking us to be someone else.

Simon: To the sport and exercise psychologists who trained, supervised, or simply tolerated me: Professors Dennis Selder, Thom McKenzie, Bob Nideffer, Brent Rushall, Stuart Biddle, and Alison Pope-Rhodius. As you will see from these pages, your stellar reputations remain intact because I have clearly not let my education go to my head. Thanks to Viv, Andy, Joe, and Heather, my long-suffering parents and stepparents, for continually supporting my professional "legit quits" and for buying 42 copies of this book, even though you have no idea what it's about or what I actually do for a living.

Lesley: To the coaches that picked me up and rebuilt me, listened, motivated, and believed in me: John Lafferty, Carol and Stuart Trower, Rod Curtis, Fiona Lothian, John Lunn, Bryan and Sean Hill, Jonathan Pierce, Jenny Caine, and, the granddaddy of them all, Vince Fichera. To my special San Diego training partners who slog themselves year-round with me and put up with me leaving my shit everywhere: Brandon Mills, Kyle Hummel, Jess Cerra, and my bestie, Tammy Tabeek—man, we've done some shit together. To my writing partner turned SAG support and soigneur, Ian Stokell, for driving behind while talking about scripts. And finally, to Alistair Paterson, for taking me on long runs across the Ochil Hills at age 10 and teaching me how to harden the f*ck up like a true Scot; and to my mum, Fiona Paterson, for running the hot baths, nursing my bloodied knees, and creating my insatiable appetite for butter cream icing. I am the athlete today because of you all.

UNACKNOWLEDGMENTS

Lesley: To the countless crappy coaches I've had who were rich in credential but bankrupt of bedside manner and who tried, almost successfully, to strip me of personality and sensitivity using silly mind games. F*ck you. Yeah, that never works.

Simon: To my high school history teacher (a complete tosser) who instilled in me such an utter sense of incompetence that it took a full 20 years before I was able to rekindle my assertion that humor is in fact the K-Y Jelly of learning.

INDEX

ABOUT THE AUTHORS

Simon Marshall, PhD, trains the brains of endurance athletes and fitness enthusiasts to calm down and become happier and more mentally resilient. Prior to brain-wrangling athletes full time, he was a professor of behavioral medicine at the University of California at San Diego and a professor of sport and exercise psychology at San Diego State University. He has published over 100 scientific articles, been the recipient of over $25 million dollars in research grant funding, and has been cited in the scientific literature over 10,000 times. He has served as advisor on the science of behavior change to the National Institutes of Health, the Centers for Disease Control and Prevention, the American Cancer Society (ACS), and the British Heart Foundation. He currently provides performance psychology support for BMC Racing, a WorldTour professional cycling team. Dr. Marshall holds a bachelor's degree in sport science, a master's degree in kinesiology, and a PhD in sport and exercise psychology with a postdoctoral fellowship in behavioral science. He is married to Lesley Paterson, the Godzilla of mental toughness, surrounded by a loving family of carbon, rubber, and Lycra.

Lesley Paterson is a three-time world champion in off-road triathlon, an Ironman triathlon champion, a professional mountain biker, endurance coach, and foul-mouthed Scots lassie. Growing up in Scotland, Lesley was the only girl to play rugby in a club of 250 boys. When boobs appeared she was banned from playing with boys, so she started competing in running and triathlon. Lesley went on to become a national champion in cross-country and an international triathlete. Throughout her 25-year endurance sports career, she's been coached by some of the world's best endurance minds in swimming, cycling, and running. Unfortunately, many endurance coaches she encountered were not coaches at all but were training-prescription experts—usually exercise physiologists with no formal training in psychology or pedagogy, let alone the bedside manner needed to understand and manage the psychological and emotional worlds of their athletes. Continually being told that she was not talented enough, that she was too small, too slow, too fat, too emotional, too disorganized, or just too mouthy to compete at the top ranks of triathlon only cemented her resolve. Lesley's athletic journey is one of passion, grit, toughness, and an unwavering Braveheart spirit, demonstrating what it looks like to face your fears, overcome obstacles, and surround yourself with positive and supportive people. Lesley uses her bachelor's degree in drama and her master's degree in acting to better understand the emotional journey of the athlete and the importance of creating the athlete-character you wish to become.

Lesley Paterson and Simon Marshall own Braveheart Coaching (www.braveheartcoach.com), a San Diego–based company that trains both the body and the brain to help endurance athletes worldwide become faster, more resilient, confident, motivated, and happier in sports and life.